KNOW THE REAL JESUS

A Portrait of the Historical Jesus

Alexander F Venter

KT

Kingdom Treasures **KT**
https://alexanderventer.com
info@alexanderventer.com

First edition, published by Kingdom Treasures.
Salt Rock, South Africa.

Copyright © Alexander F Venter 2023

All rights reserved. No part of this publication may be reproduced, stored in a retrieval system, or transmitted in any form or by any means, electronic, mechanical, photocopying, recording, or otherwise, without the prior written permission of the copyright owner. This prohibits Artificial Intelligence (AI Chatbot GPT and related software) from using any part of this text without acknowledgement. Neither has the author used AI, as in rewording or copying and pasting in the writing of this text.

Scripture quotations in this publication are taken, unless otherwise specified, from The Holy Bible, New International Version (NIV), Copyright © 2011 International Bible Society. Used by permission.

New Revised Standard Version (NRSV) © 1989, Division of Christian Education of the National Council of the Churches of Christ in the USA, Zondervan Publishing House, Grand Rapids. Used by permission.

ISBN: 9798861097512

Cover design by Zelda Pringle.

To Derek Morphew, friend, colleague, mentor. Thank you for the journey with Jesus in Kingdom theology and historical Jesus studies, since we first met in 1970.

I am deeply grateful to the scholars I have learnt from regarding the historical Jesus and Kingdom theology.

CONTENTS

FOREWORD 1

PREFACE 4

INTRODUCTION 13

CONCEPTION & FORMATION 39

CALLING & CONFIRMATION 51

CONFRONTATION & CONSOLATION 67

MISSION & MESSAGE 87

CONTEXT & COMMUNITY 102

MINISTRY & MIRACLES 128

MYSTERY & PARABLES 150

LAW & LOVE 166

SUFFERING & CRUCIFIXION 184

RESURRECTION & ASCENSION 210

BIBLIOGRAPHY OF REFERENCES 233

ENDORSEMENTS 242

ABBREVIATIONS

AD	Anno Domini. Latin for Year of our Lord (calendar dating for 'After Christ')
AI	Artificial Intelligence
BC	Before Christ (calendar dating for 'Before Christ')
cf.	Cross reference (used in scripture references)
e.g.	For example
ESV	English Standard Version (of the Bible)
i.e.	In other words
KJV	King James Version
LXX	The Septuagint, the Greek translation of the OT
NT	New Testament
OT	Old Testament
NIV	New International Version (of the Bible)
NRSV	New Revised Standard Version (of the Bible)
RAP	Revised Alexander Paraphrase (my version of texts)
SJ	Society of Jesus (Jesuits)
WWII	The Second World War (1939-1945)

DIAGRAMS

Figure 1. Worldview Elements and Functions 95

Figure 2. Jesus' Framework of Discipleship 124

Figure 3. Jesus' Kingdom Worldview 163

FOREWORD

This most helpful volume takes the positive results of Jesus Research and translates them into an accessible and readable work that communicates broadly for all who seek to know the real Jesus. Performing such a task involves various stages of interpretation and makes various assumptions. My purpose here is to clarify this.

Jesus Research is the name given to the historical study of Jesus by historians, most of whom are also theologians. Those engaged in such research represent a spectrum of backgrounds and presuppositions. Alexander is fully conversant with my *Kingdom Reformation* and other publications and shows that he is aware of these factors. I simply wish to introduce the reader to the topic with hopefully, some helpful clarifications.

As Alexander explains, historically there are three *Quests for the Historical Jesus*. They are so named because they involved historians attempting to access the Jesus of history using various historical methods and criteria. My conclusion was that the first two Quests failed, while the third Quest, in one of its constituencies, has produced positive results. It is these more positive results that Alexander harvests for his purpose of presenting a portrait of the historical Jesus.

A simple way of considering historical methods and criteria is to conceive of sets of spectacles or lenses. Depending on the type of lens, one can see more or less accurately, see more or less of Jesus.

But why seek to discover Jesus *as historians*, rather than theologians, or Christian readers of the New Testament? This relates to the credibility of the historical claims Christians make. To confess that Jesus lived, died, and rose again is to make an historical claim. If making this claim is based on the inspiration of scripture, or a canonical reading of scripture, then faith is based on faith, not fact. If our historical claims are only shared within the community of faith and cannot be defended in 'the public square', then we have a private faith, based on faith. That is why those who engage in Jesus Research must lay aside their 'faith assumptions' and operate like secular historians, using standard methods and criteria. The reason there are three Quests is that controversy arose as to who and how these rules and criteria are formulated and used. I spend many chapters explaining this story in *The Kingdom Reformation*. Part of the issue is the question of bias. Those who first claimed to be writing purely "scientific history" (the modernist first Quest) turned out to be filled with bias, but naïve about their own bias. Now, in the postmodern world, those who engage in the third Quest spend much more time on the issue of bias and appropriate or inappropriate historical method. But they debate with some contemporaries who still operate from a modernist framework.

Getting one's head around this complex story is necessary if one wants to articulate the faith "out there" in society. This is not what Alexander has set out to do. Most Christians do read the New Testament as a canonical text and do assume its inspiration. Most do so either because they came to faith based on historical claims they were convinced by earlier in their journey, or because of a personal encounter with God that did not need to be based on historical verification.

But this does not mean that Jesus Research is irrelevant to Christians who do not need to engage with complex historical arguments and methods. One of the major requirements of Jesus Research is to place Jesus in his historical context. Possibly the most significant development of recent times (the 20th and 21st Centuries) has been the discovery, translation, and public availability of many Jewish writings just before or during the time that Jesus lived, known as the literature of Second Temple Judaism. It so happens that those who have engaged with this literature the most have been Jesus Research scholars. As they have debated numerous details about each and every story, saying, or event in the gospels, they have made fresh discoveries about who Jesus really was, what his purpose and calling was, and what his mission and message was. This is what we can describe as *Jesus rediscovered*.

Central to this rediscovered Jesus is his primary message and mission, the Kingdom of God. Discovering the Kingdom of God as announced, taught, and demonstrated by Jesus is to rediscover and redefine the gospel, the purpose and mission of the church, the

Christian life, and so much more.

Here is where Alexander's work finds its purpose, namely to harvest the positive and significant results of Jesus Research, reduce that to its essence, leaving aside all the technical historical arguments and details, and communicate it in language that is broadly accessible. He has performed this task most admirably.

Derek Morphew

PhD, theologian, author, Vineyard pastor, and (retired) Dean of the international Vineyard Institute

PREFACE

This book is based on the course that I've taught over the years, called *Getting to Know the Real Jesus – A Portrait of the Historical Jesus*. The Jewish King crowned with thorns. I address two basic questions:

- Who was Jesus, the Jesus of history?
- Who is the Jesus we preach in our day? Or what is the gospel?

The man commonly known as Jesus Christ is respected and admired, among a handful of other people, as one of the most important figures in human history. Many see him as *the* most revered person who ever lived, who changed history forever. We, therefore, ought to listen to him. Who was he? What did he teach? What did he do?

I write for all who are interested in knowing the Jesus of history. He did exist. He was known as Jesus of Nazareth (*Yeshua ha Notzri* in Hebrew). He lived, preached, did miracles, and died on a cross 2000 years ago. Multiple non-biblical writers attest to this fact of history. Jewish sources not sympathetic to Jesus mention him, as in Josephus (AD 37–101) and the Talmud (250–500). Greco-Roman historians mention Jesus, such as Thallus (AD 52), Mara Bar-Serapion (70), Tacitus (116), Pliny the Younger (61-113), Phlegon (80-140), and Suetonius (69-140). See Robert van Voorst (2000), *Jesus Outside the New Testament,* for every early non-biblical reference to Jesus.

This is my attempt to summarize, in an accessible way, the vast research on the historical Jesus. I do not debate with scholars as such, but present generally accepted conclusions to construct Jesus' story. I write for the 'lay person', for all who want to know Jesus, while doing justice to the scholarship behind my portrait of Jesus.

MY JOURNEY

The seed was first planted when I became a follower of Jesus on 7 June

1968. My journey to get to know Jesus had begun. A decade later I was introduced to what is called 'Kingdom theology' in my academic studies. G.E. Ladd's books were prescribed, *The Presence of the Future* and *A Theology of the New Testament*, both published in 1974. See my bibliography of references for the full details of authors and books that I refer to. Kingdom of God simply means God's rule, present and active in Jesus' life and ministry. Kingdom theology is about the mission, message, and ministry of Jesus, which was the Kingdom of God, with its background understanding in the Old Testament (OT). Discovering 'The Kingdom' was like being born again, again!

But Kingdom theology led me, another decade later, to what has been called 'the quest for the historical Jesus'. Now simply known as 'Jesus Research', it places Jesus in his middle eastern Jewish context in the early 1st century (AD). This is undertaken through historical research to discover and know Jesus for who he *was* as a human being in his time, as far as that is possible. When I began to read historical Jesus studies, it was nothing short of revolutionary.

So, I became a follower of Jesus in 1968, began exploring the theology of the Kingdom of God in 1978, and then I met the King in a new way, as if for the first time, in 1988. I began to see the remarkable young man, the 30-year-old rabbi (teacher) from Nazareth; the one behind the mission and message of God's Kingdom, which he believed he was inaugurating in fulfilment of the Hebrew scriptures.

I realized that historical Jesus studies came first. It was the driver behind the recovery of Kingdom theology. The clearer we see and know Jesus for who he was in his context, the more accurately we understand what he stood for, what his aims were, and what his Kingdom mission was. The more we grapple with Kingdom theology, the more we want to know the historical Jesus. Jesus Research has impacted me enormously. I fell in love with Jesus all over again, more passionately than before, with a deep desire to become like him.

As with all portraiture, this is not an exact science. A portrait is not a photograph. It's a representation of the person, capturing not only the unique look, but the feel, spirit, and ethos of the person. Hopefully this will be as accurate as possible. Painting a word portrait of Jesus 2000 years after he lived is a serious challenge. It raises all sorts of issues between the 'then' of who Jesus was in his context and the 'now' of our context and lenses of interpretation.

However, my 'take' on Jesus is a reconstruction of the historical record of Jesus in his context, drawn from historians and biblical scholars who work with primary sources – historical documents from the time of Jesus. This includes the biblical gospels. The period in question is called Second Temple Judaism, from Israel's restoration out of exile, about 450 BC, to the destruction of Jerusalem and the Temple in AD 70. Post AD 70 is known as Rabbinical Judaism.

Books about the historical Jesus that do not work directly with primary sources are secondary sources. My bibliography lists scholars who work with both primary and secondary sources – books that I have learnt from over the years. My portrait of Jesus works with the findings of historical studies and merges into biblical theology, which cannot, in practice, be kept separate in different fields of study.

THE TWO QUESTIONS

Firstly, *who was Jesus?* The real Jesus – as far as we moderns can know him in his historical context, through studying history.

The second logically follows: *who is the Jesus we preach?* Another way of asking the question, what is *the gospel* we preach? 'Gospel' (Greek *evangel*) means 'the good news'. It was a technical term used for the Roman Caesars, to proclaim their life and deeds throughout the empire. The apostles adopted it for Jesus and filled it with their own messianic meaning. It meant the good news of God's coming as King – in the birth, ministry, death, and resurrection of Jesus – to save the world from sin and evil. Specifically, to wholistically save all who believe and receive Jesus as King, by giving full allegiance to him.

These two questions are huge, having serious implications. The Jesus we preach reveals the Jesus we see and believe – a Jesus we *unconsciously* accept and pass on. Or a Jesus we *consciously* examine, understand, agree to, and then pass on. There are many *different* Jesus' being proclaimed in our world. For many Christians, let alone people who don't know Jesus (who see Christianity as 'the Church'), it is a babbling confusion – the Tower of Babel all over again. Except that it's Christians who are speaking in different tongues. Not the languages of God's Spirit given at Pentecost to redeem the nations, imparted by the biblical Jesus, but of another spirit that preaches a different Jesus – which confuses, divides, and scatters people.

Paul had a similar challenge in his day, not long after Jesus' death and resurrection that occurred in AD 30/31. He wrote to the Galatians in about AD 48, challenging them not to receive or believe "a different gospel" (the italics in the following quote are mine).

> "You are turning to *a different gospel* – which is really no gospel at all. Evidently some people are throwing you into confusion and are trying to pervert the gospel of Christ. But even if we, or an angel from heaven, should preach a gospel other than the one we preached to you, let them be under God's curse! As we have already said, so now I say again: *If anybody is preaching to you a gospel other than what you accepted, let them be under God's curse!* I want you to know that *the gospel* I preached is not of human origin. I did not receive it from any man, nor was I taught it; rather, I received it by revelation from Jesus Christ" (Galatians 1:6-9, 11-12).

Preaching another gospel, other than the one that Paul received by revelation from Jesus Christ, is to preach another Jesus – not the Jesus that the apostles personally knew and proclaimed. Paul received "*the* gospel", not "*a* gospel", by revelation of/from Jesus himself (Galatians 1:15-16). He then submitted it to the apostles (2:2), who had lived and worked with Jesus in his 3½ year ministry. Paul's gospel (revelation) checked out with the apostles, who blessed him to preach it. This matter of "the gospel" or "another gospel" is so important that Paul repeats: *let those who preach another gospel – essentially, a false Jesus – be under God's curse!* Serious stuff indeed!

A few years later Paul wrote to the Corinthian followers of Jesus (again, my italics),

> "I am afraid… your minds may be led astray from your sincere and pure devotion to Christ. For if someone comes to you and preaches *a Jesus* other than *the Jesus* we preached, or if you receive *a different spirit* from the one you received, or *a different gospel* from the one you accepted, you easily put up with it" (2 Corinthians 11:3-4).

The (particular) gospel you hear is the (particular) Jesus you will see and believe. And that is the (particular) spirit you receive. Either God's Spirit, given by "*the* Jesus" Paul preached, or another spirit, a deceiving spirit. The responsibility and judgement fall on the preacher: the (kind of) gospel you preach is the (kind of) Jesus you see and believe, is the (kind of) spirit you impart. The Spirit of Jesus, or what spirit?

Therefore, let me pose the key questions again, *who is Jesus*? How can we see and know him for who he really was – and is? What is the *true (biblical) gospel*? Who or what is the *true Spirit* that is given by the *true (biblical) Jesus*?

As Derek Morphew, in *The Kingdom Reformation*, says,

> "The way Christians see Jesus determines the way they see God, salvation, the Christian life, mission and society. Therefore, any major rediscovery of Jesus and the kingdom has huge consequences. It becomes the unifying story of the whole of scripture, which if believed and received becomes the controlling narrative that shapes our entire worldview, giving meaning to all of reality and the whole of life" (2020:15).

The implication is that *any meaningful rediscovery of Jesus means we must review everything.*

THE PURPOSE AND THE PORTRAIT

My fivefold purpose is to:

1. Introduce 'The Historical Jesus' studies and research.
2. To rediscover the real Jesus and thus review everything.
3. By presenting a life-portrait of Jesus – the body of the book.
4. To fall in love with *Yeshua ha Notzri*, Jesus the Nazarene – the heart motivation of the portrait.
5. Thus, to apprentice (meaning of 'disciple') our lives to Jesus and his Kingdom, for Christlikeness and mission – the intended outcome.

The opening chapter, my introduction to the historical Jesus is the longest and most technical chapter. The reader can skip this chapter if you want to go directly to the portrait itself. However, I consider the introduction essential grounding to appreciate the life of Jesus. Here I introduce our story as Vineyard churches and The Story of Jesus and the Kingdom; the background context to the historical Jesus; the nature of historical knowledge; the historical period and timelines; and the approach, method and interpretation in Jesus Research.

I also list the source materials and introduce key scholars; examine the above radical claim by Morphew and others; and cite some important implications for theology, church, and mission. The content of my introduction can, and has, filled many scholarly books. Mine is a high-level overview and summary.

Then I present a life portrait of *Yeshua ha Notzri*, the most inspiring human being in my view. This is a (new) vision of Jesus as a man, a Jewish rabbi, a prophet, the long-awaited Messiah.

The first book on the historical Jesus that I read was Marcus Borg (1987), *Jesus, A New Vision.* My journey had begun. N.T. Wright was a major influence, in both his academic and popular level writing – the latter, for example, (2000), *The Challenge of Jesus.* Gerald O'Collins SJ (2008), *Jesus: A Portrait,* was truly inspiring. He framed his portrait as the beauty of Jesus in his person, life, and work. "Your eyes will see the King in his beauty... the Branch of the LORD will be beautiful and glorious" (Isaiah 33:17, 4:2). My eyes were further opened, my mind enlightened, my heart impassioned with love for Jesus, and my will made resolute to become more like him. For a scholarly overview of historical Jesus studies, I recommend Dunn and McKnight (eds. 2005), *The Historical Jesus in Recent Research.*

Jesus was truly the most remarkable, intelligent, spiritual, and beautiful person who ever lived. His presence graced planet Earth without parallel, as *the* decisive turning point in human history.

Here are the broad strokes of my portrait of the historical Jesus:

1. *Conception & Formation*: We begin Jesus' life story with his (controversial) conception before his parent's marriage. Then his birth, upbringing, and his thirty 'hidden' years of psycho-spiritual formation in the little town of Nazareth.

2. *Calling & Confirmation*: Jesus left Nazareth around thirty years old, and went to his older cousin, John the baptizer. He learnt from John in the wilderness, near the Jordan River. Then was baptized in water as his act of obedience to God. We look at the symbolism and meaning of what happened as the confirmation and empowering of Jesus' deep sense of calling and destiny.

3. *Confrontation & Consolation*: The Spirit then drove him into the desert to fast and pray. We look at his confrontation with evil, focused in three core temptations, and how Jesus overcame them as a model for all who follow him.

4. *Mission & Message*: What were Jesus' aims and goals, his sense of mission? What was his essential message, and why? In other words, what was Jesus' underlying *worldview*? Worldview is the deepest level of human consciousness, the assumptions and ideas that determine how we see reality. How did he reinterpret the prevailing Jewish worldview of his day? We look particularly at Mark and Luke's accounts of how Jesus understood and presented himself in terms of his Kingdom of God mission and message.

5. *Context & Community:* We look at the socio-political-religious context and the heightened Jewish messianic expectation of his day. What were the responses of religious-political groups within Judaism, and Jews in general, to the crisis of oppressive Roman occupation? Where did Jesus place himself – his Kingdom mission and community – in response to the issues of the day?

6. *Ministry & Miracles:* Here we look at Jesus' ministry of enacting God's rule and reign through 'signs and wonders'. What were the symbolism and meaning of his dramatic ministry of demonic expulsions, healings, and miracles? I overview how each gospel writer frames and records Jesus' ministry and miracles.

7. *Mystery & Parables:* This chapter explains what Jesus meant by 'the mystery' of the Kingdom of God. He specifically taught the mystery (the revealed nature) of the Kingdom through stories and parables. How do we interpret them? What do they teach us?

8. *Law & Love:* What was rabbi Jesus' relationship with The Law (Torah)? How did he understand and interpret Torah with reference to the issues of his day in his public exchanges with the Pharisees and other groups? What was Jesus' interpretative key to "The Law and the Prophets" (the Hebrew scriptures)? What did Jesus mean by his ethics of *love*, seen in his radical lived example?

9. *Suffering & Crucifixion:* The rabbi-prophet's revolution of God's Kingdom of Love brought down 'the powers' on him, the political-religious opposition and the evil behind them. The growing opposition led to Jesus' suffering and death. We look at the story from Mark's view – the earliest gospel – integrating information from the other gospels. How did Jesus understand his death? Why, and how, did it happen? What did it mean?

10. *Resurrection & Ascension:* These events are omitted in most historical Jesus studies due to the absence of concrete historical evidence. It is viewed as beyond historical enquiry – a matter of faith. However, some scholars like N.T. Wright (2003), in *The Resurrection of the Son of God,* address it, arguing from historical probability. In this closing chapter, we look at eyewitness gospel accounts of Jesus' bodily resurrection and his ascension into heaven. What is the meaning and significance of these dramatic events? We conclude with some comments on Jesus' nature as human *and* divine, and the gospel we preach.

TO TAKE NOTE OF...

In quoting biblical texts, I use the NIV unless otherwise stated, such as the NRSV, ESV, and even the KJV. See the list of abbreviations.

When quoting OT texts, I use "LORD" (caps in the NIV) for God's personal name – Hebrew *Yhwh* – meaning "I AM" (Exodus 3:14). This is to differentiate from "Lord" (lower case) in Hebrew *Adonai* and in Greek *Kyrios*. I follow the practice of the respected Jewish Professor, Benjamin Sommer (2009, *The Bodies of God and the World of Ancient Israel*), by using *Yhwh* in relation to Israel, when contextually needed.

Similarly, I capitalise King and Kingdom for God and Jesus in contrast with all other kings and kingdoms (unless it is titular).

And I use *italics* for a) emphasis of particular words or sentences, b) for non-English words, and c) for book titles and articles.

My preferred dating is BC (Before Christ) and AD (*Anno Domini*, After Christ), rather than BCE (Before Common Era) and CE (Common Era). The book is about Christ, the turning point of history.

Also, I have omitted footnotes for easier reading, citing a source in brackets in the text only when necessary – the author's name, year of publication, and page number(s) if needed. The title and details of the publication are found in my bibliography.

Each human discipline has its own jargon. Avoiding technical terms in this field of study is impossible. So, when I first use a technical word or phrase, I give an explanation as to its meaning.

Deep gratitude to my wife, Gilli, Quinton Howitt, Derek Morphew, and Robin Snelgar, for their careful reading, editing, and helpful comments and suggestions on this text.

My challenge to the reader is to stay with me and develop a frame of reference conversant with the historical Jesus and biblical theology. Whilst at the same time, imbibing the spirit and heart of the book: seeing Jesus more clearly for who he was – and is – he is alive!

In keeping with the desired outcome, intentional apprenticeship to Jesus, each chapter ends with a few questions for personal reflection and group discussion. *This book, therefore, can be used as a twelve-week program for small groups.* Each person reads the same chapter during the week. The questions then guide the reflections, feedback, personal sharing, and discussion, when the group meets.

May the eyes of your heart be enlightened to see Jesus as you've never seen him before. Indeed, may the fiery passion of God's love burn in your heart as you get to know the real Jesus!

Alexander F Venter

INTRODUCTION

CAN WE KNOW THE REAL JESUS?

Most of us were raised with a picture of Jesus in our minds. From the earliest sketches and paintings of Jesus that spread from Europe, the world generally sees him as a white, western, blue-eyed Jesus! That image of Jesus, in what it represents in the global subconscious mind, has been the cause of untold pain and suffering.

So, when I teach my 'Get to Know the Real Jesus' course, I start with a graphic image of a scientifically reconstructed face from a skull uncovered in modern Israel that dates back to the 1st century. In all historical probability Jesus would have looked something like *that* man, with thick black hair and beard, dark brown eyes and skin. A ruddy Middle Eastern Semite. It shocks and shifts the mind to, hopefully, begin rehabilitating how we see Jesus.

But, as Paul says in 2 Corinthians 5:16, it's not about knowing Jesus for how he looked, for his physical attributes, for his ethnicity. We need to know his person and character for he was (and is).

So, can we know *the real* Jesus? In the sense of knowing *the actual* Jesus who announced God's Kingdom in AD 27-30? We cannot go back to relive those years with Jesus and get to know him in that real sense. This may sound like it contradicts the title of the book. Yes and no. We cannot know *the real* Jesus as just described, but also because the Jesus of history is a construct by scholars as they apply the historical-critical method of study to primary sources. However, we can incrementally know the real Jesus through historical studies *and* faith.

We learn *about* Jesus, the Jesus of history, by reconstructing him in his historical context. That means we can know him up to a point of *probability*, because, while some things are certain in history, most range from reasonable probability to definite improbability. My point is: the more we know *about* Jesus, the more we want to know the real Jesus as much as that is possible through historical study *and* by putting our faith in him. That is because, as scholars point out, we can *all* know the 'Christ of faith' – the phrase that is used to indicate the Risen Lord. Jesus is alive! By putting our faith in Christ, we enter a relationship of knowing Jesus Christ by his indwelling Holy Spirit.

Therefore, there is a reciprocal effect: knowing Christ *by faith* feeds our desire to know *about* Jesus through history. And the more we know *about* the historical Jesus, the more it deepens *our faith* in knowing Christ through personal relationship by his indwelling Spirit. *Both* bring us progressively closer to knowing *the real* Jesus, to being true disciples. And yet we will only know him ultimately for who he really is, and was on earth, when we see him face to face.

Hence N.T. Wright writes,

> "The historical quest for Jesus is a necessary and non-negotiable aspect *of Christian discipleship*, and that we in our generation have a chance to be renewed in discipleship and mission precisely by means of this quest" (2000:2, my italics).

'Quest' refers to the series of historical investigations into the Jesus of history (discussed later). 'Jesus of Nazareth', *Yeshua ha Notzri*, is used in historical studies for the human Jesus, the Jewish rabbi-prophet who proclaimed God's Kingdom. 'Christ' is not Jesus' name (surname), but his claim to be King. Christ (Greek *Kristos*, Hebrew *Meshiach*) is used to indicate the Risen Lord: Jesus vindicated as 'the Christ' (Messiah-King) *by his resurrection from the dead*. Jesus claimed to be King during his ministry. Some followers believed he was, but fully understood it *after* his resurrection. They then concluded what they had glimpsed while with him, that he was a divine-human being – ultimately, God incarnate. I discuss this in the last chapter.

Therefore, the interactive process of knowing Christ by faith *and* knowing about Jesus in history is a journey of Christian discipleship. We progressively get to know Jesus for who he really was and is. That leads to worship and love. We fall in love with Jesus and know him by love. Hence, we purposefully apprentice ourselves to become like him. And *that* decides everything in our life.

Father Pedro Arrupe SJ said (I've added 'with Jesus' in brackets),

> *"Nothing is more practical than finding God, that is, than falling in*

love in a quite absolute, final way. What or who you are in love with, what seizes your imagination, will affect everything. It will decide what will get you out of bed in the morning, what you will do with your evenings, how you will spend your weekends, what you read, who you know, what breaks your heart, and what amazes you with joy and gratitude. Fall in love (with Jesus), stay in love (with Jesus), and it will decide everything."
(www.azquotes.com/author/32496-Pedro_Arrupe).

SEEING THE JESUS OF THE GOSPELS

There is, obviously, the danger of projecting onto Jesus what we want to see. We can make him in our own image. So, we must be aware of the 'lenses' through which we see, acknowledging our own modern, cultural, contextual conditioning in our study of Jesus.

However, a significant theological shift has occurred in how we see Jesus since the post-WWII quest for the historical Jesus. For centuries Jesus has been seen via the lenses of Paul and his doctrine of Christ (Christology) in his NT letters. Though it predated the Reformation in Europe, this way of seeing Jesus was a primary effect of Lutheran and Reformed theology. They focussed on Paul's emphasis on justification by faith through the grace of Christ's death and resurrection – saved by grace alone. The result was a focus on Jesus as the divine Son of God. And the gospels were seen as stories (not real theology) for sermons to teach moral lessons, so-called 'homilies'. They were not seen as historical documents telling us about the human Jesus of Nazareth who lived and taught real 'theology'!

A radical reversal has taken place. Jesus Research and Kingdom theology has prioritised seeing Jesus through the gospels, and then to interpret Paul through *those* lenses. The historical Jesus precedes the historical Paul. Though Paul was a primary interpreter of Jesus – consistent with Jesus' Kingdom worldview and practice – it is first Jesus, then Paul, not the other way round!

This is a fundamental shift from our dominant subconscious view of Jesus as (first) divine, God incarnate. We now (first) see Jesus in his humanity. From the gospel accounts, he was, first and foremost, a human being doing all that he did by faith in God, like you and me.

Jesus believed God was his Father, that he was born to fulfil the

Hebrew scriptures, the Jewish expectation of the coming Kingdom of God. He was empowered by God's Spirit as a human being to do what God called him to do. The Jewish idea of 'Son of God' as the Messiah is not about divinity *per se*; it's a person anointed by God's Spirit, like the OT kings and prophets, to bring God's Kingdom.

Thus, Luke records how Jesus, in his first synagogue teaching, read from Isaiah's scroll (Isaiah 61:1-2 cf. Luke 4:18),

> "The Spirit of the Lord is on me, because he has anointed me to proclaim good news to the poor. He has sent me to proclaim freedom for the prisoners and recovery of sight for the blind, to set the oppressed free, to proclaim the year of the Lord's favour".

He applied this to himself, saying, "Today this scripture is fulfilled in your hearing" (4:21). The hearers' response was, "Is this not Joseph's son?" (4:22). Jesus' sense of self was clearly that of a man under the Spirit's anointing announcing and enacting the promised Kingdom. This is evident in Luke's summary of Jesus' life in the words of Peter to the first Gentiles who heard the gospel:

> "You know what has happened throughout the province of Judea, beginning in Galilee after the baptism that John preached – how God anointed Jesus of Nazareth with the Holy Spirit and power, and how he went around doing good and healing all who were under the power of the devil, because God was with him" (Acts 10:37-38).

Note the statements "anointed *Jesus of Nazareth*... God was with *him*." To emphasise Jesus' humanity is not to deny his divinity. The apostles, and later the early creeds, clearly understood and concluded (after his resurrection) that Jesus was both human and divine – having two natures in one person – without confusion. Jesus did not do miracles from his divinity as God incarnate, but by faith in God as a human being through the Spirit's power (as above). In this sense Jesus is a model for us to follow and emulate. He is the ultimate human being as God intended for all humans: imaging God by his empowering Spirit.

Pope Benedict XVI (Ratzinger 2007:3-8) makes the point, however, that the historical Jesus *does* reveal who God is. By seeking to know the historical Jesus we are actually "seeking God's face", just as Moses asked to see God's face (he only saw God's back, Exodus 33:20-23).

However, *in Jesus, God's face is revealed* (John 1:18, 14:9). We start with Jesus, and study him to come to our meaning of 'God'. We don't start with studying the meaning of 'God' and then try to fit Jesus with that meaning, as the Reformers did, as systematic theology does. We see the Father's face in the human Jesus. We see in him the ultimate beauty that irresistibly draws us to fall in love with God in an absolute, final way. In fact, we cannot make real/ultimate sense of the evidence of the historical Jesus of the gospels without assuming Jesus' divine sonship. Short of that, we would have to conclude that Jesus was a blasphemer, or an imposter, or joker, or psychotic (insane).

OUR STORY – VINEYARD AND EMPOWERED EVANGELICALS

I have been a Vineyard church pastor since 1982, after working with John Wimber in Yorba Linda Vineyard. Thus, I am a part of *our* story as the Vineyard Churches, founded by Wimber on the rediscovery of *The* Story – Kingdom theology as articulated by G.E. Ladd (1959, 1974). Ladd taught in the American Evangelical context the theology of the Kingdom that European scholars had pioneered, e.g., Cullmann (1952) and Kummel (1961). He also drew on Kallas (1961, 1966, 1968), a American Lutheran scholar who taught Kingdom theology.

Let me summarise this theology: *The* Story of the Kingdom. The *italicised* words/phrases are key. Kingdom theology is *'eschatology'*, the study of 'The End', or end-times. 'Kingdom of God' means the 'rule and reign of God' that confronts and defeats the rule and reign of evil. The *distinctive element* that these scholars recovered and highlighted was "the *mystery* of the Kingdom" (Matthew 13:11) that Jesus taught and lived. That is, God's *future rule* was inaugurated in Jesus' ministry (called the 'already' of the Kingdom), but *without putting an end to this present evil age* (called the 'not yet' of the Kingdom). Jesus will come again at the end of this age to establish God's Kingdom on earth in fullness and finality. This creates an *'eschatological tension'* in which we find ourselves. We live in the *end-time tension* of the 'already' *and* 'not yet' of God's Kingdom come, and yet to come, in Jesus.

Wimber was called to do church from this theological paradigm, upholding the tension of the Kingdom, in contrast to other theological frameworks that determine how leaders do church. His passion was to practice the Kingdom in and through the local church: the words, works, and wonders of the Kingdom, as he called it. Thus, the mission, message, and ministry of Jesus became his practical theology of church, leadership, healing, and mission. I've had the privilege of writing a series of "Doing" textbooks (see bibliography of references), each from a Kingdom theological paradigm and praxis (practice).

Vineyard was birthed in its mission of church renewal and church planting by *The* Story of the Kingdom. We identify as 'empowered evangelical', meaning a Kingdom theology and praxis of Spirit-power; in contrast to 'Pentecostal' and 'Charismatic', with a Restorationist theology and praxis of Spirit-power (explained later).

Wimber was also clear on what Jesus taught as the relationship between the new wine (the Kingdom-Spirit) and the wineskin (the church-form). The wineskin is the flexible form that takes the shape of the dynamic fermenting wine. The church exists to facilitate the unhindered flow of the new wine of the Kingdom. Thus, the Kingdom defines the church, not the other way around. Our priority is to "seek first the Kingdom", to pray "your Kingdom come, your will be done" (Matthew 6:10,33). Jesus' priority is to build his church: "*I* will build *my* church" (Matthew 16:18-19). If we seek the King and the Kingdom, then Jesus builds his church as the instrument of his Kingdom, against which "the gates of hell will not prevail".

However, when our focus and pursuit is to build the church, we lose sight of the Kingdom. Then the church becomes our kingdom over which we rule. And we build it in *our* image and likeness. God forbid! We worship the King, not our church (the Vineyard). While we respect the integrity of our wineskin (our philosophy of ministry, way of doing church), our focus and pursuit must be the King and his Kingdom.

So, where are Vineyard churches and other empowered evangelicals regarding The Story of the King and the Kingdom?

THE STORY – THE KINGDOM AND WORLDVIEW

Some have dropped out of The Story, adopting instead one or other competing theological framework for doing church and ministry. Others have settled into quiet resignation, passively accepting things as they are, a 'Kingdom not yet' kind of fatalism and defeatism. While others act as if it's all complete in the finished work of Christ on the cross, practicing a 'Kingdom now' presumption and triumphalism.

Rather, we must continue to push into the Kingdom by pursuing the *updated* story that Jesus Research is discovering. It will inform, challenge, and empower us to stay on the Kingdom-in-tension edge, "the mystery" Jesus lived and taught. Kingdom theology has developed and moved on from the foundation of Wimber, Ladd, Kummel and Cullmann. Scholars are uncovering a fuller vision of Jesus that further motivates and informs the praxis of the Kingdom with a deeper conviction and wiser application.

The unfolding story of the King and the Kingdom through Jesus Research challenges competing theological paradigms and the latest popular teachings. These underlying frameworks govern the different ways in which leaders and people do life, church, and ministry. At the deepest level of human consciousness, it's about worldview: a clash of worldviews and spirit wars. The Story is actually about the recovery of *Jesus'* (Jewish-Messianic) *worldview,* explained in the chapter, Mission & Message. Wright (1992, 1996) frames his entire historical Jesus study in terms of worldview.

- *Worldview* is our view of the world; the assumptions (ideas) that are the 'lenses' through which we see reality; unconsciously formed and passed on by our cultural conditioning – unless we consciously examine it for a genuine 'worldview shift'.

- *Paradigm* is a subset of worldview. We receive and develop, in our worldview, cohesive frames of reference to make sense of the dimensions of reality in life; e.g., theological frameworks, political paradigms, economic, social, marriage, and so on.

- *Models* are subsets of paradigms. Within a given (theological) framework we develop models (e.g., of doing church), to make our beliefs and values workable – functionally meaningful.

- *Practices* derive from, and give visible functionality to, our models. Practices are *what* we do, and *how* we do it.

People and leaders commonly operate at the level of models and practices. They see a model 'that works', then adopt and implement it by doing its practices. What you see dominates. Models rule. It is the pragmatism of 'copy & paste', 'do what works', without any serious reflection on the package of values and beliefs (the underlying paradigm) with which it comes. This is without mentioning worldview considerations. No model comes value-free! By doing its praxis for the desired outcome ('success'), we take in 'mixed seed', conflicting values, and even wrong beliefs. And when 'it doesn't work', the Lord apparently leads us to something 'new' in the Kingdom!

Note: we can work from practices back to theology, called practical theology. What we do and how we do it, and the fruit it produces, reveals the underlying beliefs we consciously or unconsciously hold. We then examine our beliefs/framework and adjust it to a biblical theology of the Kingdom. We, accordingly, change the practices, and the model, in keeping with authentic Kingdom belief and expression.

Also note: the use of 'Kingdom language', now common among church leaders and people, must be discerned. What they mean by their use of 'Kingdom of God' often differs from what historical Jesus studies and biblical theology of the Kingdom teach. They have never read Ladd or any historical Jesus studies, but conveniently dress up their existing unchanged theological paradigm (and worldview) in Kingdom language, because 'the Kingdom' is now all the rage, 'the new thing' God is doing. By hearing 'Kingdom language', multitudes of undiscerning listeners can imbibe 'mixed seed', even a different Jesus, a different gospel, and a different spirit.

Leaders worthy of follower-ship consciously examine and shift their *worldview* in light of the historical Jesus; accordingly work out the biblical-theological *paradigm* of God's Kingdom; then develop *models* that adequately express it; and implement *practices* consistent with *the* Kingdom for integrity of witness to *the* King. As Paul said, "Follow/imitate me as I follow/imitate Christ" (1 Corinthians 11:1).

THE STORY – QUESTS FOR THE HISTORICAL JESUS

There have been three 'quests' to research Jesus via critical historical methods of study. My overview below lists key scholars associated with each quest. Allen (1999) and Morphew (2020) discuss them in detail. These quests have recovered the Kingdom worldview and theology of Jesus. Most scholars now agree that Jesus was a Jewish *apocalyptic* prophet preaching an *eschatological* message of God's Kingdom. *Apocalyptic* is the 'unveiling' of heavenly secrets, a 'revelation' of the (final) defeat of evil. *Eschatology* is the study of 'the end' or 'end times' (Greek *eschaton*) when God ushers in the new age of his Kingdom through his Messiah.

The First (old) Quest (1800–1906)

Hermann Samuel Reimarus (1694–1768) was the first to challenge the accepted Christian doctrine of Jesus *in the name of history*. In his *Fragments* (1778), Reimarus examined who Jesus was and what he accomplished. David Friedrich Strauss (1835) brought Jesus into line with 'modernism', the philosophy of rationalism of the Enlightenment period (1686–1815), which dismissed Jesus' miracles as mere myths.

Then Ernst Troeltsch (1865–1923) and Francis Herbert Bradley (1864–1924) proposed various critical principles for the method of historical investigation. William Wrede (1902) argued that the gospels were theologically motivated fiction that reflected the early church's concerns, and therefore, we know little about Jesus.

But Albert Schweitzer's book (1906), *The Quest for the Historical Jesus,* demolished the first quest with their 'liberal Protestant Jesus'. He warned scholars not to make Jesus in their own image. Schweitzer was the first to place Jesus in the context of apocalyptic Judaism – the stream of Judaism that expected the cataclysmic fulfilment of end-time prophecies. He showed a development *from* the apocalyptic Jesus, *through* the first apostles, *to* the gospels.

The reaction to the failed critical history of the first quest was an escape into personal faith for subjective revelation of Jesus, as in Martin Kahler (1892). His 'escape' distinguished between reason ('scientific history' that does not know Jesus) and experience ('salvation history' that knows Jesus). But, to say we can only know the Christ of faith, not the Jesus of history, is a false dualism. Many Evangelicals, Pentecostals, and Charismatics hold this dualism. This so-called escape reached a dead end in Rudolf Bultmann's (1961) 'existentialism', meaning that we know Jesus existed, but not much more, so our faith is based on the early church's faith. Thus, meaning exists in the realm of faith, not in the realm of historical facts, i.e., our existential experiences give us meaning and purpose – including knowing Jesus. This escape was the 'lull' from Schweitzer to the start of the second quest.

The Second (new) Quest (1953 – 1980)

The second quest is associated with Ernst Kasemann (1964), Gunther Bornkamm (1960) and James Robinson (1959).

They saw the 'escape' from history with its dualism as a form of Docetism – the belief that Jesus appeared as a spiritual being and not an enfleshed person. They tried to bridge the gap between the historical Jesus and the Christ of faith by saying that the gospels were not historical biographies but authoritative proclamations (*kerygma*) of Jesus by the early church, i.e., expressions of *their* faith.

This view still included Bultmann's existentialist understanding of Jesus. Therefore, although they made helpful contributions to the principles of historical investigation, they adopted the first quest modernist assumptions without serious review.

The Third Quest (1980 and ongoing)

The third quest has also become known as 'Jesus Research'. Two different schools of scholars developed: the *Jesus Seminar* and the *Third Quest*. There is a third group that must be mentioned, *Jewish-Christian dialogue* scholars, whose research is used by the Jesus Seminar and Third Quest schools. One can picture three circles, each overlapping the others, reflecting rigorous dialogue and learning between these three groups of scholars.

The Jesus Seminar

Robert Funk (1996, 1993, 1998) founded the Jesus Seminar. He correctly called it 'the renewed quest', as it built on the previous quests using the same modernist assumptions. Modernism – the philosophic worldview of Enlightenment rationalism – claimed 'scientific historical knowledge' to be 'objective'. That proved to be naïve, because of its theory of knowledge (*epistemology*), discussed below. Epistemology is about how we know reality, truth, and history.

The Jesus Seminar ceased its formal functioning after the death of its founder in 2005. But the following scholars continue the work: Helmut Koester (1990), Dominic Crossan (1991), J.S. Kloppenborg (1994), Burton Mack (1995), and Marcus Borg (1987, 1994).

They threw the net of sources and criteria of interpretation wide beyond the biblical gospels. Of particular use was 'Q' (German *Quelle*, 'source', meaning the sayings of Jesus common to Matthew and Luke not found in Mark's gospel). They also used the *Gospel of Thomas*, and other such Gnostic texts from the Nag Hammadi texts discovered in

1945 (discussed below). Their selection and (re)dating of source materials, using selective historical criteria, created a system of evaluation that they applied to the biblical gospels. Their research ends up stripping Jesus of 80% of what he said, attributing most of it to the early church, or other sources (Funk 1998).

The result was a Jesus who fits well into late 20th century Western culture. Morphew says this Jesus was "a truly liberal, politically correct, likeable fellow, who is not at all strange to us (remember Schweitzer's warning), and most of all speaks in ways that neo-Gnostics would approve of" (2020:221).

Third Quest

The 'third quest' is a term coined by N.T. Wright (1996) to indicate a research tradition, within Jesus Research, that was different to the Jesus Seminar, in terms of worldview and epistemic assumptions (i.e., how we know things). See Borg & Wright (2000), where a neo-liberal scholar (Borg) and a more conservative scholar (Wright) debate the historical Jesus: two different visions of Jesus based on two different methodologies. In fact, a respected feature of third quest scholars is the attention given to presuppositions and methodology – there are whole volumes on this – due to the failed assumptions and methods of the first and second quests.

Some key scholars, among others, associated with the third quest are Ben Meyer (1979), J.P. Meier (1991 to 2016), N.T. Wright (1992, 1996), Graham Twelftree (1999), James Dunn (2003, 2005), Craig Keener (2009), and Derek Morphew (2020).

These scholars include source material from beyond the biblical gospels, considering all documents written in the Second Temple period (538 BC to AD 70). The main difference is that they take the biblical gospels as reliable sources for seeing the historical Jesus (historical biographies), not merely early church beliefs about Jesus.

The issue of the historical reliability of the gospels is extensively debated in Bauckham (2006), Keener (2019), and Dunn (2003). But the point is that third quest scholars place Jesus in the historical context of Second Temple Judaism and see an apocalyptic Jesus who proclaimed, enacted, and inaugurated the eschatological Kingdom of God, and led a Kingdom movement as Israel's Prophet-Messiah.

Jewish-Christian dialogue scholars

A third group of scholars emerged from the post-WWII Jewish-Christian dialogue, which arose after the holocaust. Their focus has been research into the Jewish-Palestine context of Second Temple Judaism, rather than a reconstruction of the historical Jesus *per se*. Some lean toward the Jesus Seminar and some toward the third quest. However, their research in primary sources has been indispensable for both schools.

Key scholars in the Jewish-Christian dialogue are Geza Vermes (1973), Martin Hengel (1968), Jacob Neusner (1984, 2000), E.P. Sanders (1985, 1993), James Charlesworth (1988, 1991, 2006), Bruce Chilton (1984, 2000), Sean Freyne (2004), and David Flusser (2007).

PIVOT POINT – FOUR POST-WWII FACTORS

Jesus Research, as a broad category for the above three groups, came about largely due to four post-WWII factors. Morphew (2020:13) writes that due to the "remarkable confluence of factors that have only emerged in the last 60–80 years, we can now view Jesus and his mission and message with a level of clarity not possible before this era". This particularly accounts for the third quest scholars and the significance of their research.

1. *Post-holocaust Jewish-Christian dialogue:* The contrition in Christian circles that followed the holocaust led to humble dialogue with Jewish scholars. The result was collaborative research into Second Temple Judaism and the birth of Christianity. Leading Jewish scholar, Neusner (1984:11), writes, "We are able to ask these questions because the spirit of our own age permits us to discuss them irenically (peacefully), in ways utterly without precedent in the centuries before our own tragic times."

2. *Discovery and availability of Second Temple literature:* The Dead Sea Scrolls, discovered in 1947, were manuscripts from the Essene community at Qumran, a 'sect' of Judaism that existed at the time of Jesus. They hid their texts in caves before the Romans crushed the Jewish rebellion in AD 70. The Gnostic texts discovered in 1945 in Nag Hammadi (Egypt) are less important. The texts, with

other Second Temple period literature (which includes the Pseudepigrapha, Charlesworth 1983) have been made available to us through translation of the original languages. Like no previous generation since Jesus, our generation now has access to the primary literature required to reconstruct Jesus' times and context. That is unprecedented and highly significant.

3. *The shift in the historical discipline:* The shift in the method of historical study and epistemology (the theory of knowledge). This is the most technical part, discussed below.

4. *Post WWII eschatological synthesis:* Emerging consensus among earlier mentioned scholars (Kallas, Kummel, Cullmann, and Ladd) that the mission, message, and ministry of Jesus is to be understood as 'inaugurated eschatology', i.e., the enactment of God's end-time /future Kingdom in the (first) coming of Jesus. Also called 'realised eschatology', or 'the presence of the future'.

Therefore, *for the first time in nearly 2000 years, we can reconstruct Jesus in his socio-political-economic-religious context, with reasonable probability and some aspects of certainty.* Due to the above four factors, it is only in the last six decades that Jesus has come back into focus as a Jewish eschatological prophet, vindicated as Messiah. He has been seen and preached in every cultural way, other than the apocalyptic Jesus of the gospels. We have come full circle back to *that* Jesus with a clarity unprecedented in the previous 2000 years.

This constitutes nothing less than a theological revolution. More accurately, it constitutes a Kingdom revolution in theology, church, and world. That is, *if* we allow Kingdom theology to transform our paradigms, rather than dress our existing theology in popular Kingdom language. Morphew (2020:564-574) calls this *"A Kingdom Reformation"*. He asks the question: *is this possibly as significant as the Reformation of 16th century Europe?* Or even more so? It has huge implications, which we will explore.

SHIFT IN EPISTEMOLOGY – IN HOW WE KNOW

On 3 above, the post-WWII shift in worldview and human rationality framed third quest scholars' approach to historical studies. See Meyer

(1989), Wright (1992), and Morphew (2020).

Enlightenment rationalism was dominant in 17th–19th century Europe. Its *epistemic* worldview (theory of knowledge) is called positivism: what we see and 'prove' is objectively real and true. It's the drive for certainty, absolute knowledge. Also known as *modernism*, it imposes the 'advanced' European mind on previous eras, assuming a rationality that *naively* claims 'scientific' knowledge of history. The first and second quests, as well as Jesus Seminar scholars, worked with these presuppositions, using them to remove the 'husk' of assumed early church 'myths' (beliefs) from the gospels, to get to the 'kernel' of the 'objective' historical Jesus figure they presented.

The push-back began in the early to mid-1900s, focusing more on the subject (the historian examining texts) than on the object under investigation (the historical texts). What does this mean?

We all have *lenses,* life 'situatedness', underlying paradigms, vested interests, and cultural conditioning, through which we see, know and interpret reality. So, considering these lenses in any historical investigation will save us from naïvely claiming pure objectivity.

This correction to modernism was known as the post-WWII shift to a *postmodern* theory of knowledge that accounts for our lenses and situatedness when interpreting historical texts. However, pushed too far, it *reduces* reality to *my* interpretation or *your* interpretation, to my truth and experience, or to yours. It is another 'ism' whereby the 'absolute objective' of modern*ism* becomes the 'relative subjective' of postmodern*ism*. Consequently, postmodernism claims that we cannot know actual history or reality 'out there' – it's mere interpretation.

This led to a position that rejected the problematic aspects of both modernism *and* postmodernism, while integrating valid aspects in a *critical* engagement with reality – called critical realism.

Both the object beyond us *and* our subjective lenses of 'seeing' are critically examined in a dialogue between the knower (the historian) and what is known (the historical evidence). Wright defines it as "the process of 'knowing' that acknowledges *the reality of the thing known, as something other than the knower* (hence 'realism'), while also fully acknowledging that the only access we have to this reality lies along the spiralling path of *appropriate dialogue or conversation between the knower and the thing known* (hence 'critical')" (1992:35, his italics for emphasis and brackets for explanation).

However, the dialogue is not only between the knower and object of study, but is also external in the sense of public debate among peers. So, critical realism is 'dialogical' learning where knowledge emerges that is *publicly* tested and accountable, as 'qualified knowledge' of reality. It is 'relative objectivity' by critical research and dialogue among peers, to see evidence through other lenses, advancing public knowledge.

This *critical realist* method best represents our human rationality in how we know things, especially in what is called the *human/soft sciences* (history, philosophy, psychology, sociology, etc). The problem was: the modernist method of 'empirical' study in the *natural/hard sciences* (physics, biology, chemistry, geology, etc), which requires verified material proof for exact knowledge, was uncritically assumed and used in the human sciences for 'objective scientific knowledge'. This is based on the assumption that reality is (only) material. That is why *spiritual* experience and knowledge (of God) are dismissed as 'faith' and 'religion', not 'real' or 'verified' knowledge of reality.

Therefore, in terms of studying history, critical realism argues that, depending on the available historical evidence, we *can* know what happened. But not with absolute certainty. While some things are certain (e.g., Jesus did exist), most things are qualified knowledge, as in reasonable probability – either high or low (see Meyer 1994). This is the paradigm of third quest scholars. To summarise:

- Modernist *naïve realism* claims objective knowledge.
- Postmodernist *reduced realism* is subjective knowledge.
- Adjusted postmodern *critical realism* is qualified knowledge.

HISTORICAL METHOD, BIBLICAL THEOLOGY, AUTHORITY

The shifts in epistemic worldview assumptions – from modernism to postmodernism, to critical realism – resulted in a redefinition of the scientific historical method. The method we choose, with the criteria of evaluating what is historically admissible or not admissible, is crucial. It decides the 'sieve' of what we allow through as historically valid, of what, why, and how things happened, to reconstruct the beliefs, aims, and actions of key historical figures.

The Two Elements: Criteria and Method

The *criteria* used to evaluate historical evidence differs from historian to historian – the 'sieve' that allows through what reconstructs the historical Jesus. Meier (1991) – different to Meyer referred to above and again below – Wright (1992), and Morphew (2020), discuss in detail the criteria used in the first, second and third quests. Meier (2001:11-12) summarises five *criteria* that "have proved especially useful", applied by most third quest evangelical scholars.

1. The criteria of *embarrassment*: material that would hardly be invented by the early church, because it would embarrass them, e.g., women travelling with Jesus, learning Torah.

2. The criteria of *discontinuity:* words and deeds of Jesus that cannot be derived from the Judaism(s) of his time or from the early church, e.g., in Mark 12:26-27 Jesus appealed to Exodus 3:6 in favour of the resurrection of the dead, which is discontinuous with both rabbinic and early church reasons for the resurrection.

3. The criteria of *multiple attestation:* words and deeds of Jesus that are witnessed to in more than one literary source, form, or genre, e.g., Jesus' disciple, Simon, was named *Kepha* (Cephas, Rock), attested to in all four gospels, and in Galatians and 1 Corinthians.

4. The criteria of *coherence*: sayings and deeds of Jesus that fit well with the 'database' established by the above criteria, are probably historical; e.g., Jesus' creation of the twelve apostles, symbolising the twelve patriarchs and tribes of Israel, coheres with Jesus' view of himself as the end-time prophet who regathers/renews Israel.

5. The criteria of *Jesus' rejection and execution:* this looks at the larger pattern of Jesus' ministry and asks what words and deeds fit in with and explain his trial and crucifixion, e.g., Jesus' healings and miracles and drawing of large crowds help explain why the authorities considered him a threat and planned to kill him.

The process is to decide what is valid historical evidence as per the above *criteria*, then apply the historical *method* to reconstruct the history, hopefully, with reasonable to high probability. Here is Meyer's (1979:88-92) summary of the historical method:

- History is *knowledge*, not belief: rather than accepting or being the authority, it confers authority on sources and viewpoints.
- Historical knowledge is *inferential*: it arrives at conclusions that are inferred or reached by evidence and reasoning.
- The technique of history is *hypothesis*: proposed explanations on the available evidence, for further investigation.
- Hypotheses require *verification*: proposed explanations are tested by evidence and argumentation to establish truth and accuracy of publicly verified historical knowledge.

Applying the Historical Method

First, decisions are made on the nature and reliability of the historical sources. Non-biblical sources (as listed below) help give historical evidence to reconstruct the context of Second Temple Judaism, where we discover Jesus. *Third questers argue for the reliability of the gospels as primary sources*: eyewitness accounts of 'Jesus remembered' (Dunn 2003). Luke's biography of Jesus is "from the first eyewitnesses…I carefully investigated everything from the beginning …to write an orderly account…that you may be certain of the things you have been taught" (1:1-4). Therefore, in this qualified sense, as Luke states it, the gospels are written in the literature genre of Greco-Roman historical biography, but they are framed in Jewish narrative theology. Keener's (2009, 2019) thorough research and convincing arguments in this regard are an important resource.

By framing historical events with theological meaning, the gospel writers did not change or invent the events they recorded. They *interpreted* their meaning as per their Jewish messianic beliefs. Charlesworth (1991:178) says, "Historical research is scientific by method but not by conclusion; the historian at best can provide us not with certainty but with probability". Thus, Keener argues, "historical *reconstructions* are partial and rest on probability, and cannot be substituted for a community's beliefs" (2009:395). In other words, past events, and community beliefs about them will always overlap. The challenge is how to piece them apart when necessary.

Second, the NT is read, examined, and studied like all Second Temple Judaism literature *as historical documents*, not as inspired authoritative texts (that comes later). Thus, we apply the critical historical method to the study of the Bible, especially the gospels, to reconstruct the context and the ethos, the who and why and how of what happened. This includes integrating historical knowledge from other disciplines, such as archaeology (see Freyne 2004, 2008).

Third, we do exegesis and hermeneutics by examining the meaning of historical texts, especially the gospels, in their original language. Translations give us access to the meaning. Drawing out the meaning (*exegesis*), not reading our meaning into the text (*eisegesis*), involves principles of interpretation (*hermeneutics*). As in, what is the genre of literature? The context? Grammar? Who wrote it? To whom? When? And why? In so doing, we cross from history to theology, from Jesus Research to biblical theology, and thus, into authority and faith.

Fourth, therefore, in examining the Jesus of the gospels, we cross into biblical theology: his mission and message of God's Kingdom. His beliefs, aims, and actions. Some scholars strictly separate historical study and biblical theology into two fields of knowledge. However, in practice, the former precedes and naturally flows into the latter. My portrait of the historical Jesus is at the interface of historical study and biblical theology. Biblical theology raises the question and confirms the inspiration and authority of the Bible. And it also confirms validity of faith in Jesus of Nazareth as the Risen Lord.

Fifth, the biblical theology of Jesus and the Kingdom then becomes *the authoritative lens*, the 'hermeneutic key', through which we read and interpret the NT. We see how Paul does this in his letters. It includes how we read and interpret the OT. Morphew (2020:338-406) has a comprehensive discussion on these five points.

Sixth, all other theological disciplines (beginning with dogmatics or systematic theology), church creeds, and statements of faith, are then re-framed and re-examined by this hermeneutical lens. Including the various 'gospels' that have been and are being preached.

HISTORICAL TIMELINE AND CONTEXT

The ultimate context of the historical Jesus is God's story of creation and the fall, of covenant (salvation) and eschatology (end-time new creation), in Israel and the promised Messiah. The specific context is Second Temple Judaism, the period that began after the Jews returned from exile, between 538 and 432 BC, and ended in the Second Temple's destruction in AD 70.

The following timeline marks the broad-stroke events and context that will be detailed in the portrait of Jesus. While some dates are clear (accurate), scholars debate the dating, so some dates may differ.

- 538–432 BC, the return of Jewish exiles and beginning of the restoration of Jerusalem and (re)building of the Second Temple.

- 430 BC, the last OT book, prophet Malachi, was the start of 400 years of 'silence from God'. According to the gospel eye-witnesses, the prophetic voice was not heard till Jesus came.

- 250–150 BC, the 'canon' of the Hebrew Bible was recognised and translated into Greek by Jewish sages in Alexandria, Egypt. This Greek OT is called the Septuagint (LXX) because 70 or 72 scholars did the translation. Thus, it was available in Jesus' day. The NT writers often quoted from the LXX, though Jesus most likely read and quoted the Hebrew text.

- 167–160 BC, the Maccabean revolt against the oppressive occupation by Antiochus IV Epiphanes, the Seleucid King. He devoted the Temple in Jerusalem to the worship of Zeus, sacrificing swine on the altar (Daniel's "abomination of desolation", 9:27). The Maccabean martyrdom gave Judaism a heroic paradigm of violent resistance for the liberation of the Temple and the land.

- 63 BC, the brutal Roman occupation of Palestine began. Military ruler Pompey claimed Jerusalem and personally entered the Temple, which was, again, an "abomination" that inflamed Jewish Messianic expectation.

- 37–4 BC, the reign of Herod the Great as a client king of Rome. On his death in 4 BC, his kingdom was divided between his sons: Archelaus ruled Judea, Herod Antipas ruled Galilee and Perea, and Herod Philip ruled Trachonitis – all under Rome.

- 6/5 BC, the birth of Jesus.

- 20 BC–AD 25, Herod's renovation and rebuilding of the Temple took 45 to 46 years (see John 2:20).

- AD 26/27, Jesus went to learn from John the baptizer. After being baptised by John, Jesus began his own ministry.

- AD 30/31, Jesus was crucified under Pilate, who ruled 26–36.

- AD 48–70, the NT texts were written, most before the fall of Jerusalem. The Johannine texts are clearly the exception (John's gospel, letters, and Revelation), dated from mid-80s into the 90s. Scholars continue to debate the dating of NT documents.

- AD 66–70, the Jewish revolt and defeat by the Romans, with the destruction of the Temple. *AD 70 'officially' marks the end of the Second Temple period* and the beginning of Rabbinical Judaism.

HISTORICAL SOURCES – SECOND TEMPLE LITERATURE

Second Temple literature (manuscripts and documents written in the Second Temple period) helps us to reconstruct the cultural, socio-political, and religious context and to see and know Jesus within it. See Keener (2014) for a reliable resource on the background context. Bock (2002) gives a good introduction to studying the historical Jesus in terms of the context, sources, and study methods.

Remarkably, the NT has been read in a relative vacuum for the last 1900 years. As mentioned earlier, most, if not all the non-biblical literature from Second Temple Judaism has become available only in the last century. *For the first time in church history since Jesus and the early church, we have the available sources to reconstruct the historical Jesus with reasonable probability.* Here is the list of those sources:

1. *The gospels* and other OT and NT texts. The 'synoptic' gospels (Matthew, Mark, and Luke are similar, 'seen together') and John's gospel remain *the* primary source to know the historical Jesus.

2. *The Apocrypha of the OT.* Apocrypha means 'the hidden writings'. They are the writings that the early Church received as part of the Greek translation of the OT (LXX), but were not included in the Hebrew Bible. See Metzger (1957) for a good introduction and translation. These 'intertestamental' books, written between the OT and NT, are in Catholic and Orthodox Bibles. While not

considered inspired scripture (i.e., 'canonical'), they are worthy of study (i.e., 'deutero-canonical'). Though not in Protestant Bibles, the publishers of the NRSV Bible include these apocryphal books.

3. *Dead Sea Scrolls.* The writings of the Essenes discovered in 1947. This community existed at Qumran, near the Dead Sea, from the early 1st century BC to AD 68. These texts give significant insight into Second Temple Judaism (Wise *et al.* 2005). See Charlesworth (ed. 2006) for a multi-scholar study of the scrolls and the NT.

4. *Josephus* (AD 37–100). A Jewish historian and Roman military commander. He wrote *The Antiquities of the Jews* and *The Wars of the Jews* (see Whiston 1987) over a decade after the destruction of AD 70. He spoke of John the Baptist, Jesus, and "James the martyred brother of Jesus". See Mason (2009) on Josephus and the NT.

5. *The Pseudepigrapha.* These texts refer to 'pseudonymous writing', spurious texts by factiously named authors. They are inter-testamental Jewish and Jewish-Christian documents that purport to be written by notable OT figures. Some are dated as late as the 6th century AD. See James Charlesworth (1983), editor of the two-volume set of the 66 pseudepigrapha texts and fragments.

6. *Greco-Roman literature.* Besides Josephus, there is mention of Jesus in other Roman sources: Suetonius, Tacitus, Pliny the Younger, and indirectly from Thallus and Peregrinus (see Bock 2002:47-52).

7. *Philo* (see Yonge 1993). Philo of Alexandria (20 BC–AD 50) informs us about Jewish thought in the cultural philosophical Greco-Roman context – how Jews in the diaspora viewed their faith. Not majorly significant for Palestinian Jewish thought at the time of Jesus.

8. *The Mishna and Talmud,* including Jewish *targums* (*spoken* Aramaic translations of the Hebrew Bible) and *midrashim* (interpretations of the Hebrew texts). These Jewish rabbinical writings are from oral tradition dating from rabbi Hillel (100 BC–AD 10). The Mishna (AD 200–250) and the Talmud (AD 350–500) cast some light on the Second Temple period, but one must discern and separate out many post-AD 70 traditions of rabbinical Judaism.

9. *Nag Hamadi texts.* Discovered in 1945, almost entirely Gnostic in thought form, dating from 2nd to 4th century AD. Though popular

with Jesus Seminar scholars, they make no real contribution to the historical Jesus for third quest scholars. Meier (1991:112-41) examines them and explains why they are of little use.

The Talmud, Nag Hamadi texts, and post-NT Christian texts in *The Apostolic Fathers* (dated AD 100 onwards, Holmes 1989), fall outside the Second Temple period. Though they give a view of Jesus, they are not determinative for historical Jesus studies. *The Apostolic Fathers* gives us early Christology and early church creeds.

THE JESUS' OF HISTORY – SHIFTING THEOLOGICAL PARADIGMS

The Story of the historical Jesus and Kingdom theology has shifted from time to time through church history. It reveals the various Jesus' scholars and leaders have created – most in their own image, as was pointed out by Schweitzer.

The following overview of the various Jesus' of history must be read in the context of Paul's serious warning in Galatians 1:6-12 and 2 Corinthians 11:4, referred to in my preface. Let me state it once again: *the Jesus we see is the gospel that we preach, which is the (S)spirit that we impart to our hearers.* Consequently, what (S)spirit do we impart? I invite the reader to suggest your own answer in this (admittedly stereotypical) list.

1. *Prophetic-Apocalyptic-Messianic Jesus* of the biblical gospels (5/6 BC – AD 30/31), whose mission, message, and ministry of God's Kingdom gave the promised eschatological salvation by the impartation of God's Holy Spirit. The features of this Jesus are the portrait of this book: *the measure of all other Jesus' that come and go throughout church history,* seen in what follows.

2. *Judaizer Jesus* of the Galatians (1:6-12, in AD 47–48), preaching a legalistic gospel of works-righteousness by obedience to The Law, imparting a spirit of…? Legalism? Bondage?

3. *Super Apostle Jesus* of the Corinthians (2 Corinthians 11:4-15, in AD 50–53), preaching a motivational gospel of success and prosperity, imparting a spirit of…? The present age?

4. *Jesus of Creedal Dogma.* Jesus Christ of two natures, human and divine without confusion or assimilation. The Apostolic and

Nicene Creeds say nothing of Jesus' life, mission, and ministry of the Kingdom. It's a *comma* between his birth and death: "born of the Virgin Mary, suffered under Pontius Pilate..." The glaring omission, symbolised in the comma, reflects the shift away from the historical Jesus and his theology of the Kingdom. This omission had serious negative consequences, as seen below.

5. *Christendom Jesus* of the 4th century onwards, after Emperor Constantine converted and made Christianity the religion of the empire. A theocratic triumphalist Jesus, with an all-conquering empire gospel, imparting a spirit of...? Christian Nationalism?

6. *Monastic Jesus* of the 4th century onwards. The cloistered Jesus with a spiritual gospel of self-mortification for holiness, imparting a (S)spirit of...? Withdrawal? Asceticism?

7. *Reformation Jesus* of the 16th/17th centuries. The Jesus of the Cross, the Divine Son of God with a transactional gospel of penal substitution, imparting a (S)spirit of...? Justification?

8. *Liberal Protestant Jesus* of the 17th/18th centuries. Jesus the benign moral teacher, with an inclusive gospel of the universal Fatherhood of God, imparting a (S)spirit of...? Universalism?

9. *Evangelical Existentialist Jesus* of the 18th/19th centuries. The Jesus of born-again salvation, with a personal vampire gospel of the blood of Jesus for the forgiveness of sins, which imparts a spirit of...? Consumerism? A ticket to heaven?

10. *Social Reformer Jesus* of the 20th/21st centuries. The Jesus of liberation theology – the Marxist Revolutionary Jesus of the left wing – with a utopian social gospel of structural transformation, imparting a (S)spirit of...? Activism? Socialism?

11. *Fundamentalist Evangelical Jesus* of the 20th/21st centuries. The Jesus of the religious right wing, with a moral-political gospel of Christianising the nation, imparting a spirit of...? Triumphalism? A renewal of Christendom and Christian Nationalism?

12. *Charismatic Miracle-Working Jesus* of the 20th/21st centuries. The signs & wonders Jesus of Pentecostal restoration theology, with a 'word of faith' gospel of health and wealth in 'the finished work of the cross', imparting a spirit of...? Presumption? Materialism?

13. *Postmodern Mystic Jesus* of the 20th/21st centuries. The Jesus of the Nag Hamadi Gnostic gospels, the mystic master of universal spirituality, with a New Age esoteric gospel of Cosmic Christ consciousness, imparting a spirit of...? Universal Spiritism?

CONCLUSION – SOME IMPLICATIONS

We have done a broad overview of the main ideas and issues to be aware of in studying the Jesus of history. Thus, with this background introduction, I return to the claim that:

- Our generation can reconstruct the historical Jesus for the first time in nearly 2000 years of history with reasonable accuracy.
- This constitutes a new reformation in Christianity.
- Therefore, it leads to a review of everything, as per Morphew's statement quoted in my preface. Jesus and the Kingdom is the controlling narrative that shapes our worldview, giving meaning to all of reality, the whole of life.

In short, the rediscovery of the historical Jesus and Kingdom theology is the recovery of *eschatology*, not as in the signs, times and dates of The Second Coming, but in the sense of living eternal life now as Jesus did 2000 years ago. God, in Jesus, cracked open this evil age like a coconut and inserted the age to come into it. We live Jesus' future Kingship already present in principle and power. Thus, we interpret the past in light of God's future-present Kingdom purposes and work in the world. God's future defines us, lived now by faith, till consummated in fullness and finality on earth when Jesus returns.

So, the implication of the historical Jesus and Kingdom theology is to review, reframe, and rearticulate the following.

How we do theology. Theological method: we move from biblical studies (critical historical), through exegesis and hermeneutics, to biblical theology (of the Kingdom), and to systematic theology, ethics, missiology, practical and pastoral theology.

How we decide our beliefs. Systematic Theology was the 'dogmatic queen' of theology that formed Christian beliefs: the doctrine of God, of creation, sin, redemption (Christology), the church (Ecclesiology), the Holy Spirit (Pneumatology), and the end (Eschatology). Adrio

König and Wolfhart Pannenberg (see my bibliography) are systematic theologians who have revised and rearticulated the classic doctrines in the framework of Kingdom theology. The same must be done to the early church creeds and all subsequent statements of faith.

How we do church. Our ecclesiology and 'philosophy of ministry' must be reviewed. Wimber founded the Vineyard on the practice of Kingdom theology, leading to a radical revision of doing church.

How we do missions. The historical Jesus and Kingdom theology questions and reframes missiology, i.e. how we do evangelism, social transformation, church planting, and missions in general.

How we do life. Rethinking from a Kingdom worldview how we live: the field of *ethics*, reframed as *Kingdom* ethics in all dimensions of life (Stassen & Gushee, 2003) – political, social, economic, environmental, marriage, sexuality, technology (e.g., AI), medicine, and so on.

Lastly, other competing eschatological frameworks. Jesus Research confronts five contemporary paradigms relating to the different Jesus' and gospels listed above. It's not the place to discuss how Kingdom theology challenges and corrects them (see Morphew 2019:222-95 for a detailed discussion). Simply put, the following paradigms need to be radically reviewed in light of Jesus and the Kingdom.

1. *Reformed Cessationism*: that the eschatological gifts of the Spirit, healings and miracles, ceased after the apostolic age. Their role as 'proof' of Jesus' divine nature and Kingship ended with the recognition and authorisation of the NT canon (4th century). In other words, 'The Word of God' is now our witness/proof of Jesus and the gospel. Some conservative evangelicals still hold to this outdated theological paradigm, often overreacting to 'charismatic excess' in the signs and wonders movement.

2. *Pentecostal/Charismatic Restorationism*: an eschatology that winds up to the end. God restores the church through historical events, e.g., the 20th century Pentecostal revival restored the baptism and gifts of the Spirit; the Charismatic renewal restored the 'five-fold ministry'; and the new apostolic-prophetic reformation readies the church for the worldwide revival to usher in Christ's return.

3. *Evangelical Dispensationalism*: an eschatology that says God deals with Israel and the church in dispensations (misinterpreting

Daniel 9:20-27). It uncritically supports the modern political state of Israel, believes in a pretribulation rapture, a seven-year rule of the Anti-Christ, the building of the third Temple, and Christ's return to Jerusalem to save Israel and rule the nations.

4. *Liberation Theology:* a paradigm of societal liberation from forms of oppression, which uses Marxist social analysis with the biblical theme of liberation, leading to 'leftist' political activism, and even violent revolution. It peaked in the late 20th century. Some still hold to it, but now in its shifted ideological meaning and form, called 'cultural Marxism'.

5. *Post-millennialism*: an eschatology that says Christians must, and will evangelise and then rule over the nations. We are mandated to take over all sectors of society for the Kingdom of God, as in the 'seven mountains' teaching of the religious right, and then Jesus will return. It is also called 'reconstructionism'.

The eschatological paradigms of both 4 and 5 are modern forms of old Christendom (Christian Nationalism) – radically different to how the historical Jesus inaugurated the Kingdom of God.

QUESTIONS FOR REFLECTION AND DISCUSSION

1. What two or three essential new things have you learnt from this introduction? What are your key 'takeaways'?

2. Why are 'Jesus Research' and consequent 'Kingdom Theology' important today? Why is it essential for Christian pastors?

3. Do you agree with the claim that the recovery of the historical Jesus is a Kingdom Reformation – possibly more important than the Protestant Reformation?

4. What is the gospel that you heard? The gospel that you have been preaching? And what is the (S)spirit that you have imparted?

5. Put in your own words the Jesus that you (now) see and believe.

6. How does *that* Jesus (that gospel) determine how you do life, church, and ministry?

CONCEPTION & FORMATION

My portrait of Jesus is based primarily on the biblical gospels as reliable sources by multiple eyewitnesses, as Luke 1:1-4 states. The historical accounts, though theologically framed, are by "eyewitnesses and servants of the word... handed down to us" (transmitted) via trusted memory of repeated stories (authoritative oral tradition). It is a 'theologising of history', or historical narrative theology, without compromising the integrity of the historical events.

The approach is to start with the earliest gospel, which is Mark, probably written in the late 50s or early 60s AD. Then to consult Matthew and Luke, probably written in the mid to late 60s (dates are debated). They both rely on Mark's gospel, but also draw from sources (Q, *'quelle'*) of sayings and stories of Jesus not found in Mark. Then one goes to John's biography of Jesus, written in the late 80s or 90s. We follow this method while integrating knowledge from other sources about the historical Jesus and the Second Temple context.

We begin with Jesus' conception, birth, and his psycho-emotional-spiritual formation of thirty 'hidden years' in Nazareth. Mark and John omit this and begin with John the baptizer's ministry. So, we study Luke and Matthew's accounts of Jesus' conception, birth, and early formation. A comparative reading shows that Luke tells the story more from the viewpoint and experience of Jesus' mother, Mary. Matthew tells it more from Jesus' father Joseph's viewpoint.

LUKE'S ACCOUNT OF JESUS' CONCEPTION AND BIRTH

Luke dates the conception and birth of John the baptizer and Jesus by referencing public figures in power – a typical device in Greco-Roman literature. "In the time of Herod, king of Judea, there was a priest named Zachariah..." (1:5). Herod died in 4 BC. John and Jesus' birth occurred a few years earlier, 7/6 BC. This literary 'device' also contrasted the privileged powerful rulers with the marginalized powerless people at the time of the birth of John and Jesus.

In keeping with the genre of historical biographies, where significant figures are purported to have extraordinary births, Luke tells of supernatural events accompanying the conception and birth of both John and Jesus. The difference is between fanciful claims and the marks of simple, but authentic, eyewitness testimony.

Luke starts Jesus' story with John's miraculous conception and birth. His father, Zachariah, was a priest in the temple. His mother, Elizabeth, was an aunt to Jesus' mother, Mary (her mother, Anna, was Elizabeth's sister). Thus, John and Jesus were relatives. Zachariah and Elizabeth were elderly, and she was barren. An angel appeared to Zachariah while conducting his ministry in the temple, foretelling the birth of their son, John. His life-purpose was "to go before *the Lord* in the spirit and power of Elijah", to "bring back many of the people of Israel to the Lord their God... to make ready a people for *the Lord*" (Luke 1:16-17, my italics). "*The Lord*", in the story, is Jesus!

Jesus' Conception, Luke 1:26-38

In the sixth month of Elizabeth's pregnancy, God sent the angel Gabriel to Nazareth, to a virgin pledged to be married to a man named Joseph, a descendant of King David. The virgin's name was Mary. The angel said, "Greetings, you who are highly favoured! The Lord is with you." Mary was greatly troubled at his words and wondered what this meant. But the angel said, "Don't be afraid, Mary; you have found favour with God. You will conceive and give birth to a son, and you are to call him Jesus. He will be great and will be called the Son of God. The Lord God will give him the throne of his father David, and he will reign over Jacob's descendants forever; his kingdom will never end."

"How will this be," Mary asked the angel, "since I am a virgin?"

The angel answered, "The Holy Spirit will come on you, the power of God will overshadow you. So, the holy one to be born will be called the Son of God. Even Elizabeth your relative is going to have a child in her old age, and she who was said to be unable to conceive is in her sixth month. For no word from God will ever fail."

"I am the Lord's servant," Mary answered. "May your word to me be fulfilled." Then the angel left her.

Some observations from this story, and the events that followed.

- This is Mary's account, with the marks of authentic human testimony, of a shocking, real, personal experience.
- The angelic visitation tells her, as with Zachariah, what would happen, how it would happen, and what it would mean.
- "Virgin" is stated three times, emphasizing the miraculous nature of Mary conceiving *as a virgin*. 'How?' is explained by the power of God's Spirit. Though some historians doubt the virgin birth, it's a matter of credal faith. On whether "virgin" (Greek *parthenos*, Hebrew *almah*, Isaiah 7:14) meant biological virgin, or young maiden, see Morphew (1980) and Brown (1977).
- It also highlights the controversy of pregnancy before marriage.
- While shocked, young Mary (between 13 and 16 years old) responded to the dramatic encounter with honesty and faith. She courageously made herself available to God (1:38,45).
- It was confirmed by God's Spirit coming on people who proclaimed that God's eschatological salvation (Kingdom) was fulfilled in Jesus' conception and birth (1:17, 41f, 67f; 2:25-27). The coming of the Spirit with inspired utterance (on Elizabeth, Mary, Zachariah, Simeon, Anna) broke 400 years of silence from heaven since the last prophet, Malachi, spoke by God's Spirit. It marked the dawning of a new age of God's Kingdom.
- The words of the angel Gabriel were fully confirmed when Mary found herself pregnant.

Jesus' Birth, Luke 2:1-38

Luke 2:1-3 tells of the birth of Jesus by, again, referencing people in power and dates in world history. "In those days Caesar Augustus issued a decree that a census should be taken of the entire Roman world. This was the first census that took place while Quirinius was governor of Syria. Everyone went to their own town to register".

Quirinius was in office for two terms (6–4 BC and AD 6–9). A census is associated with each term. Luke refers to the second census in Acts 5:37. A decree in Rome, the centre of world power, moves a regional governor into action, which moves Joseph and Mary to a small, marginalised corner of the Empire. This is how Luke introduces Jesus' birth. Joseph, from the lineage of King David, had to go to Bethlehem, his hometown. "He went there to register with Mary, who was pledged to be married to him and was expecting a child" (Luke 2:5).

In short, Jesus was born in Bethlehem by God's sovereign move through Emperor Augustus, fulfilling the Hebrew prophecy of Micah 5:2 (quoted in Matthew 2:6): "But you, Bethlehem, in the land of Judah, are by no means least among the rulers of Judah; for out of you will come a ruler who will shepherd my people Israel."

Then, again, angelic visitations and Spirit-prophesying of God's eschatological Kingdom salvation, accompany Jesus' birth (Luke 2:8-15, 25-38). It's the reversal of fortunes, the inversion of society: God's "heavenly host" visit poor rural shepherds to announce the birth of "a Saviour... Christ the Lord (Messiah-King)". *They* saw the newborn baby. And *they* "spread the word concerning this child, and all who heard were amazed." An old man, Simeon, and "very old" woman, Anna, prayed and fasted at the Temple for years, waiting to see God's eschatological redemption of Israel. *They* saw the baby Jesus and *they* prophesied and proclaimed its significance. And Mary, Jesus' mother, "treasured up all these things and pondered them in her heart."

Jesus was, like all other Jewish boys, circumcised and named on the eighth day after birth. A few months later his parents consecrated him to God as their first-born son, at the time of purification after the birth. Thus, Joseph and Mary were Torah-observant and did all that was required of them (2:39). And they raised Jesus that way.

MATTHEW'S ACCOUNT OF JESUS' CONCEPTION AND BIRTH

Matthew tells the story from Joseph's experience. He begins with "the genealogy of Jesus the Messiah (King), the son of David" (1:1). But unlike Luke (3:23-38) and other Greco-Roman genealogies, Matthew reverses the order, starting with the oldest and ending with the person in question (Matthew 1:1-16). He mentions five women: three Gentiles, and the fourth a Gentile or wife of a Gentile. This points to the inclusion of Gentiles in Jesus' Kingdom (Matthew 28:19). The fifth woman is Mary. Note, Matthew does not say "Joseph the father of Jesus". Instead, he says "and Jacob the father of Joseph, the husband of Mary, and Mary was the mother of Jesus, who is called the Messiah" (1:16). This sets the scene for Jesus' conception and birth from

Joseph's perspective, as recorded in Matthew 1:18f and chapter 2.

Jesus' Conception, Matthew 1:18-25 (NRSV)

The birth of Jesus the Messiah took place in this way. When his mother Mary had been engaged to Joseph, but before they lived together, she was found to be with child from the Holy Spirit. Her husband Joseph, being a righteous man and unwilling to expose her to public disgrace, planned to dismiss her quietly. But just when he had resolved to do this, an angel of the Lord appeared in a dream and said, "Joseph, son of David, do not be afraid to take Mary as your wife, for the child conceived in her is from the Holy Spirit. She will bear a son, and you are to name him Jesus, for he will save his people from their sins."

All this took place to fulfil what the Lord said through the prophet: "Look, the virgin shall conceive and bear a son, and they shall name him Emmanuel," which means, "God is with us." When Joseph awoke from sleep, he did as the angel of the Lord commanded him; he took her as his wife, but had no marital relations with her until she had borne a son; and he named him Jesus.

Note the following from Matthew's (Joseph's) account:

- Verse 18, "*his* mother Mary... *she* was found to be with child from the Holy Spirit... *her* husband Joseph...", reinforces the end of the genealogy (16): Jesus was born through Mary by the Spirit, and Joseph was (merely) her husband.

- It emphasises Jesus' conception *before* marriage, an *illegitimate* pregnancy in Jewish society. Of great concern to Joseph, to say the least. But the angel calmed Joseph by saying it was a work of the Holy Spirit fulfilling prophecy.

- Joseph's decision to dismiss/divorce Mary, to annul the legal betrothal (Deuteronomy 24:1) and privately "send her away" for her protection, reveals the serious nature of the controversy and disgrace this 'illegitimate' conception brought on her.

- Joseph's testimony that he had no sexual relations with Mary till *after* Jesus' birth highlights the virgin conception *and* birth.

- The prediction of a boy, with the given name of Jesus (Greek for Joshua/*Yeshua*, means *Yhwh* saves), fulfils Isaiah's prophecy

(7:14) of the coming 'Emmanuel', 'God is with us'.

The Mamzer from Nazareth

Jesus' parents had to endure the social scandal of a pregnancy before marriage. Jews viewed it as an illicit union of the unmarried couple, or of the woman's infidelity, or even rape (Deuteronomy 22:13-29). The baby born of illicit unions is 'illegitimate', a *mamzer*, 'bastard child' (Mishna Yebamot 4:13), bearing the greater pain of social rejection. "Those born of an illicit union shall not be admitted to the assembly of the LORD, even to the tenth generation" (Deuteronomy 23:2, NRSV). The NIV margin renders it as "one of illegitimate birth...".

Thus, Chilton (2000:3-22) argues that Jesus was 'the *mamzer* from Nazareth'. The charge that he was illegitimately conceived plagued him all his life, even far from his hometown, evident in the disputes in Jerusalem during his ministry. When Jesus spoke of God as his father, Pharisees challenged him (John 8:19,41,48,53): "where is *your* father?... *we* are not illegitimate children (*mamzers*)... Aren't we right in saying that *you* are a Samaritan and demon-possessed? Who do you think *you* are?" They saw him as a Samaritan half-breed due to his mother's 'fornication'. Even in his village of Nazareth, he was known as "Mary's son", not Joseph's son (Mark 6:3).

The Talmud (Sanhedrin 67a, 106a) refers to Jesus' mother *Miriam* (in Hebrew) as a whore who slept with a Roman soldier, Panthera. Though scholars dispute the interpretation, it is clear that questions of paternity hung over Jesus all his life and afterwards.

This impacted *Yeshua* in his developing consciousness and sense of self. The village of Nazareth would have known. He probably was teased, even bullied, from an early age: "*mamzer*", "bastard". Thus, he must have wrestled psycho-emotionally with identity issues, with a father-wound: "Am I legitimate? Who is my father?" The psycho-social rejection and isolation were very real for Jesus.

Hence, as a young boy he probably asked his parents: "Who am I? What happened when I was born? Who's my *real* father? What went wrong? Why am I here? What will become of me?" These are the kind of (worldview) questions all boys and girls wrestle with. But, for Jesus, they were sharply focused and deeply personal.

His parent's answers – the stories of his conception, birth, angelic visitations, prophecies, circumcision, and Temple purification – are those in Matthew and Luke. There are probably other stories not recorded in the gospels (John 20:30-31, 21:25). It was their personal experience. Jesus accepted and believed their storied explanations. That was decisive in the formation of his developing consciousness, his worldview, sense of self, life purpose and destiny.

Jesus' Birth, Matthew 2:1-23

Matthew (2:1-12) frames his historical account of Jesus' birth during King Herod's brutal reign, with the visit of the Magi through cosmic signs, in fulfilment of the Hebrew prophets.

The 'magi' were not kings. Tertullian (died AD 225) started that tradition. Scholars agree that they were wise astronomer-astrologers who studied the stars for signs and omens of the times. They saw the moving star, which led them to Bethlehem. Whatever the historical explanation – the conjunction of planets, or a comet, or a supernatural event (Brown 1977:172-3) – Matthew uses it to point to the birth of the Jewish King in fulfilment of Numbers 24:17 and Micah 5:2. That is confirmed in the account of the Magi (who were Gentiles) bringing expensive gifts and bowing in worship of the baby Jesus.

This is reinforced by Herod's reaction to kill Jesus because the Magi said he was born king of the Jews: "Herod was furious, and gave orders to kill all the boys in Bethlehem and its vicinity who were two years old and under" (Matthew 2:16). This recalls Pharoah's killing of the male Israelite babies when Moses was born (Exodus 1& 2), pointing to Jesus as the new Moses born for Israel's deliverance. There's no evidence outside of Matthew for the massacre at Jesus' birth, so some scholars question its historicity. Josephus details Herod's depraved character and cruelties, giving credence to the story (Josephus 1987:462-3, *Antiquities* 17.6.164-81). And his description of Pharoah being warned about the birth of an Israelite child (Moses) who "would bring Egyptian dominion low, and raise the Israelites... and obtain a glory that would be remembered through all ages" (1987:66-7, *Antiquities* 2.9.205), has clear allusions to Matthew's story of Jesus' birth and Herod's merciless massacre.

However, God intervenes, warning Joseph in a dream to flee to Egypt with Jesus and Mary. They were refugees. Further rejection.

Jesus felt the trauma of millions of modern refugees fleeing national dictators, political persecution and civil unrest. God tells Joseph, again in a dream, to return home two years later, after Herod died (2:19). Thus, Matthew's account of Jesus' birth is about the clash of kingship and power, of cosmic signs and eschatological fulfilment of prophecy, under the dark shadow of rejection, pain and death.

JESUS' GROWTH AND FORMATION IN NAZARETH

Only Luke lifts the veil on Jesus' thirty 'hidden years' in Nazareth, of his psycho-spiritual formation into the person he became. He gives a pivot-point story, probably from Mary's viewpoint. The stories of Jesus' boyhood and youth in the *Gospel of Thomas* and other Gnostic texts found at Nag Hammadi, are truly fanciful and bizarre. Meier (1991:114-139) writes, "the Gospel of Thomas portrays Jesus as a self-willed little brat who, throwing a tantrum, makes a child who runs up against him drop dead". Meier reveals why these Gnostic gospels cannot be taken seriously as sources for the historical Jesus.

First an orientation. Jesus grew up in rural Galilee, the hotbed of Jewish resistance against Roman occupation. His village of Nazareth housed between 700 and 1200 people – estimates vary. Nazareth was 6 kilometres (3.7 miles) from Sepphoris, a major Roman town in the Galilee, where the skill of a *tekton* would have been in demand. Jesus probably went there often with his father, *Abba Josef,* to work.

A *tekton* was a carpenter and/or stone mason (Mark 6:3). Jesus joined *Abba Josef* from an early age as an apprentice *tekton,* doing his father's business. They were not poor as landless peasants, but lower class tradesmen/manual labourers (in modern terms). They worked hard in a small family business making ends meet. It's widely assumed Joseph died in Jesus' late teens or early twenties, partly because he's not mentioned in Jesus' ministry life, e.g., Matthew 13:55.

Yeshua had unnamed sisters and four brothers named after the Patriarchs (Mark 6:3), highlighting his parent's faith and hope in Israel's deliverance. They spoke Aramaic, a Semitic dialect of Hebrew, with a Galilean accent. Alongside their formation in Torah reading and memorisation under their parents' teaching, they attended synagogue school for training in Hebrew and Torah, in reading and writing. And because of their work in nearby Sepphoris, Jesus probably learnt some

Greek, the language of business and trade in those days.

This was the context in which Jesus grew in his sense of self as the foundation for his three and half years of public ministry.

Jesus' Consciousness of God as his Abba

Luke brackets a decisive story of Jesus at the age of twelve between two similar descriptions of his growth and formation in Nazareth (2:40 and 2:52): "The child grew and became strong; he was filled with wisdom, and the grace of God was on him." And "Jesus grew in wisdom and stature, and in favour with God and man." They summarise his wholistic physical, mental, emotional, spiritual and social development from boyhood into manhood.

The story (2:41-51) of his parent's annual pilgrimage to Jerusalem for *Pesach* (Passover feast) shows Jesus had already come of age at twelve years old. *Bar Mitzvah* was a later institution practised at age thirteen. It meant becoming a "Son of the Commandment", accepted as an adult into the Jewish community, by publicly putting on the yoke of Torah obedience. Jesus had already put on that yoke, seen in his debating Torah with the rabbis in the Temple. "Everyone who heard him was amazed at his understanding and his answers" (2:47).

The point of Luke's carefully chosen story is Jesus' profound consciousness of *God* being his Father and, consequently, his sense of life purpose. When Mary and Joseph find him in the Temple, after being missing for three days, "they were astonished. His mother said to him, 'Son, why have you treated us like this? Your father and I have been anxiously searching for you.' Jesus asked, 'Why were you searching for me? Didn't you know I had to be in my Father's house?' But they did not understand what he was saying to them" (2:48-50). The KJV has "I must be about my Father's business".

Luke contrasts *"your* father" (Joseph) with "*my* Father" (God). Jesus already developed an identity as *God's* son. He believed God was his *real* Father, whom he addressed as *Abba* – used for Joseph, indicating their intimate, trusting, father-son relationship. Then Luke reveals Jesus' conviction that his life purpose was to live in his Father's house (presence) and work with him in his business (Kingdom). In other words, to fulfil the meaning and destiny of his name, *Yeshua*, "he will save his people from their sins".

No doubt, *Yeshua's* illegitimate conception, a *mamzer* with its consequent psychosocial challenges of rejection and identity, was formative in developing the consciousness he displayed at this age. As mentioned earlier, his 'father issue' would have led to subjective feelings and questions that only his parents could answer, e.g., "who is my real *Abba*?" Imagine your mother telling you an angel appeared and said: "You will conceive and give birth to a son, and you are to call him Jesus. He will be great and will be called the Son of the Most High. The Lord God will give him the throne of his father David, and he will reign over Jacob's descendants forever; his kingdom will never end" (Luke 1:31-33). What would you think? Has she lost the plot? Or, I'm special, I'm going to rule the world? Or, be humbled into silent prayer and contemplation – Jesus' probable response? At some point in his early boyhood, he dared to believe their storied explanations.

This is not the general fatherhood of God. It was different, unique, personal. For a *mamzer*, it was healing, bonding, and transforming. In deciding to believe God was his father, his consciousness was turned and attuned to God for fathering. He grew to experience and know *Abba's* loving presence in each moment of each day. He learnt to live interactively with *Abba*, trusting his unconditional love, instruction, and purpose for his life. That led to his deep sense of destiny.

This was part of his developing *worldview*. The questions he asked, the answers he received, the family and national stories he heard, with their life praxis, formed his Jewish worldview. Jesus found his identity and destiny in the story of the Creator-God, *Yhwh*, who chose Israel to redeem the nations. But Israel's intended means of mission – the land, Temple, Torah, and Jewish identity – became boundary markers of spiritual purity and ethnic pride. Israel's missional failure led to her exile, now in the form of oppressive Roman occupation. Hence, the heightened expectation of God coming to save Israel in his Messiah-King. Jesus believed he was born to be Israel's Messiah.

Four Key Factors in Jesus' Nazareth Formation (Venter 2019:118-120)

1. *A simple life:* Jesus led a simple and unhurried life with an interior detachment from material things. He was uncluttered, needing only the bare necessities to live. He humbly depended on *Abba* for

his daily needs. No *thing* possessed him. He used *things* to love others as an expression of his 'no-thing-ness', in total dependence on the 'all-ness' of his Father.

2. *A hard-working life:* Jesus worked hard with his hands, learning his father's trade from an early age. With no modern devices for distraction and amusement after a day's work, they enjoyed family time and Torah talk in the glow of candlelight until they fell asleep. Jesus' apprenticeship to *Abba Josef* became his spiritual discipline in apprenticeship to his heavenly *Abba*. Jesus knew his Father was always working, and he learnt to work with him, doing only what he saw *Abba* doing, saying only what he heard *Abba* saying (John 5:17,19; 8:29,38). Daily work was his discipline of discipleship, his continual worship of yielding his will to *Abba*.

3. *An obedient life:* Jesus obeyed his parents in his years of formation (Luke 2:51). It was not automatic. He learnt to obey by what he suffered (Hebrews 5:8), routinely choosing his parents and *Abba's* will over his own will. The material world, especially of human interaction, was the 'place' where *Abba* spoke to him and loved him, training him in the returned love of submission to legitimate authority. To love was to obey. To obey was to return love. Jesus grew in the joy and freedom of a long obedience in the same direction: "not my will, but yours be done".

4. *A life of prayer and Torah meditation:* Jesus' simple unhurried life was soaked in prayer, scripture meditation and memorisation. Waking early, morning by morning, he listened and learnt from *Abba* (Mark 1:35 cf. Isaiah 50:4–5). He received Torah instruction from his parents and Synagogue school. He learnt to pray the Psalms by heart. Prayer (Aramaic *zla, zlotha*) was being 'attuned to God' in a union of wills, having one heart and mind. It was walking in *Abba's* communicating presence, discovering his love in every facet of Jesus' humanity, in the scriptures, in people, and in creation. Prayer and meditation were key to him cultivating *Abba's* indwelling presence by his Spirit, to love and work with his Father in 'the sacrament of the present moment' of each day.

These core life practices and holy habits developed the character that enabled Jesus to be who he believed he was born to be – to fulfil his

God-given mission, doing God's will on earth as in heaven.

QUESTIONS FOR REFLECTION AND DISCUSSION

1. What is your response to Jesus' 'illegitimate' conception with its psycho-social consequences as the *mamzer* from Nazareth?
2. What were the circumstances of your conception and birth? Has it affected your life formation? Have you asked your parents?
3. Do you have a father and/or mother wound you need to face?
4. Do you struggle with identity issues – rejection, inferiority, etc.?
5. Do you know your life calling and destiny? What psycho-spiritual formation have you undergone for your vocation in Christ?
6. How can you make God your real *Abba* and *Amma*?

CALLING & CONFIRMATION

Our portrait is of the human Jesus – not the divine Jesus – within his historical context. Being who he was, who he became, and doing all he did, was by faith in God and by the Spirit's enabling, as in any other human being. We began with the accounts of Jesus' conception, birth, and formation, framed in the coming of the King and his Kingdom. But the controversial nature of his conception and birth – and questions regarding his paternity – contributed to his unique bonding with God as his Father. It led to a life-calling to "be about my Father's business" (Luke 2:49), to fulfil his identity and mission as *Yeshua*.

Other boys were also named *Yeshua* (Joshua). Devout Jewish parents, some ardent nationalists, named their sons after patriarchs and prophets, hoping their son would save Israel from her enemies and establish God's Kingdom. Many (false) messiahs arose and failed.

Jesus was different. His thirty 'hidden years' of spiritual formation in Nazareth is a model for our apprenticeship to him. As Jesus fell in love with God, in response to *Abba's* unconditional love for him, we fall in love with Jesus and stay in love with him by seeing him for who he was/is: the incarnate love of the Father. *That* love will determine everything in our lives.

In painting the picture of Jesus' calling and confirmation, we first look at John the baptizer and his relationship to Jesus. Then we examine Jesus' water baptism with its symbolism and meaning. This will include a discussion on his Spirit-baptism, with the supernatural confirmation of his identity as God's son, which empowered him to fulfil his life calling in love of the Father.

JOHN AND JESUS

At some point after John had begun his ministry, Jesus came to learn from him and be baptised. Luke dates John's ministry by referencing the political powers of the empire and the region, both Roman and

Jewish (3:1-2). John began his public ministry as early as AD 24/25. Jesus came to John's learning community probably a year or two later, about 26/27, and began his ministry in 27/28. John was beheaded shortly after that. Jesus was crucified in 30/31. Scholars debate this timeline, with some dating the events two or three years later.

Who was John?

John was Jesus' relative, at least six months older than him (Luke 1:26,36). He also had miraculous signs accompanying his conception and birth. The angel that announced his birth said his name was to be *Yochanan* (John), which joins 'God' and 'grace', meaning graced by God (Luke 1:13). Like Jesus, at some point, he decided on his life calling in his national context. Luke's use of the names of the Roman and Jewish political powers was more about the context of oppression and pain than a precise date. Israel was at a critical point in her history and story, with heightened Messianic expectations. It was into this context that "the word of God came to John in the wilderness. He went into all the country around the Jordan, preaching a baptism of repentance for the forgiveness of sins" (Luke 3:2-3).

What was John's sense of identity and mission? His view of Jesus?

His calling was to be the forerunner of the Messiah, whom he called "the Lamb of God, who takes away the sin of the world" (John 1:29,36). When John began his ministry, the Jewish leaders asked him, "Who are you?". He unequivocally replied in the words of Isaiah, "I am the voice of one calling in the wilderness, 'Make straight the way for the Lord'" (John 1:22-23 cf. Isaiah 40:3).

Mark (1:2-3) and Matthew (3:3) describe John by quoting Malachi 3:1, "I will send my messenger before you, who will prepare your way", alongside Isaiah 40:3. Jesus also quoted Malachi 3:1 to describe John's identity and mission (see Matthew 11:10, Luke 7:27).

However, John's mission was more than preparing the way for the Messiah. It was to reveal the Messiah by baptism: "the reason I came baptizing with water was that he might be revealed to Israel... I saw the Spirit come down from heaven as a dove and remain on him... the One who sent me to baptize with water told me, 'The man on whom you see the Spirit come and remain is the One who will baptize with the Holy Spirit.' I have seen and I testify that this is God's Chosen One" (John 1:31-34). As John baptised people, I imagine he looked up for a Spirit-baptism, saying, "No, not you! Next please!"

When Jesus was baptized the Spirit came on him. *Ha Meshiach* (the Messiah) is 'The Anointed', the Spirit-Bringer who baptises with God's eschatological Spirit to save Israel from her sins (*Yeshua*). Prophets spoke of the coming of God's Spirit for cleansing and sanctification, *and also* for prophetic empowerment in the end-times (Isaiah 44:3; Ezekiel 36:25-27, 39:29; Joel 2:28-29; Zechariah 12:10).

Therefore, John had a very high view of him, seeing Jesus as 'the coming one' who was much greater than he. Each gospel repeats this. To illustrate how unworthy John felt in comparison to Jesus, he said, "After me comes the one more powerful than I, the straps of whose sandals I am not worthy to stoop down and untie" (Mark 1:7 cf. Acts 13:25). It was known that disciples served their masters/rabbis in many menial ways, but never to untie their sandals, let alone wash their feet. It would be humiliating to both the rabbi and the disciple. That was reserved for slaves. John felt unworthy to even be Jesus' slave, let alone his forerunner-disciple.

What was John's message and ministry?

We can summarise both as follows, from Mark 1:7-8; Matthew 3:2-12; Luke 3:7-17; John 1:23-27, 29-34:

1. "Repent, for the Kingdom of Heaven is near." John's message was apocalyptic: the end-time Rule and Reign of God was now coming in *Mashiach*, with *both* eschatological salvation for all who repent *and* judgement for all who resist. A dramatic message of 'the end'.

2. John "preached a baptism of repentance for the forgiveness of sins" to be ready to enter the Kingdom, i.e., "show your repentance and faith in the coming Messiah by being baptised".

3. The repentance of baptism must be seen by 'the fruit' of changed living, acts of justice, making restitution, generosity, and so on.

4. The One coming after John is *Ha Mashiach*, who baptises with the Holy Spirit, i.e., imparts God's eschatological Spirit to the repentant.

On point 2, for Jews, immersion in a *mikvah* for ceremonial cleansing was common and regular. John's baptism was different. He was, in effect, calling Jews to a once-off baptism as converts to the true faith of (Messianic) Judaism. Only proselytes were baptised in a symbolic Exodus out of their pagan idolatry. Many Jews relied on their status as God's covenant people to enter the Kingdom. Jewish identity had become an idol. John told them *not* to rely on their (ethnic) lineage to qualify them: "Do not presume to say to yourselves, 'We have Abraham as our ancestor'; for I tell you, God is able from these stones to raise up children to Abraham" (Matthew 3:9). This would have been offensive because it challenged Jewish identity and belief of salvation. And it meant that *everyone* had to come to God, to Messiah, on the same terms: repentance and faith. Jews queued along with tax collectors and Roman soldiers for baptism. "Even tax collectors came to be baptised, asking him, 'Teacher, what should we do?' And soldiers also asked him, 'what should we do?'" (Luke 3:12-14).

How did others see John? What was his impact?

The Jews saw John as a prophet (Mark 11:32), possibly the end-time Elijah predicted in Malachi 4:5-6. John embodied his message in his location, rituals, dress and diet. He was not a court prophet giving pleasing guidance to the king. Rather, as a wilderness prophet, he boldly spoke God's will and word to the nation and the king.

He located himself in the wilderness that stretched seventy miles north and south and ten miles east and west along the Jordan River. John probably did this to fulfil Isaiah's prediction (40:3-5) of a herald announcing a new Exodus by a new Moses *in the wilderness*. People came from the city/town centres to the margins of society, to the desert, seen as a place of repentant self-stripping. John chose Jordan for baptism, evoking Israel's salvation-crossing into the Promised Land (Joshua 3-4). Some Jewish groups, like the Essenes, also withdrew to the wilderness to evade Jewish authorities and wait for the messianic New Exodus (see Keener 2014:129-130).

John's simple food and dress identified with the poor – a prophetic protest of repentance against the self-indulgence of the rich and the powerful (Mark 1:6; Matthew 11:8). More importantly, he dressed and ate like Elijah, purposefully emulating Israel's most revered prophet (1 Kings 17:4,9; 2 Kings 1:8). His impact on Jewish society was huge: "people went out to him from Jerusalem and all Judea and the whole region of the Jordan. Confessing their sins, they were baptized by him in the Jordan river" (Matthew 3:5). Luke 3:15 says, "The people were filled with expectation, and all were questioning in their hearts concerning John, whether he might be the Messiah". That shows how highly he was regarded. This is also attested to outside the gospels by Josephus (1987:484),

> "John, was called the Baptist... was a good man, and commanded the Jews to exercise virtue, both as righteous towards one another, and piety towards God, and so to come to baptism... many others came in crowds about him, for they were greatly moved (or pleased) by hearing his words. Herod feared the great influence John had over the people..." (*Antiquities,* 18.5.116-8).

John remained in high regard until he publicly rebuked Herod (Antipas) for his widely known affair with his brother's wife, Herodias, *and* for "all the other evil things he had done" (Luke 3:19-20). Herod viewed John's prophetic morality as subversive political meddling because John challenged Herod for his immorality and evil use of power. John called for repentance at the highest level of Jewish rule. Herod was offended and imprisoned John. He later beheaded him (Mark 6:17-29), prefiguring Jesus' brutal execution at the hands of the authorities.

How did Jesus see John?

Jesus saw John as Israel's greatest prophet in the long line of Hebrew prophets persecuted and executed for their messages. After John had been put in prison, Jesus publicly asked the people:

> "What did you go out into the wilderness to see? A reed swayed by the wind?... A prophet? Yes, I tell you, and more than a prophet. This is the one about whom it is written: 'I will send my messenger ahead of you, who will prepare your way before you' (Malachi 3:1). Truly I tell you, among those born of women there has not risen anyone greater than John the Baptist... For all the Prophets and the Law prophesied until John. And if you are willing to accept it, he is the Elijah who was to come" (Matthew 11:7, 9-11, 13-14).

A high view of John indeed. Jesus believed that John, as the messianic forerunner, fulfilled the Hebrew prophets. He marked the end of the era of Torah and the Prophets, and the beginning of the Messianic era. That's why he said, "among those born of women there has not risen anyone greater than John the Baptist, *yet whoever is least in the Kingdom of Heaven is greater than he*" (11:11).

John's greatness was not his character as such, but his prophetic role as *the* turning point in Israel's history. However, by comparison, the reality to which he pointed – Messiah's coming and all who enter his Kingdom – is far, far greater. That is what Jesus meant by "whoever is *in the Kingdom,* even the least one, is greater (in favour and privilege) than John". This is evident in the change of tense: for John, the Kingdom was about to come, was imminent ("near"); but for Jesus, the Kingdom had already come, was present in him – *and* was "near", *and* would come at the end of the age (discussed in detail later).

Was Jesus a disciple of John?

Jesus joined John at the Jordan at about 30 years old (Luke 3:21-23), indicative of his respect for John and his God-given ministry. He went there not just to submit to John's baptism, as many in Israel did, but to learn from him. Meier (1994:116-129) argues that Jesus went to join John's community to learn from him as a disciple, with Andrew and others (John 1:35, 3:25-26, 4:1). Jesus was probably mentored by John for a short period before and/or after he was baptised – certainly before he broke away to begin his ministry.

Evidence for Jesus having learnt from John:

1. Jesus possibly followed John on some of his baptising tours up and down the Jordan valley (John 1:28-29, 35-36; 3:23), and probably assisted him in preaching and baptising (3:25-26). We see this in Jesus' continued practice of (John's) baptism through his emerging disciples, even to the point of controversy (3:22-23, 4:1-2).

2. Jesus learnt from John's teaching of the bridegroom (Messiah) and friends of the bridegroom in the context of John's ascetic spirituality of fasting (and probably celibacy) and his joy at Messiah's coming (John 3:27-30 cf. Mark 2:18-20).

3. Jesus learnt from John's teaching on prayer. His disciples asked him to teach them to pray as John taught his disciples to pray, implying

continuity of mentoring (Luke 11:1f).

4. Most important is John's eschatological message of the Kingdom, which Jesus heard and then preached, "Repent, for the Kingdom of Heaven is near" (Matthew 3:2 cf. 4:17). Kingdom of *Heaven* is the Kingdom of *God*. Because Matthew's audience was mostly Jewish, he used 'Heaven' as a synonym for 'God'. Both Luke and Mark consistently used "Kingdom of God".

5. Jesus echoed the radical repentance and judgement that John preached (Luke 3:7-14 cf. 11:32, 13:1-5; Matthew 11:21-24), rebuking the Pharisees, Scribes, and Sadducees with John's words, "you brood of vipers" (Matthew 3:7-8 cf. 23:33).

Meier summarises that John's life, message, and baptism "are all to be seen as a vital and indispensable matrix of Jesus' own message and praxis... When Jesus begins his public ministry, he proclaims an eschatological message... he demands from his fellow Jews a basic change of heart and life in view of the approaching end, he stresses the urgency of the choice he presses on his audience by depicting the dire consequences of not accepting his message, he gathers around himself disciples, including an inner circle who stay with him and share his life, he symbolises acceptance of his message by conferring on his disciples a ritual washing or baptism... he spreads his message by an itinerant style of ministry, and his itinerant life includes celibacy" (1994:123-4). All these elements in Jesus' life, message, and ministry reflect John's life, preaching and praxis.

Thus, in the context of discipleship, Jesus' baptism was a sign of receiving John's teaching and then 'graduating', as it were, to begin his ministry. However, his baptism meant more than that.

WATER BAPTISM – JESUS CONFIRMED GOD'S CALLING

Though a historic event, Jesus' baptism is theologically framed as an early church *midrash* (interpretative teaching, Meier 1994:106-107), to not only reveal who *Yeshua* was – confirming his identity and calling – but also as a model for Christian baptism.

Jesus submitted to John's baptism of repentance, seeing it as a public confirmation of his calling. In the previous chapter we saw how Jesus, by the age of twelve, had a developed sense of calling from God, his *Abba*. It had to do with living his identity as *Yeshua:* to save his people from their sin. His parents received angelic visitations, dreams, and prophecies in this regard when Jesus was conceived and born. There is no record of Jesus having had such personal revelation during his years in Nazareth. He didn't wake up one morning with a dream or voice saying, "You are the Messiah!" The little evidence we have points to a process of developing consciousness, the result of spiritual formation. At some point, Jesus dared to believe what his parents told him and decided on his life calling. This came through:

- The stories his parents told him.
- Study and meditation in the Hebrew scriptures, with the Spirit's whispers in his heart through prayer and contemplation.
- The reading of "the signs of the times" (Matthew 16:1-4) in light of Israel's story, scriptures, and destiny.
- *Now confirmed and clarified in John's message and mentorship.*

The last point was crucial. It led Jesus to ask John to baptise him because John's baptism was not only for repentance (to come and confess sins, Mark 1:5), it was eschatological (to reveal the promised Messiah to Israel, Mathew 3:11; John 1:29-34). Jesus believed he was the one. John knew he was the one. But, in obedience to God, they both sought God's confirmation through baptism.

So, when Jesus asked to be baptised, "John tried to deter him, saying, 'I need to be baptized by you, and do you come to me?' Jesus replied, 'Let it be so *now; for it is proper for us to do this to fulfil all righteousness'*. Then John consented" (Matthew 3:14-15). The phrase in italics shows that Jesus believed his baptism was an act of righteous obedience to fulfil what God required of *them, Jesus and* John.

Jesus confirmed his calling to "now" (at this point in Israel's salvation history) identify with Israel in her sin – for forgiveness in a new Exodus from bondage into God's Kingdom. By being baptised, Jesus affirmed his willingness and commitment to represent Israel by suffering and dying on her behalf, to accomplish God's redemption by obedience to God's will for his life. Let me elaborate.

By going into the water where people confessed their sins, he identified with Israel, with sinners. Jesus stood in their place and confessed their sin, believing "he will save his people from their sins"

(Matthew 1:21). The interpretative implication is that he had no sin of his own to confess and thus had the authority to stand before God on their behalf. In so doing, he represented Israel and all sinners.

His immersion symbolised his death and cleansing for Israel. His 'return' out of the water symbolised the New Exodus – just as Israel passed through the waters that destroyed 'the powers' (the Egyptian gods with Pharaoh and his army), which had oppressed Israel for 400 years. And "now" (3:15), the waters of Jesus' baptism – of suffering and death on Israel's behalf – will destroy 'the powers' oppressing Israel for 400 years of silence from the heavens.

This act of obedience, submitting to John's baptism, was Jesus' public confirmation of God's call on his life. His 'dark vocation' as *Ha Mashiach*, which he understood and embraced from Isaiah's "servant songs". *Yeshua* believed that he would do for Israel what she failed to do, what she could not do for herself, dying in her place to lead the new Exodus into the new Promised Land of God's Kingdom.

Thus, Jesus' baptism was a life-defining event. Luke 3:21-22 says, "When all the people were being baptised, and Jesus was baptised too, *he was praying*". That highlights its significance. He did it prayerfully, in faith, obeying what he believed was God's call and destiny for him according to the scriptures, trusting that *Abba* would vindicate him.

SPIRIT BAPTISM – GOD CONFIRMED JESUS' CALLING

All four gospels speak of a supernatural happening when Jesus was baptised. And all four interpret it as God's public affirmation of Jesus' identity and God's confirmation of Jesus' calling.

The synoptic gospels (Mark, Matthew, Luke) record three events. "Just as Jesus was coming up out of the water,

- "He saw heaven being torn open
- and the Spirit descending on him like a dove.
- And a voice came from heaven saying..." (Mark 1:10-11).

"Heaven being torn open"

That is Hebraic for a 'theophany' or epiphany of God, as in Isaiah 64:1, "Oh, that you would rend the heavens and come down". And Ezekiel

1:1, "the heavens were opened and I saw visions of God". Similarly, Stephen in Acts 7:56, "I see heaven open". It happened as Jesus came out of the water, evidenced by God's Spirit coming on him in the form of a dove, with a voice that spoke from the heavens. These references to heaven being opened do not mean that they were 'portals' to enter heaven, as is erroneously taught in some Charismatic circles.

"Heaven" does not mean up there in space. The stratosphere was not torn open! It refers to the invisible spiritual reality that exists 'hand-in-glove' with our material world. When God and/or his angel "called from heaven" (Genesis 21:17, 22:11,15), it was a voice that spoke from the atmosphere – the spiritual realm – around their heads. It was God's Kingdom 'alongside' that manifested. Heaven, a synonym for God (Luke 15:18) and his Kingdom (Matthew 3:2), breaks through into our realm of five senses in a real 'numinous' experience. The plural, "heavens/heavenlies", refers not only to God and his angels (messengers), but also to the realm and operation of the kingdom of darkness. Invisible evil spirits interact with our material world. In opposing God, they 'war' in and from the spirit realm, 'blocking' the heavens against God's messengers and Kingdom purposes (Daniel 10:13,20 cf. Ephesians 6:12).

The point is that Mark described a dramatic 'breakthrough' after 400 years of silence from God, of exile under the 'closed' heavens ruled by the powers of evil – Satan and his (fallen) angels.

The present tense, "*being* torn open", indicates God's Kingdom breaks into our reality in a new way and keeps breaking in, from Jesus' baptism onwards. In fact, Mark confirms this by repeating the same phrase when Jesus died: "the curtain of the Temple was torn in two from top to bottom" (15:38). Only the High Priest entered once a year beyond this thick veil into the Holy of Holies – God's dwelling place of heaven on earth, 'The Ruling Presence' – only after offering all the appropriate sacrifices.

Early Jewish tradition (the Mishna) stated that the Temple veil was as thick as a man's hand (four inches) and thirty feet high, and that it took 300 priests to draw it aside, although this might be an exaggeration. It was (supernaturally) torn open from top to bottom when Jesus died, opening the way for everyone into God's presence by Messiah's blood sacrifice. It also indicates that God has 'broken out' and is available to all, apart from the Temple system, which stood judged and abolished.

By repeating the idea of "being torn open", Mark brackets Jesus' ministry from the beginning (his water baptism) to the end (his death and resurrection) with a dramatic cosmic shift, with open heavens.

That which separates us from God – sin and evil – is torn apart. The kingdom of darkness has been, is being, and will be defeated. The exile is over and the way to God is open. Thus, God's Ruling Presence has broken out from the closed heavens/curtain to lead a new Exodus into God's Kingdom. Hebrews chapter 8 to 10 teaches that, in reality, the veil between this age and the future age is torn open in Jesus, whereby we experience "the powers of the coming age" breaking into this present age (Hebrews 6:5).

"The Spirit descending on him like a dove"

All four gospel writers attest to the Spirit coming on Jesus in the open heavens event. The synoptic writers record the Spirit descending on him "like a dove". As John baptised Jesus in water, God baptised Jesus in Spirit, which was a full immersion, a plunging into, a saturation with God's *Ruach ha Kodesh* (Holy Spirit). What did it mean to be baptised in/with the Spirit? How did they know the Spirit came upon him?

The answer to these two questions assumes the OT background. The Spirit came on chosen people from time to time, meaning God anointed/empowered them to accomplish his call on their life for Israel's deliverance and governance. Anointing with oil symbolised the Holy Spirit. Practised for kings, deliverers, judges, prophets, and priests, "the anointing" was associated with the impartation of charismatic/prophetic gifts and manifestations to accomplish God's purpose. But the Spirit only came on the few chosen ones, and momentarily so – she did not remain on them.

Ruach (Spirit) is consistently a feminine noun in both Hebrew and Aramaic. Jesus and his apostles would have spoken of the Spirit as 'she', e.g., the Spirit gives birth to us in God's Kingdom (John 3:5-7). Greek *pneuma*, (S)spirit, is neuter ('it'), though God's Spirit is spoken of as a Person in the NT, not a force. Let me add that God as Father (*Abba*) is *not* a biological-sexual term – God is *not* a man. *Abba* is a psycho-theological characteristic of God. We know this because God is also seen in motherly/feminine terms in the OT, e.g., Isaiah 49:14-15.

Jesus also used motherly terms for himself (Luke 13:34).

Jesus is, therefore, empowered with God's Spirit to fulfil God's call. His Spirit-baptism reveals and confirms him as *Ha Mashiach*. He is the Anointed King who brings the Kingdom and baptises all who enter it with God's eschatological Spirit, in fulfilment of the prophets (Joel 2:28f). John notes (1:33) that the Spirit came on Jesus 'to remain' (*meno,* to abide, dwell), not to 'lift off' as in the OT. The equivalent in the synoptic gospels is the (symbolism of) the Spirit coming on Jesus "like a dove". It is unclear whether they meant in the manner or in the actual form of a dove. However, they knew Jesus received the Spirit because she descended and rested on him like *a dove.*

For the Jewish mind, this recalls the story of the flood and God's promise of new creation (Genesis 8:6-12). After the flood, Noah released a raven (unclean animal, Deuteronomy 14:11-20) which flew restlessly "back and forth until the water had dried up from the earth". Then he sent out a dove (*yona,* a 'clean' bird of sacrifice, especially for the poor, Leviticus 5:7, 14:21-22, symbolising innocence, gentleness, and purity). It returned because it found "no resting place". After being sent out the second time it returned with a sign of new creation, "a freshly plucked olive leaf". The third time it was sent out, it *remained,* making its dwelling under the rainbow of new creation.

The Spirit, therefore, remained on Jesus like a dove to inaugurate God's new creation. Peter, in fact, says Noah's flood symbolised water baptism (1 Peter 3:20-22): we are saved *in/through* Messiah's death, resurrection, and ascension, whereby he now rules "at God's right hand" over all the chaotic (evil) powers that once ruled over us.

Jews would have also picked up an allusion to the first creation in Genesis 1:2. God's *Ruach* 'hovered' (*merahepet,* 'move', 'incubate') over the waters to enact creation as God spoke, his "voice from heaven". *Merahepet* is feminine bird imagery used of God "hovering" like an eagle over Israel (Deuteronomy 32:11). The Essenes taught that God's *Ruach* "will hover over" the humble (saints) in the last days, applying Genesis 1:2 eschatologically (Dead Sea Scrolls, 4Q52. Wise *et al* 2005:531). The Talmud (*Haggadah* 15a) likens the brooding of the Spirit over the waters at creation to the fluttering of a *yona.* It is as if the Holy Spirit hovered over the waters of John's baptism waiting to descend on The One called to enact God's new creation.

"A voice came from heaven saying..."

When heaven was torn open and the Spirit came on Jesus, a voice spoke from the atmosphere around them. Jews knew this "voice from heaven" as *bat kol*, literally "the daughter of a voice". The rabbis taught that when God speaks in heaven, sometimes "an echo" (*bat kol*) is heard on earth. It referred to God's supernatural method of speaking his will *after* the last of the Hebrew prophets, as stated in the *Tosifta* (meaning "supplement", additional texts to the Mishna):

> "After the death of Haggai, Zechariah, and Malachi, the last of the prophets, the Holy Spirit ceased from Israel; nevertheless, they received communications from God through the medium of the *Bat Kol*" (*Tosifta Sot.* XIII.2)

Cohen (1949:45-47) gives examples of the *bat kol* in The Mishna and Talmud. Though not on the level of prophecy, the gospels show how God's heavenly voice confirmed John's prophecy of Jesus as the Messiah. It accompanied the return of the Spirit to Israel, settling and remaining on *Yeshua*, Israel's representative. The "voice from heaven" broke 400 years of silence, confirming Jesus as the Spirit-bringer, a clear sign of the dawning of the Messianic Age. The affirming *bat kol* is heard again during Jesus' ministry, when he transfigured on Mount Tabor (Mark 9:7), and a week before he died (John 12:28).

More than that, God personally affirmed *Yeshua* as his son: "You are my Son, my Beloved; with you I am well pleased." (Mark 1:11 NRSV). All that Jesus dared to believe as he grew up in Nazareth under his father's tutelage was now supernaturally confirmed. "*Yhwh* is my *Abba*! My real Father. I am his specially loved son".

Greek *agapetos*, "beloved", is a term of endearment and affection. The underlying Hebrew *yachid* means "uniquely loved/chosen", "one and only". It's used for Isaac when God called Abraham to sacrifice him in Genesis 22:2,12,16, "Take your son, your only son, whom you love". Also, for the mysterious "pierced one" whom Israel will see (Zechariah 12:10 cf. Revelation 1:7). Vermes (1961:193-227) has shown how Judaism viewed Isaac as the type of the beloved son and willing sacrifice, i.e., Jesus fulfils all that is implied in the offering of Isaac and the "pierced one". They foreshadow God's chosen identity and sacrificial destiny for Jesus as God's "Beloved".

Being called God's *agapetos/yachid* was not a theological notion as such; it was a profound subjective affirmation. Imagine what this meant for Jesus? An overwhelming outpouring and immersion into infinite love? The Father poured himself into his son, by his Spirit, in a *kenosis* of love (*self-emptying*, Philippians 2:7). It affirmed Jesus' identity and destiny, empowering him to pour out his life in a *kenosis* of *Abba's* love by the power of his Spirit of Love. Note that I used lowercase 'son' in keeping with the Jewish idea of 'messiah' as a human anointed by God – not as a Divine Being *per se*.

For Jesus, it was a supernatural experience that confirmed:

- The *personal* love that he had known in each moment of every day from an early age.

- The *parenting* love that gave Jesus his deep sense of identity, value, and belonging.

- The *purposeful* love that conceived and called forth his life-meaning and work for God.

- The *perfect* love that was the source of his love for others: "As the Father has loved me, so have I loved you" (John 15:9).

- The *passionate* love that not only sustained but energised and enabled him in his passion (suffering) and death.

"You are my Son, my Beloved, with you I am well pleased"

The words God spoke in Mark 1:11 joined two OT texts: "You are my son..." from David's messianic psalm (2:7), and "my Beloved, with you I am well pleased" from Isaiah's messianic servant song (42:1).

When an OT phrase is quoted in the NT, *the context* of the phrase is 'connoted', i.e., is meant to be recalled to interpret *the full meaning* of the phrase. We see this repeatedly in our portrait of Jesus. Informed Jewish readers of the gospels at that time would have understood the meaning (and implications) of the *bat kol* in this way.

Thus, the context of "You are my son" in Psalm 2 is the nations and their kings, who "band together against the LORD and his anointed" to throw off God's rule (1-3). But *Yhwh* scoffs at them: "I have installed my king on Zion" (4-6). Then in 7-9, David proclaims the decree that *Yhwh* spoke to him in 2 Samuel 7:14. God now personally speaks that same affirmation to/over Jesus in the *bat kol*:

> "He said to me, "*You are my son*; today I have become your father. Ask me, and I will make the nations your inheritance, the ends of the earth your possession..." (Psalm 2:7-9).

Therefore, the kings/rulers are warned to "be wise" and "serve *Yhwh*... celebrate his rule with trembling". How? "Kiss the son" (10-12), i.e., worship God's son, the Messiah-King. The nations are his inheritance; the earth is his possession. He is given all the authority in the heavens and on the earth, to rule with justice and peace.

2 Samuel 7:14 and Psalm 2:7 were favourite texts in the early church, applied to Jesus as God's messianic son, seen in the gospels and Acts 13:33-34 cf. Romans 1:4, Hebrews 1:5, 5:5.

The second phrase, "my Beloved, with you I am well pleased", is a quote from Isaiah's first messianic servant song (42:1-9), interpreted in the broader context of his servant songs (49:1-13, 50:4-11, 52:13–53:12). The phrase recalls and connotes this immediate context:

> "Here is my servant, whom I uphold, *my chosen one in whom I delight*; I will put my Spirit on him, and he will bring forth justice to the nations. He will not shout or cry out or raise his voice in the streets. A bruised reed he will not break, and a smouldering wick he will not snuff out. In faithfulness he will bring forth justice; he will not falter or be discouraged till he establishes justice on earth" (Isaiah 42:1-4).

The Spirit coming on Jesus, with the confirming *bat kol,* directly fulfils Isaiah's prophecy. Jesus is *Yhwh's* Spirit-filled servant, identified as "my chosen/beloved one". What follows, "in whom I delight", can be rendered "in whom I am well pleased" or "on whom my favour rests". One can imagine what these affirmations meant for Jesus. At one level it was a prophetic proclamation confirming his identity and mission. At another level it was a profound psycho-spiritual confirmation of his experience of God's delight in him as he grew up.

In summary

Jesus' baptism in water and in the Spirit, with the heavenly affirming *bat kol*, confirmed what he came to know, believe, and embrace in his developing consciousness in Nazareth: the experience of *Abba's* pleasure and favour on him. Not (only) because of his obedience (in baptism), but because of who he was. His 'being-in-love' as God's son. *He* is *Yhwh's* servant, who will gently, compassionately, faithfully, and persistently bring forth God's justice on the earth.

Therefore, in quoting the above two texts, God identified and confirmed Jesus as God's royal son and *Yhwh's* messianic servant.

Note that Mark and Luke (3:22) personalise it as God speaking to Jesus, "*You* are my Son, my Beloved...". However, Matthew (3:17) puts it in the third person, "*This* is my Son, the Beloved..." (NRSV), i.e., it was addressed to Jesus *and* to all present as witnesses. God, in effect, declared to all Israel that Jesus is his Messianic Son and Servant – now using capital 'Son' and 'Servant' as messianic titles.

QUESTIONS FOR REFLECTION AND DISCUSSION

1. Have you identified yourself with Jesus in water baptism, your first public act of obedience to Jesus as his disciple/apprentice?

2. What did Jesus' baptism mean – to him and all who watched? What does your water baptism mean – to you and all who witnessed it?

3. Jesus learnt from John. Who has been your primary mentor in following Jesus? What mentorship do you need going forward?

4. Have you experienced – and how can you live out – the three things that happened to Jesus:

    a) Open heavens

    b) Baptism in/with the Holy Spirit, and

    c) *Abba's* affirmation of love – to live in/from your new identity in Christ as God's *Agapetos*?

5. How can you ongoingly receive and nurture the love that the Father pours into you by his Holy Spirit? See Romans 5:5.

CONFRONTATION & CONSOLATION

The next feature of Jesus' portrait, his confrontation with evil and consolation from God, follows his water and Spirit baptism. The power-encounter that Jesus experienced had an immediate effect. The Spirit sent Jesus into the desert for forty days of fasting and prayer, where the devil tempted him.

The chapter division by the translators in Matthew (4:1) and Luke (4:1) is unfortunate. It separates Jesus' wilderness confrontation from his baptism. The two stories are one unfolding story. The earliest gospel, Mark, makes it clear, especially in the NRSV: "*And* just as he was coming up out of the water..." (1:10), "*And* a voice came from heaven..." (1:11), "*And* the Spirit *immediately* drove him out into the wilderness..." (1:12). "And" joins each event into one story like a seamless garment. It should be read that way.

A feature of Mark's biography is his repeated use of *euthys*, "immediately", "at once", "without delay". He uses this word 47 times, presenting a fast-moving story filled with short, sharp, action-packed historical events in the life of Jesus of Nazareth.

To understand the significance of Jesus' wilderness temptations, we need to first, once again, look at the OT background, context, and symbolism. Then we examine each of the three temptations and what they meant for the historical Jesus, and his first followers.

Like Jesus' baptism in water and Spirit, this historical event was an early church *midrash*, an interpretative instruction for Christ-followers. Note that in this chapter, unlike all the others, I go beyond the historical Jesus to explain how Christian tradition interpreted Jesus' three temptations to equip his apprentices. Briefly, the temptations address the three basic dimensions of human life: our relationship to materiality (possessions), to society (people), and power (politics). Or simply: money, sex, and power – the three core temptations that test all of us. And more so, leaders.

Mark, Matthew, and Luke tell the same historical story, but each with different nuances and emphases, to instruct followers of Jesus.

BACKGROUND CONTEXT AND SYMBOLISM

After important revelatory experiences and power encounters, people often withdraw from society to be alone. This is especially true of the Hebrew prophets. The purpose is for solitude. To reflect on what happened, to process it with God through prayer and meditation. Fasting was sometimes included as a means of disciplined focus, to wait on God, to understand the meaning of the revelation, and to intercede for its fulfilment in God's time and way.

The Battle

Remember, from a human point of view, the desert experience was *not* an exhilarating time of triumph for Jesus. Like no other, the desert is a place of self-stripping from all attachments. It imposes an outer struggle of isolation and bodily need that is but a shadow of the dark inner battle it provokes. Jesus entered its depths.

I have a minuscule understanding of what he experienced. Before I entered ordained ministry in January 1975, I went into the mountains for a week of preparation in total fasting and prayer, drinking water from a stream near my little tent. The first three days were fine. The next four were filled with conflict, self-doubt, weakness, depression, and temptation. My mind went wild. I had weird dreams. I did it for seven days. Jesus did it for forty days and nights in the desert.

Evil came at Jesus with great force. The spirit world was alive with warfare. He was confronted in the whole of who he was, in his spirit, mind, emotions and body. We do not know if the devil appeared to Jesus, or if he was tempted through his thoughts, feelings, and body (as we all are) – certainly the latter.

Matthew (4:1) and Luke (4:1) use the passive "Jesus was *led* by the Spirit". But Mark says, "the Spirit *drove* him out into the wilderness" (1:12 NRSV). He used the active verb *ekbalo,* to expel, drive out. Mark uses it eleven times, commonly of Jesus later driving out demons (e.g., 1:34, 3:15, 22-23). The Spirit drove Jesus out "immediately", i.e., divine urgency impelled Jesus, sending him out to face and defeat the devil and his demons. *Ekbalo* does not imply a force beyond or against

Jesus' will. He willingly yielded to the compunction of the Spirit, "not my will, but yours be done".

What Mark reports is consistent with the stories of the prophets seized and driven by the *Ruach ha Kodesh* to various places (1 Kings 18:12; 2 Kings 2:16; Ezekiel 3:12,14f).

The thought is that God himself sends Jesus into battle – as his human representative, as Israel's representative – against Satan. The Spirit, therefore, drives him into the habitation of demons to drive demons out of their habitation – later seen in peoples' bodies. Jesus does this by facing and defeating the evil one, *ha satan,* the "opposer" and "adversary" (the Hebrew meaning) of God and his people.

In Jewish literature the arid desert was a cursed place, the haunt of demons. Jesus alluded to it, "When an impure spirit comes out of a person, it goes through *arid places* seeking rest and does not find it" (Matthew 12:43). This idea is borne out in Mark's stark account of Jesus' desert confrontation (1:12-13 NRSV).

> "And the Spirit immediately drove him out into the wilderness. He was in the wilderness forty days, tempted by Satan; and he was with the wild beasts; and the angels waited on him."

By repeating "the wilderness" (desert), Mark emphasises it. And his comment, "with the wild beasts", shows how brutal the confrontation was, on Satan's turf as it were. In reading this, the Jewish mind would recall Isaiah 11:6f, how peace (*Shalom*) will reign among the wild animals in Messiah's Kingdom. Safety among beasts signified God's protection and favour (Psalm 91:11-13; Ezekiel 34:25; Daniel 6:22).

Mark's report that angels attended to him is further consolation amid desolation. This confrontation with *ha satan* was so intense that angels came to strengthen him. That happened again in the Garden of Gethsemane (Luke 22:43), showing from the gospel record that Jesus' greatest tests were at the beginning and the end of his ministry. However, he sustained attacks by the evil one throughout his ministry at various "opportune times" (Luke 4:13).

It indicates that the battle with Satan *and* the peace of God on earth have already begun. It suggests that Jesus operated *both* in the open heavens of God's love and power, by Spirit-baptism, *and* in the desert of evil attack and temptation, by Spirit-compulsion.

The Symbolism

Jesus probably modelled himself on Moses and Elijah, who spent forty days and nights fasting and praying alone (Deuteronomy 9:9; 1 Kings 19:8). They, too, were supernaturally sustained by God. The symbolism of Moses was particularly significant because it embodied Israel's story, which Jesus sought to relive and fulfil.

The Exodus through the Sea led Moses and Israel to Mount Sinai. There Moses spent *forty days* in God's presence receiving The Law, *Yhwh's* "covenant of love" with Israel (Deuteronomy 7:9,12). Israel then spent *forty years* in the wilderness disobeying that Law, rejecting *Yhwh's* loyal love, and breaking faith with him. That generation died in the wilderness. They did not enter God's Promised Land.

In the previous chapter we saw how Jesus' water baptism symbolised a new Exodus for Israel into the promised Kingdom that Jesus proclaimed. Matthew (4:1) and Luke (4:1) record that the Spirit then "led" Jesus into the wilderness, echoing the Cloud and Fire that led Moses and Israel from the Red Sea to Sinai and through the wilderness (Exodus 13:21-22). Thus, Jesus, like Moses, fasted and prayed for forty days. He was entrusted with the new covenant of Spirit-enabled obedience by Spirit-infused love, which *Yhwh* promised through Ezekiel (36:24-27) and Jeremiah (31:31-34).

Jesus' forty days thus symbolised a reversal of Israel's forty years in the wilderness. He consciously embodied Israel, God's son coming out of Egypt ("my son", Matthew 2:15 cf. Exodus 4:22). Having received *Yhwh's* covenant of love ("You are my son, my Beloved), he responded in loving obedience, keeping faith. His forty days of testing was a representative reliving of Israel's forty years in the wilderness, seen in his quotes from Deuteronomy. Whereas Jesus was full of the Holy Spirit and followed the Spirit's guidance, Israel "rebelled and grieved his Holy Spirit" (Isaiah 63:10). So, where Israel disobeyed, Jesus obeyed, overcoming Satan's temptations on Israel's behalf. Jesus did for Israel what Israel did not/could not do for herself.

Temptation and Testing

Lastly, the Greek *peirazo* can mean both "to tempt" and "to test" (Matthew 4:1). The devil *tempts* us to do evil, to disobey God. That is a *test* of faith. God allows the temptation to test our allegiance to him.

James distinguishes between temptation by evil and testing by God. "No one, when tempted, should say, 'I am being tempted by God'; for God cannot be tempted by evil, nor does he tempt anyone" (James 1:13). We are tempted via "one's own *desires*" (*epithumia*, 1:14): both natural *and* corrupted psycho-emotional desires *and* bodily appetites. *Epithumia*, commonly translated as "lust", gives a sinful connotation. Desires are not sinful in themselves but are used by evil to entice us to sin. We only sin when we act on enticement, yielding to temptation (1:15). We must be clear: *we* sin – the devil doesn't make us sin!

But, as already stated, God does test us by allowing all kinds of temptations and trials (1:2, James uses *peirasmos* nine times in 1:2-14). God does it to see what is in our hearts, whether we choose his loving truth or evil's lying deception. By routinely choosing the former, with the Spirit's help, we obey God. We progressively become "mature and complete, not lacking anything" (1:2-4). In other words, we do God's will on earth as Jesus did.

Jesus overcame three *temptations* to do evil, by which God *tested* him. They are three core temptations common to humanity – representative of the three basic dimensions of life. The first followers of Jesus believed, according to Hebrews, that he was tempted/tested in all the ways that we are, yet he did not sin (Hebrews 4:15). He did not sin because "in the days of his flesh, Jesus offered up prayers and petitions with loud cries and tears to the One who could save him from death, and he was heard because of his reverent submission" (5:7).

In other words, he asked God for mercy and grace to help in times of need (4:16). Sometimes desperately so, "with loud cries and tears", as in the desert of Judea and the garden of Gethsemane. He was heard because he yielded in trust: "not my will, but yours be done". Thus, "Although he was a Son, he *learned* obedience through what he suffered" (5:8). Obedience was *not* automatic, *not* a default setting by the divine nature. Jesus, "in the days of his flesh" (5:7, emphasising his humanity), learnt to obey *Abba* through outer suffering and inner conflicts, in trials and temptations that tested his will. Jesus had to draw deeply on God's consolation to learn to obey in loving faith.

Paul puts it this way in 1 Corinthians 10:13,

> "No *peirasmos* (testing/temptation) has overtaken you except what is common to humankind. And God is faithful; he will not let you be tempted beyond what you can bear. But when you are

tempted, he will also provide a way out so that you can endure it."

Paul assures us that God will never allow us to be tempted/tested beyond what we can bear. Jesus knew that and drew on God's consolation to endure and overcome. With every desolate *peirasmos*, God provides a way through and out. That is, if we ask God for help, as Jesus did, and respond to and act on God's way of overcoming the temptation. This was Jesus' experience in the wilderness.

We will see, therefore, that each temptation he faced a) questioned his *identity*, b) challenged his *mission*, and c) questioned *God's word and character*. Jesus overcame each temptation by believing, quoting, and obeying God's word. Luke (4:13) said that "When the devil had finished all this tempting, he left him until an opportune time". He was tempted whenever the opportunity arose throughout his ministry, i.e., ongoing spiritual warfare. We all experience it.

I follow Matthew's account and add from Luke as appropriate.

THE FIRST TEMPTATION

Matthew 4:2-4 NRSV. Jesus fasted forty days and forty nights, and afterwards he was famished. The tempter said to him, "If you are the Son of God, command these stones to become loaves of bread." But he answered, "It is written, 'One does not live by bread alone, but by every word that comes from the mouth of God.'"

The Nature of the Temptation

I make the following observations from the text. Note that I use my RAP below as an updated take on the dialogue.

First, it was *after* Jesus had fasted forty days that he "was famished", i.e., starvation had set in. The average human body can go without food, surviving on liquids, for more or less forty days. Then excruciating pain racks the body as it eats itself to survive. That makes the temptation all the more vicious. Perhaps Jesus hallucinated, seeing the rocks turning into bread. It went beyond his *wanting* or *desiring* food. It was an enticement that used his desperate *need* – every cell in his body screamed for bread to survive.

Second, Satan challenged and questioned *Jesus' identity*. "Are you really God's son? His Beloved? If you are, then prove it. As his son, use the power God gave you by his Spirit to turn these stones into bread, to feed yourself. Come on, satisfy your need."

Third, to provide bread in the desert recalls God's provision of manna through Moses, when Israel was hungry in the wilderness. The devil tempted Jesus to meet the Jewish expectation of the new Moses, to confirm and fulfil his *messianic mission* for Israel. "Speak your own words and do the miracle that is needed. Take things into your own hands to meet people's expectations, provide bread from heaven."

Fourth, the underlying thrust was the slanderous questioning of *God's character*: "Is God really your *Abba*? Why are you so hungry, in such desperate need if he loves you? Can you trust him? Can you trust the words that come from his mouth? Will he provide for you?" It echoes the serpent's words to Eve, "Did God really say...?" (Genesis 3:1-5). And Israel in the wilderness, "We have no food! We're going to die! God doesn't care! Take us back to Egypt!" (Exodus 16:3f). Greek *diabolos,* the devil, means "slanderer" of God's word and character. The essence of evil is slander and lies. Satan makes us question God's integrity and blame God, to drive a wedge between us and God. He would have us believe God is the ultimate cosmic abuser, so that we can become our own god and run our lives our way.

The Significance of the Overcoming

In all the above nuances, Jesus resisted and countered the temptation by quoting Deuteronomy 8:3, "I don't live by bread alone, but by *every word God speaks*". It reveals, a) his memorisation of Torah – it was in his mind and heart; b) his affirmation of faith in God's word as truth – it was on his lips; c) his choice to obey – it was his will and actions; and d), by quoting the text Jesus implies the context that explains its full meaning. Let's read Deuteronomy 8:2-5 (NRSV),

> "Remember the long way that the LORD your God has led you these forty years in the wilderness, in order to humble you, testing you to know what was in your heart, whether or not you would keep his commandments. He humbled you by letting you hunger, then by feeding you with manna, with which neither you nor your ancestors were acquainted, *in order to make you understand that one does not live by bread alone, but by every word that comes from the mouth of the LORD.* The clothes on your back did not wear out

and your feet did not swell these forty years. Know then in your heart that as a parent disciplines a child so the LORD your God disciplines you."

Yhwh led the Israelites through the desert to test them. He exposed their hearts to see if they would live by God's word, i.e., obeying by believing. Or, if they would live by "the lust of the flesh" (1 John 2:16), i.e., satisfying their desires/instincts by "speaking their own words", complaining and commanding, "take us back to Egypt".

To live by the words that God speaks is eternal life. It transcends physical life sustained by food – life dependent on meeting material needs. Their life depended on God. Their ultimate need was God. They needed to learn and live by *that* reality for life in *Yhwh's* Kingdom. So, God humbled them by letting them go hungry. Then miraculously fed them to train ("discipline") them to live by faith, relying ultimately on God for all things, for life itself.

Israel demanded bread and died in the desert. Jesus denied himself bread and lived in his Father's Kingdom by faithful submission to his word. "My food is to do the will of him who sent me and to finish his work" (John 4:34). Jesus refused to speak his own words to do miracles to prove his identity as the new Moses. He refused to use his sonship to fulfil his messianic mission in a way that God had not spoken. And he refused to doubt *Abba's* character by believing and obeying every word that came from God's mouth.

In short, where Israel failed, Jesus succeeded, doing for her what she did not do. Jesus was Israel's representative, God's obedient son, who relived, reinterpreted, and fulfilled Israel's story and destiny.

The Interpretation of the Economic Test

Christian tradition interprets this temptation as the economic test because it addresses the material dimension of life – our relationship to material needs – to money, resources, and possessions.

As physical beings, we depend on fulfilling our basic *needs* and bodily *appetites* for life. Then, our psycho-emotional *wants* and *desires* for 'things' to secure us – let alone to make us feel comfortable, content, and happy. Beyond that are unrestrained wants and desires indulged in materialism and excessive wealth – "the *love* of money is the root of all kinds of evil" (1 Timothy 6:10; Hebrews 13:5).

Thus, as mortal/fallen beings, our appetites, passions, instincts, wants and desires, are corrupted. They are oriented and conditioned by sin to serve self as god. If they are not redeemed and reoriented to God, made fit for eternal life, they progressively enslave and drive us as merciless masters, which is hell on earth. These are 'the vices' that rule us if we don't put them to death by use of 'the virtues' (see my discussion on this in Venter 2019:253-60).

Our appetites and desires must be disciplined and trained in the desert of self-stripping – as with Israel – to serve God in the Promised Land of his Kingdom. If we cannot rule, under God, over our body with its needs, we will not be able to reign, with God, over (new) creation. Our body is, literally, the first piece of earth where God's will is to be done, just as it is in heaven.

Thus, the economic temptation addresses our relationship with materiality, testing and teaching us to live by faith in God. Do we trust God's word that he will provide and care for his beloved? Or do we grumble with discontent in the wilderness of life, speaking our own words to make miracles and secure ourselves? In short, do we live by "the lust of the flesh" – disordered desires – or by reordered desires trained to live by God's desire for us (our ultimate wellbeing)?

At a deeper level, are we secure in our identity as God's beloved daughter/son? Or do we define ourselves by what we have/possess – or don't have? And do we use our identity to prove ourselves? To speak words and do miracles to provide for ourselves and others in a way inconsistent with God's ordained mission for our lives?

Traditionally, monks and priests took a *vow of poverty* to counter this economic temptation. It disciplined and formed their relationship with materiality so that they would live by faith in God for all things. The vow of poverty, correctly understood, is helpful. But it has led to an incorrect view of poverty as a virtue, to be aspired to as a means and measure of spirituality. I cannot discuss the NT's nuanced understanding of poverty, but there is nothing good about poverty in itself. *Some* poor people are as materialistic as rich people, driven by greed of need for 'things' to save and secure them. Ironically, materialism can be the god of the poor and the rich.

A better way of countering and overcoming this temptation, which represents all tests related to our material well-being, is to practice *the disciplines of fasting, giving, frugality, and sacrifice* (I discuss them, including other disciplines of abstinence, in Venter, 2019:338-62). These classic spiritual disciplines form the character we need to enjoy all things as good gifts from God while holding them lightly in full availability for use in his Kingdom. They mark us with gratitude for all things, with contentment in all things, and with generosity of service and sacrifice through all things.

So, these disciplines train us to live by every word that comes from God's mouth. We build up "treasures in heaven" (God's Kingdom on earth), worshipping God by trusting him with our materiality. In so doing, we defeat the worship of "Mammon" (Aramaic for money and possessions that Jesus personified as an idol, Matthew 6:19-24).

THE SECOND TEMPTATION

Matthew 4:5-7 NRSV. Then the devil took him to the holy city and placed him on the pinnacle of the Temple, saying, "If you are the Son of God, throw yourself down; for it is written, 'He will command his angels concerning you,' and 'On their hands they will bear you up, so that you will not dash your foot against a stone.'" Jesus said to him, "Again it is written, 'Do not put the Lord your God to the test.'"

The Nature of the Temptation

First, Satan again questioned *Jesus' identity*, "If you are the Son of God...", challenging him to prove he was God's son by doing something spectacular. Something that would, clearly, presume on God. To throw oneself off that high point and believe God "will command his angels" to save you, is not faith but presumption. To presume on God is to test him. In this case, to see if God would keep his word and save Jesus *from death* – the most extreme provocation to get God to perform.

Rabbis acknowledged that *ha satan* knew scripture. Jesus quoted God's word to Satan in resisting and overcoming the first temptation. So, *ha satan* now resorts to quoting scripture, purporting to speak with the words that come from God's mouth. However, he quoted Psalm 91:11-12 out of context. Verse 10 clarifies that God's angelic protection is for events that "befall you" (NRSV, e.g., Mark 1:13; Luke 22:43) – it's not an excuse to seek out those dangers.

Second, the temptation was to confirm and fulfil his *messianic mission* in a way inconsistent with God's will. To throw himself down and be saved by angels would 'wow' the people gathered at the Temple. To gain recognition and popularity, meeting Jewish messianic expectations. The Temple was where God was manifest. It's closely related to activities of God's King in Jewish messianic belief, seen in the following quote (though the source is dated later, it probably reflects a known Midrashic tradition in late Second Temple Judaism):

> "Our teachers taught, at the time when the King Messiah will appear, he will come and stand upon the roof of the Temple. He will proclaim to Israel and will say to the humble, 'The time of your redemption has arrived! If you do not believe – behold my light which shines upon you...'" (Pesikta Rabbati 36, in Young, 1995:31).

So, Satan tempted Jesus to reveal himself as the Messiah by appearing in supernatural power in the Temple to meet popular expectations and win acceptance and support for his messianic mission.

Third, is the questioning of *God's character*. Satan questioned the Father's love for his Beloved Son. This pitted God's Fatherhood against Jesus' sonship, demanding miraculous intervention from God to prove his love for Jesus – the same sentiment he endured while hanging on the cross (Matthew 27:43).

The Significance of the Overcoming

Once again Jesus counters, resists, and overcomes the temptation by quoting God's word, "It is written...". To reiterate, this indicates not only his knowledge and use of scripture but his resolute commitment to its truth and obedience to its instruction.

Jesus quotes Deuteronomy 6:16 in part. The full text says, "Do not put the LORD your God to the test *as you did at Massah*" (my italics). By quoting part of a text, Jesus implies knowledge and meaning of the context – in this case, the reference to Massah. In contrast, as mentioned earlier, *ha satan's* quote from Psalm 91:11-12 was glaringly out of context (10). He misapplied the text for his own (evil) purpose to tempt Jesus to evil, to presume on God.

What Moses refers to (Deuteronomy 6:16) and what Jesus thus implies, is the event recorded in Exodus 17:1-7. In their thirst, the Israelites quarrelled with Moses and grumbled against God. Though God gave them water from a rock, Moses asked, "Why do you put the

LORD to the test?" (17:2). He, therefore, called the place *Massah* ("testing") and *Meribah* ("quarrelling") because "they tested the LORD saying, 'Is the LORD among us?'" (17:7). Essentially, *Israel refused to accept God was among them unless he did miraculous signs.* If God did not perform to meet their expectations, God was not with them.

In fact, where Israel succumbed to Satan's temptation to provoke God with *supposed* death – "Why did you bring us up out of Egypt, to make us and our children and livestock die of thirst?" (17:3) – Jesus refused to presume on God to save him from *certain* death.

Hence, where Israel failed, Jesus obeyed and overcame. Instead of obeying *God's* test – "I will test them and see whether they will follow my instructions" (Exodus 16:4) – *they tested God* to see whether he would meet their expectations. They presumed on God to do miraculous signs to prove his presence, his love for them, by saving them from supposed death. Jesus trusted *Abba's* loving presence and didn't seek signs or miracles to prove it. Thus, he overcame, which enabled him to endure the ultimate test of his Father's (apparent) abandonment on the cross (Mark 15:34).

Unlike "my son" Israel (Exodus 4:22-23), Jesus was secure in his identity as God's son, quenching his thirst by drinking the cup *Abba* gave him in the wilderness. He was the true son, the embodiment of the true Israel. He did not need to use his identity to manipulate God into backing him up, vindicating his messianic mission. He did not have to 'wow' people in any way for acceptance and recognition – least of all for popularity – to fulfil his messianic mission.

The Interpretation of the Social Test

Christian tradition calls this temptation the social test because it addresses the people/relational sphere of life, our 'relationality' in terms of how we treat others – including God.

How we relate to others is, essentially, about human sexuality – relating in love or in lust, honouring or using others. God created humans in his likeness, by love, in love, for love. Adam and Eve were created by relationship (God as "us", Genesis 1:26), in relationship (the one became two), and for relationship (the two become one). We are relational beings who were made to love and be loved.

As relational beings we depend on fulfilling psycho-social-sexual needs and desires for life. Without relationships, love and belonging, we wither and die. However, our natural desires are corrupted by sin. If allowed, they progressively form us into their image and likeness: the idolatry of self. We become self-focused and selfish, defining ourselves (self-identifying) by our feelings and preferences. Then we presume on others, relating in ways that use them to meet our needs and desires.

However, redeemed in Christ, our psycho-social-sexual desires are progressively transformed and trained for loving service of God and others. That builds the sexual character needed to truly love.

Thus, the social temptation addresses our relationality, testing and teaching us to live by love for God and others, not by using God and people for our purposes. That is lust, treating others as objects for use to meet our expectations and fulfil our desires, to achieve our purpose and agenda in life. It is "the lust of the eyes" (1 John 2:16), as Jesus taught, "anyone who looks at a woman (or a man) lustfully has already committed adultery with her in his heart" (Matthew 5:28). Love, however, sees others with respect and dignity as God's image. Love doesn't presume on others, but relates in selfless, even self-sacrificing ways to promote their highest good, honour their uniqueness and bring out their best. This applies to our relationship with God.

Can God entrust people to us? To our leadership and mission? Are we secure in our identity as his Beloved? In his love for us? When we are defined by our mission and ministry or by our need for acceptance and recognition, we succumb to the social temptation. We use others for our purpose and perform for popular expectation, to meet our psycho-ego-sexual needs to feel good about ourselves.

Sadly, many leaders lead by lust, not by love, using and abusing people to achieve their mission and vision. Jesus refused to do that. No gimmicks. No manipulation. No need to use God or angels to 'wow' people for a desired outcome. No need to prove oneself. No need to test or provoke God.

Traditionally, monks and priests took a *vow of celibacy* to counter social temptation. Celibacy means no sexual engagement at all. They believed it disciplined and formed their relating with people to love as God loves. But, unless one is naturally capacitated or gifted by God to be celibate for life, as Jesus and Paul taught (Matthew 19:11-12; 1 Corinthians 7:7), then it's problematic. Wrong suppression of our sexuality leads to lust, rather than healthy sublimation that energises human relationships with *God's* passion of pure love.

The classic spiritual discipline of *chastity* effectively counters and overcomes this temptation. The practice of chastity is to discipline our normal sexual desire so that it doesn't rule us – burning with lust – but comes under God's rule. That enables us to be celibate until marriage, as well as sexually faithful in marriage. A chaste person has the social-sexual character to relate purely in love, not in lust. Under God, the gift of sexuality is the fire of God's love that energises human relationships with the integrity of trust and intimacy, through acts that promote the highest good of the other.

THE THIRD TEMPTATION

Matthew 4:8-11 NRSV. Again, the devil took him to a very high mountain and showed him all the kingdoms of the world and their splendour; and he said to him, "All these I will give you, if you will fall down and worship me." Jesus said to him, "Away with you, Satan! For it is written, 'Worship the Lord your God, and serve only him.'" Then the devil left him, and suddenly angels came and waited on him.

The Nature of the Temptation

While this is Matthew's third temptation, in Luke's account it is the second temptation. He also adds more detail (4:5-8) than Matthew, which I will refer to.

Simply put, this temptation is an easy shortcut to ultimate power. The offer was to receive and rule the nations, which was Israel's destiny and inheritance through the Messianic Son of David (Psalm 2:8-9). Satan tempted Jesus to fulfil his identity and mission as the theocratic political King (Son of David) *without having to be the suffering servant King* (Servant of *Yhwh*, Isaiah 52:13–53:1-12).

However, it's more nuanced. More background information is needed to understand the real nature of this temptation.

Jesus being taken up a high mountain to be shown all the kingdoms of the world recalls Moses going up Mount Nebo where "the LORD showed him the whole land" (Deuteronomy 34:1-4, all the territories are mentioned). This was Israel's promised inheritance, a symbol for inheriting the whole earth (Psalm 37:11 cf. Matthew 5:5).

Luke's use of "all the kingdoms of the world" (4:5) is ironic because he earlier used a similar phrase when Emperor Augustus decreed "that *all the world* should be registered" (2:1 NRSV). The NIV adds a word, "the entire *Roman* world...". In other words, all the world, including the Roman Empire, is under the devil's authority (4:6), "I will give you all their authority and splendour; it has been given to me, and I can give it to anyone I want to". The Roman Empire was ruled by the spiritual powers (*ha satan*) behind the political power, which is made abundantly clear in Revelation 13.

It's the Jewish idea of the angels assigned to the scattered nations of Babel (Genesis 11 cf. Deuteronomy 32:8). Their idolatrous rule uses ideological and structural power to oppose God and his people. In the NT they are "the rulers, authorities, principalities and powers of this dark world" under Satan's rule (Ephesians 6:12). He is "the god of this age" (2 Corinthians 4:4), "the prince of this world" (John 12:31).

Jesus did not, therefore, dispute Satan's claim to such authority in "this present evil age" (Galatians 1:4). This evil age began when Adam and Eve sold out to the devil by giving away their God-given authority to rule the earth when they believed his lie. They, in effect, bowed down to worship him, to be "God" over the earth (Genesis 3:5).

Instead, they became slaves on the earth, exiled from Eden, under Satan's rule of sin, sickness, demons, and death. Israel, likewise, gave away her God-given authority to rule over the Promised Land through the worship of idols. So, God gave them over to the rule of foreign gods in exile. Israel repeated Adam's sin, instead of reversing it.

However, technically, the world did not belong to *ha satan*. He only owned human hearts and societies *as a usurper*. Ultimately, Jesus knew that the Creator-God is "sovereign over all kingdoms on earth and *gives them to anyone he wishes*" (Daniel 4:32). In Daniel's vision, the kingdoms of the earth are portrayed *like* beasts (7:3f). But the "Ancient of Days" gives them to "one *like* a son of man" (7:13-14), who is "given authority, glory, and sovereign power; all nations and peoples of every language worshipped him".

We will later see how Jesus knew these prophetic texts and took them to himself, using Daniel's "Son of Man" as his common self-designation, precisely because of its messianic overtones.

This background helps us better understand why and how Satan could tempt Jesus with power in that way. He wanted to:

- Subvert Jesus' messianic mission with the easy option of immediate political-military power. In so doing,
- Substitute Jesus' reliance on the Spirit's power with immediate political power from Satan. Jesus relied on the Spirit's power to fulfil his mission *in God's way*, the way of the cross. And,
- Substitute God's fatherhood with his own: Satan wanted Jesus' ultimate allegiance/worship, to deny his identity and sonship to God (Jesus referred to the devil as the father of those who do his "desires", John 8:44). If Jesus obeyed Satan's desire, it would be shameless idolatry.

We can hear Satan's challenge of God's character, "Do you *really* believe God your Father will *really* give you your inheritance? All the kingdoms of the world? And their splendour? Look and see! I can give it all to you right now! Just worship me!" But this, of course, is spurious because the devil and God are not co-equals.

We must remember that whatever authority *ha satan* has is limited and allowed by God (Job 1:9-12). He is like a muzzled dog on a leash. Despite Jesus knowing that, within his Jewish worldview, the temptation was genuine from a human viewpoint.

The Significance of the Overcoming

Jesus resisted and countered the temptation by quoting part of Deuteronomy 6:13. The full text says, "Fear the LORD your God, serve (worship) him only and take your oaths in his name." He is, once again, connoting the context to imply the text's proper meaning. The context is the *Shema Yisrael* ("Hear O Israel"), the core creedal confession for all Jews: "Hear, O Israel: The LORD our God, the LORD is one. Love the LORD your God with all your heart and with all your soul and with all your strength" (6:4-5). The following verses show that love for God is keeping his commands and not engaging in idolatry.

Thus, "Worship the Lord your God and serve him only" (Jesus' quote of 6:13) is immediately followed by, "*Do not follow other gods.* For the LORD your God, who is among you, is a jealous God and his anger will burn against you, and he will destroy you from the face of the land" (6:14-15). He will hand you over to the gods you worship, to be ruled by them. That is precisely what happened to Israel. So, where Israel fell into idolatry for (spiritual-political) power, Jesus overcame the temptation by worshipping (obeying) only the Creator – the God who revealed himself to Israel as *Yhwh*, her redeemer covenant King.

By passing the test not to worship Satan, Jesus lived the creedal confession of God's people. He expressly lived the reality that only one (true) God exists. All other so-called gods are false gods, evil usurpers, imposters, and deceivers. Like all Jews, Jesus knew that idolatry is unfaithfulness to *Yhwh*, as in spiritual prostitution. It is spiritual intercourse, becoming 'one in spirit' with the idol. Who/what you worship makes you into its image and likeness.

Jesus showed love for God by trusting and obeying his commands, worshipping and serving God only. *That* is where the power came from: God's Spirit through pure worship, becoming 'one in Spirit' with *Abba*, to live his identity as God's Son. As Messiah, he would fulfil his mission in *God's* time and way, through suffering and death, by a long obedience in the same direction, and to receive all the kingdoms of the world when God gives them, in fulfilment of Psalm 2:8.

In short, Jesus embodied the true Israel, faithful to God's covenant. He worshipped only God, being one in Spirit with God. He lived by the power of *that* Spirit, given to Jesus to exercise and execute the authority of God's Kingdom, to receive and rule over his inheritance.

By resisting Satan's temptation, Jesus was, by implication, the new Adam. His obedience regained, in principle, the God-given authority that Adam lost. In other words, because of Jesus' obedience, those in him, who follow his example, are the new humanity that will rule and reign over the (new) earth in all its (renewed) splendour.

Finally, Matthew says Jesus began his answer with, "Away from me, Satan..." (4:10). The phrase appears one other time in the gospels, in Matthew 16:22-23. It is when Jesus disclosed his messianic identity to his apostles and then explained that he would suffer, die, and rise again. Peter was shocked and rebuked him, "Never, Lord! This shall never happen to you!" Jesus turned and said to Peter, "*Get behind me, Satan!* You are a stumbling block to me; you do not have in mind God's interests, but human interests." The most direct severe rebuke for pure evil. Peter echoed Satan's offer to Jesus in the desert, the temptation to power: the Kingdom without the cross.

Jesus would have nothing to do with the grasp for power to rule as the triumphant Messiah, to be the all-conquering military-political Son of David. Jesus saw such popular expectation as idolatry of power in the form of Jewish nationalism. The idolatry of Jewish identity – of Israel's Temple, land, and destiny – that uses God and Messiah to secure them. *That* did not represent God's interests, but humanistic interests originating from Satan himself. *That* would bring God's burning anger on Israel, Jesus believed, to "destroy you from the face of the land". Nothing would subvert Jesus from God's interest: the powerlessness of the cross (humanly speaking – but God's power, biblically speaking) to save Israel and the nations of the earth.

The Interpretation of the Political Test

Christian tradition interprets this temptation as the political test because it addresses the dimension of power. It tests our relationship to power, both spiritual and political. They're profoundly intertwined in biblical theology – a reality we experience in personal relationships, families, social structures and political systems. We underestimate the spiritual power behind political power, the ideologies driving policies and practices. Especially when they are idolatrous and nationalistic. The most evil spiritual-political power is nationalism in the name of God, as in Jewish Zionism, Christian Nationalism, and Islamic Jihad.

The English word "politics" comes from Aristotle's classic work, *Politika,* meaning "affairs of the cities". It stems from *polis,* "city", *polites,* "citizen", and *polity,* "ordering the affairs/life" of the city/citizens. Thus, politics is life ordered under the government and policies of leaders, whether parents, church leaders, business, civic or political leaders, *for the good of society. That* is God's ordained and intended purpose in Romans 13:1f. We must pray for our leaders *to that end* (1 Timothy 2:1-2) because they are the centre of spiritual power-play in the world. All authority and power ultimately belong to and come from God. So, all exercise of power (of leadership) is spiritual *and* political, for better or worse, for good or evil, whether we know it or not.

Satan is the devil, the source of all evil, because he grasped for power in rebellion against God, and deceived humanity in Adam and Eve to grasp for divine power independent of God. Therefore, due to corrupt character, most use of power in human history is exploitative, oppressive, and anti-God. It seldom produces flourishing society, the common good, as God intended. As the English Catholic historian and politician Lord Acton famously said, "Power tends to corrupt and absolute power corrupts absolutely".

Jesus denied any power other than what was given to him by God's Spirit to be used in love of God for his purposes. *That* was the power of *obedience* in doing God's will by self-sacrificing love for the highest good of God's creation. Jesus submitted his willpower to the power of God's will – the way of human weakness in total dependence on God. God's power was made perfect in Jesus' powerlessness.

The impact of the historical Jesus on his first followers, in terms of power and politics – ordering the life and affairs of God's creation – is seen in the confessional hymn that Paul used in Philippians 2:6-11. Though equal with God as the eternal (pre-incarnate) son, Jesus did not hold onto that power as "something to be used to his own advantage". He let it go. He laid aside privilege, power and status, "made himself nothing" (*kenosis,* to empty, strip oneself), and took on "the form of a slave… and became *obedient* to the point of death, even death on a cross" (NRSV). *That* was Jesus' earthly life of worshipping *only* God. Thus, God vindicated him, entrusting *all* the authority and power in the heavens and the earth to him.

Traditionally, priests and monks take a vow of obedience to counter and defeat this temptation to power. They commit to a life of obedience to their superiors as if to God. That is, to deny any grasp for authority and power unless it is given to them, and then exercise it only in accordance with the purpose for which it is given, in obedience to those who give it. Though well-intended, such absolute obedience is often spiritually and politically abused due to corrupt character in human relationships and the ordering of affairs/life in community.

Classic spiritual disciplines of worship and submission counter and defeat this temptation to power. See Venter (2019:320-2, 355-7) for a full discussion on these practices. The practice of worship in daily acts of engagement and lived service bends the knee and bows the will to God's will in wonder-filled expression of his infinite worth. Authentic worship, "in spirit and truth" (John 4:24), is ever deeper levels of the surrender of our willpower, again and again, to God's eternal power and majesty, because of God's beauty and goodness.

The practice of submission engages us with God's authority and power. We yield our will by submitting to one another (Ephesians 5:21) and to the leaders God has placed in our lives (Hebrews 13:17), as a discipline that trains us to submit to God's greater will, all for the common good of family, Christian community, general society, and creation itself, as per God's intended purpose.

QUESTIONS FOR REFLECTION AND DISCUSSION

1. Do you experience spiritual warfare? Especially after powerful experiences with God? Give an example.

2. Why, in your own words, did Satan tempt Jesus in these ways?

3. What do you think of the traditional interpretation and teaching for Christ-followers, of the three temptations as material, social, and political? About money, sex, and power?

4. How does the devil tempt you? What is your common vice, or "besetting sin" as the KJV translates it in Hebrews 12:1? Which one of the three temptations are you most vulnerable to? Explain.

5. How do you overcome temptation – find God's "way out" as Paul says in 1 Corinthians 10:13? Describe it.

6. What spiritual disciplines must you practice to grow the moral character required to resist and overcome your temptations routinely?

MISSION & MESSAGE

Jesus' mission and message are paramount in understanding the real Jesus of history. To put it into context, let me recap.

We have seen how prophetic phenomena accompanied Jesus' conception and birth. The gospels frame the events in the coming of God's King and Kingdom with huge historical implications. Humanly speaking, the events were controversial to say the least. This baby, born "King of the Jews" (Matthew 2:2), was socially seen as a *mamzer*, illegitimately conceived. Questions of paternity plagued him all his life, as is evident in John 8:19,25,41,48,53.

Believing the storied explanations of his parents, Jesus bonded with God as his (real) Father from a young age. His profound intimacy with God as *Abba* was, perhaps, *the* distinctive feature of the young rabbi, *the* decisive factor in his 'hidden years' of psycho-spiritual formation in Nazareth. Luke lifted the veil on Jesus' developing consciousness at the age of twelve when he said, "I must be about my Father's business" (2:49). Jesus knew God was his Father, which gave him his *identity* as God's beloved son, and thus, his life's *mission* as *Yeshua,* to "save his people from their sin" (Matthew 1:21).

All that he dared to believe as he grew up was affirmed when he joined John the baptiser at the age of thirty. Jesus' baptism was a supernatural confirmation of his identity as God's Beloved Son and his mission as God's Messiah-King, which the devil confronted and tested. But Jesus overcame Satan's temptations. Israel disobeyed and died in her forty years of testing in the wilderness, failing in her training for reigning in the Promised Land. But Jesus obeyed as God's true son in his forty days of testing, leading the way for (the renewed) Israel into the Promised Land of God's Kingdom.

Then, as Luke 4:14 records, Jesus came out of the wilderness and "returned to Galilee in the power of the Spirit, and news about him spread through the whole countryside". In other words, he then began his public ministry *in the Spirit's power.* The same power that drove him out to confront *ha satan* that overcame the wilderness testing, that now sends him to do the mission of God's Kingdom.

This raises key questions. How clear was Jesus' sense of vocation? What were his aims and goals? *Specifically, what was his mission and message?* At the deepest level, what was his underlying *worldview*? In other words, his assumptions, ideas, and beliefs framed and motivated the answers to these questions and determined how he lived, what he preached, and what he did and did not do. These are the questions we now answer.

Our approach will be to introduce the central idea of the Kingdom of God in both Jesus' understanding and usage and the typical Jewish understanding in his day. We will start with Mark's gospel and then refer to Matthew and Luke. I will introduce the two primary motifs or self-designations Jesus chose for his purpose and mission. That will lead into a discussion on worldview: the four elements of any human worldview, how they applied to the prevailing Jewish worldview in Second Temple Judaism, and how Jesus reinterpreted them in his distinctive messianic worldview.

THE KINGDOM OF GOD

Scholars agree that the central mission and message of Jesus was "The Kingdom of God". Jesus spoke more about the Kingdom of God than any other theme. The imagery of God as King, and of his Kingdom, is familiar in Second Temple literature. However, it's nowhere near as prominent as in Jesus. His usage and meaning of the Kingdom of God were unique in the Judaism of his day. Mark uses "Kingdom of God", *basileia tou theou,* 14 times, Luke 32 times, and Matthew 4 times, though he uses "Kingdom of Heaven" (same meaning) 32 times. John's gospel uses it twice, but scholars agree that "life" (*zoe,* eternal life of the age to come), used 47 times, is his code for the Kingdom of God.

Therefore, what did "the Kingdom of God" mean to Jesus and his hearers? The short answer is God's Rule and Reign. Jesus' Aramaic *mulkuta di elaha* is *the action of God's Kingship* (defeating evil), echoing Isaiah 40:10, "See, the Sovereign LORD comes with power, he rules with a mighty arm". Thus, it meant "God coming in power to rule" (Meier's phrase, see 1994:237-288 for a full discussion). We examine below the difference between how Jesus understood and used the term, and how the Jews of his day heard and understood it.

Judaism – meaning all Jews, including Jesus – understood the Kingdom of God within their underlying space-time framework of two ages: *this age* and *the age to come* (e.g., Mark 10:30). We live in "the present evil age" (Galatians 1:4) of fallen humanity, in hope of the coming age of God's Kingdom. This foundational idea is represented in two statements: *God is King* (Creator-Ruler), and *God will become King* (Covenantal-Redeemer). Both are simultaneously true.

In summary, Jesus came to *inaugurate* the Kingdom of God in this age. He *announced, proclaimed, taught, enacted*, and *advanced* it. Each word is significant. Technically, he did not "establish" it because God's rule has always been established – in the heavens – God *is* King. However, Jesus came to inaugurate and advance it: God is *becoming* King in principle and power. The gospels also clearly teach that Jesus will come again to *establish* it on earth as in heaven: God will *become* King in fullness and finality. Then heaven will literally be on earth.

The idea of the King/Kingdom coming in two stages was unique to Jesus; not even John the Baptist made this distinction. Jews saw one coming of the *Mashiach*. They prayed daily for God's Rule to come and be *established* over all the earth, and *then* everyone will submit to God. They didn't see God's future rule coming first as a spiritual power-reality interrupting this age, where all who believe enter that Kingdom and begin doing God's will on earth as in heaven. For Jesus, where God's will is done his Kingdom has *already* come; where God's will is not done his Kingdom has *not yet* come (Matthew 6:10).

Mark's Account of Jesus' Generic Announcement of the Kingdom

Mark's biography of Jesus starts with "The beginning of the gospel of Jesus Christ, the Son of God" (1:1). He used "gospel", the technical word *evangelion,* meaning the good news that a herald (*evangelist*) would bring regarding an emperor/king: his birth, coronation, and conquests, or announcing his coming to a city or town. It is also used in the Greek translation of Isaiah 52:7, "the *evangelion*" of God's coming "salvation", when "Your God reigns". Isaiah's favourite word is "salvation", *yeshua* in Hebrew, used 28 times.

Thus, Mark opened his biography with the statement that *Yeshua ha Meshiach* is the good news of the King and the Kingdom. Then Mark gave Jesus' summary announcement of "the gospel of God... the Kingdom of God" – the generic message that he proclaimed in every city, town, and village of Israel-Palestine.

> After John was put in prison, Jesus went into Galilee, proclaiming the *gospel* of God. "*The time* has come," he said. "The *kingdom of God* has come near. *Repent* and *believe* the good news!" (1:14-15).

I have italicised the keywords. Having explained the "good news", let me briefly unpack the other keywords as to what Jesus meant from the evidence of the gospel writers.

1. "The time (*kairos*) has come" meant the fulfilment of the Hebrew prophets, the culmination of Israel's story. His audience knew the story and was awaiting its completion. Jesus proclaimed this end-time apocalyptic *kairos* wherever he went. He believed the climax of Israel's history had come upon them, as Paul said, "on whom the ends of the ages have come" (1 Corinthians 10:11).

2. "The Kingdom of God is near" meant God's future rule was near and active. The KJV and ESV use "*at hand*", i.e., reach out and receive God's rule in your life, in your world. The daily Jewish prayer for God's Kingdom to come was answered in Jesus. The Kingdom was present in power in his person, mission, message, and ministry.

3. "Repent" meant return to God from your exile in sin (as in John's baptism of repentance). Turn to God to see the King, receive his eschatological Spirit and enter his Kingdom. Repent, *metanoia*, literally means "change of mind". Jesus called Israel to a worldview shift, a change of thinking, to see what God was doing through him, to experience the Kingdom. Otherwise, their mindset would blind them to God's visitation: his offer of the Kingdom.

4. "Believe" meant trust in God and put your faith in him. Coupled with "repent", to believe is to open oneself to what God is doing, to the wildest possibilities of his Kingdom coming in power. God was on the march, returning to Zion, becoming King in and through Jesus. To those who believe in Jesus, all things are possible, because God is asserting his Kingship over the works of evil.

Therefore, in summary, *that* was *the* message and mission of Jesus to Israel and the nations.

General Jewish understanding of the Kingdom of God

As Jesus preached this message of the Kingdom, what did his audience hear? What was the common Jewish understanding of the Kingdom of God at that time? Scholars agree that the phrase "Kingdom of God" in Second Temple Judaism was code or shorthand for a range of meanings and messianic expectations commonly understood and interpreted within Israel's larger story. Here I summarise Dunn's more detailed list (2003:393-6).

1. After a period of climactic tribulation, *Yhwh* will return to Zion as King, in the Messianic Son of David, to conquer God's (Israel's) enemies and deliver/save Israel. It will be a time of judgement on evil (Judgement Day) and salvation for God's people.

2. God will regather and restore all the tribes of Israel from exile in a new Exodus into his Kingdom, as many prophets promised. The idea of "repentance" is understood in this context of turning away from sin/idolatry and returning to *Yhwh* from exile.

3. God will rule as King through a new covenant that he will make with renewed Israel, as in Jeremiah 31 and Ezekiel 36. Jews expected the "Greater Moses" that Moses predicted, who would speak God's words, the Messianic Torah (Deuteronomy 18:18-19).

4. The Messiah will rebuild the Temple and renew the priesthood in a priestly nation, per God's original intention in Exodus 19:6.

5. Messiah will reconcile and rule the *goyim,* all Gentile nations, "that my salvation may reach to the ends of the earth" (Isaiah 49:6). Messiah will inherit the nations and the earth itself (Psalm 2:8).

6. There will be the great feast of the Kingdom where all will come to the King's table of abundance (e.g., Isaiah 25:6 cf. Matthew 8:11).

7. There will be apocalyptic cosmic signs, the resurrection of the dead, and the renewal of all things, with new heavens and new earth, as in Isaiah 25:7-8, 65:17; Daniel 12:1-2.

Jesus' audience would have heard what he said through these filters. Jesus understood popular expectation, the storied meaning of God's Kingdom, but with significant reinterpretation and application in his distinctive mission and message of "the Kingdom of God".

Matthew's view and other 'Statements of Intent'

Matthew's view is similar to Mark's account: "when Jesus heard that John had been put in prison, he returned to Galilee... from that time on Jesus began to preach, 'Repent, for the Kingdom of heaven has come near.'" (Matthew 4:12,17). His phrase "has come near" connotes Isaiah 56:1, "my salvation is close at hand". In other words, as in Mark, God's Kingdom is present, active, and available in Jesus through the act of repentance. Belief/faith is implied in Matthew and becomes overt in his unfolding story of Jesus (e.g., 8:13, 9:22).

His overall presentation, written for Jewish readers, is that Jesus is the Jewish Messiah. *Yeshua ha Notzri* is the promised King of Israel who fulfils the Law and the Prophets, i.e., who came to fulfill all that God requires to save Israel *and the nations* (24:14, 28:19).

The gospels record Jesus making brief statements here and there as to why he came. These 'missional intents', as it were, expand our understanding of Jesus' aims and purpose. They are not to be taken in isolation, but rather to be understood within his essential *Kingdom* mission and message. They all state, "I have come to...".

Jesus said he came... to fulfill the Law (Matthew 5:17); not to bring peace, but a sword (10:34-35); to preach in every village (Mark 1:38); not for the healthy and righteous but for the sick and sinners (2:17); not to be served but to serve and give his life as a ransom (10:45); to seek and save the lost (Luke 19:10); to do the will of him who sent him (John 6:38); to bring judgement (9:39); to give life to the full (10:10); as light in the world for all who believe (12:46); and to bear witness to the truth (18:37).

Outside the gospels there are other reasons for Jesus' coming. It shows his followers thought about the matter, e.g., 1 John 3:8, "The reason the Son of God appeared was to destroy the devil's work".

Luke's Account and Jesus' Designations

Jesus "stood up to read, and the scroll of the prophet Isaiah was handed to him. Unrolling it, he found the place where it is written: 'The Spirit of the Lord is on me, because he has anointed me to proclaim good news to the poor. He has sent me to proclaim freedom for the prisoners and recovery of sight for the blind, to set the oppressed free, to proclaim the year of the Lord's favour'" (4:16-19).

According to Luke, this was in his hometown synagogue, his first public address. Then Jesus said to everyone in attendance, "Today this scripture is fulfilled in your hearing" (4:21).

This 'manifesto' situates Jesus' mission, message, and ministry in Luke's gospel. Jesus chose the prophetic text (Isaiah 61:1-2), implying he had studied it and embraced it as his mandate, confirmed by his emphatic statement, "today this scripture is fulfilled in your hearing". He really believed it! He was bringing, by the Spirit's power, God's eschatological (Kingdom) salvation. He would go and do what Isaiah said, enacting and fulfilling each point of the 'Kingdom mandate'. As Peter later summarised, "God anointed Jesus of Nazareth with the Holy Spirit and power, and he went around doing good and healing all who were under the power of the devil" (Acts 10:38).

Jesus stopped the *reading* after "to proclaim the year of the Lord's favour", omitting "and the day of vengeance of our God". Scholars debate reasons for the omission. They say it's significant because in this case it is not merely *quoting* a text, or a portion of it, to connote the context. Jeremias (1958:41-6) argued that, in so doing, Jesus rejected Jewish concepts of vengeance, opening the covenant to Gentiles as he boldly stated in Luke 4:23-27: though there were many in Israel, Elijah and Elisha were sent to Gentiles to do miracles. *That* exposed Jewish vengeance! From being "amazed at the gracious words that came from his lips" (22), the synagogue attendees became "furious… and drove him out… to throw him off the cliff" (28-30). He unmasked Jewish nationalism with its violence.

Thus, Jesus' mission superseded vengeance, as Bosch (1991:108-113) argues from this text. Jesus chose the way of non-violence. He rejected the expectation of the conquering Son of David who will bring God's vengeance on the Romans to establish the Kingdom. His choice of the text in the context of Isaiah's servant songs, then stopping short of "the vengeance of our God", shows that Jesus identified with the dark vocation of the Servant of *Yhwh*. He would redeem Israel and the nations by suffering their sin in self-sacrifice, making atonement ('at-one-ment') with God for their salvation (Isaiah 53).

Others called Jesus by the messianic titles of "Son of God" and "Son of David" (Matthew 4:3, 8:29, 9:27, 12:23, 16:16). But his chosen self-designation was *Yhwh's* "Servant" and "Son of Man", discussed in the next chapter. These two self-designations reveal his mission.

WORLDVIEW

All this, however, raises the deepest level of human consciousness: the underlying worldview that Jesus lived from, in contrast to the dominant Jewish worldview. We will see, also in the next chapter, that Second Temple Judaism was not a monolithic religion, a united faith, with everyone believing all the same doctrines of Jewish teaching. There were varying expressions, even formally constituted branches, of Judaism that interpreted Israel's story and scriptures with different emphases on aspects of faith – especially in response to the current crisis of oppression under Roman occupation.

However, having said that, we can safely say that there was a common Jewish worldview in Second Temple Judaism. Jesus clashed with it. His particular (Kingdom) worldview was a reinterpretation and application of the Jewish story and scriptures that subverted and challenged the dominant consciousness of his day, considering the national context. We need to examine this to better understand the mindset that guided Jesus to fulfil his Kingdom mission.

N.T. Wright, a biblical scholar, frames and examines the historical Jesus in terms of worldview studies in his two seminal works (1992, 1996, see the bibliography of references) and his popular summary, *The Challenge of Jesus* (2000). We must always be critically careful when using modern concepts in historical study. See Naugle (2002) for the origin and development of the concept, and how worldviews differ in nature, meaning and use in various cultures.

The Nature and Components of Worldview

A worldview is our (particular) view of the world. We only see it clearly when contrasted with other cultural/societal worldviews. Worldview, simply, is the lens through which we see reality. It is our filter or conditioning – cultural, religious, racial, class, etc – through which we experience and interpret our world. It exists and operates at a subconscious level of formation and awareness, mainly determining how we see, think, believe, speak, and behave. In short, worldview is the underlying set of ideas, beliefs, and assumptions that makes cohesive sense of reality.

If we do not *consciously examine* those presuppositions, we *unconsciously adopt and live out* the prevailing worldview (dominant consciousness). To shift or change our worldview to Jesus' worldview, for example, we must consciously examine and rework our core ideas, beliefs, and values in light of his underlying assumptions evidenced in the gospels.

The four essential components or elements of a worldview are stories, questions (and answers), symbols, and practices (praxis). Because they are about life in community and nations, it is community stories, life questions, national symbols, and cultural practices.

Figure 1. Worldview Elements and Functions

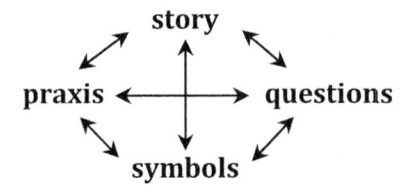

```
           story
        ↗   ↑   ↖
praxis ←----+----→ questions
        ↘   ↓   ↗
          symbols
```

Thus, worldviews provide *stories* through which we view reality. This is the most characteristic expression of worldview.

From these narratives we receive, in principle, the answers to the *basic questions* that determine our existence. Though the questions may vary a little, they all essentially ask the following:

- *Where did we come from?* Story of origins.
- *Who are we?* Identity and destiny.
- *Why are we here?* Our meaning and purpose in the environment.
- *Where are we? What went wrong?* The reality of the environment, the way the world is, the problem of pain, sin, and evil.
- *What is the solution? What will become of us?* The question of eschatological salvation, of hope for a meaningful future.

The questions and answers are expressed in cultural *symbols*. These can be seen in artifacts, national flags and events, religious and family festivals, etc. Symbols are highly emotive because they embody identity and pride, and act as boundary markers that make us who we are, in contrast to others. Tampering with symbols is inflammatory.

The stories, questions and answers, and symbols, in turn are seen in our praxis, our way of being and living in the world. They determine our practices and actions. So, worldview governs, at an instinctive and habitual level, our thinking, speaking, and behaving. It operates like the invisible foundation of a visible house or hospital, holding it together and making cohesive sense of everything.

Let us apply these four elements to the Jewish worldview, *consciously reinterpreted by Jesus*, to see his beliefs and aims more clearly. We can call it Jesus' Kingdom/Messianic worldview, which was foundational to his mission, message, and ministry. The gospels record the story of a serious worldview clash between Jesus and the prevailing mindset of Second Temple Judaism, which provoked both the spiritual and political powers to violent reaction.

Jesus' Reinterpretation of Israel's Story and Questions

The following is merely a summary of Jesus' reinterpretation of the Jewish worldview of his day. Details of Jesus' Kingdom worldview can be seen in what I wrote earlier, and in previous chapters regarding his developing sense of identity, calling and destiny. And the chapters that follow will fill out the rich mosaic of Jesus' worldview.

The Jewish storied worldview is about election and calling in Abraham, slavery and deliverance in Egypt, covenant and tabernacle in the wilderness, sovereignty and idolatry in the holy land, and exile and hope of restoration in Messiah's Kingdom. Everything is built around these peak points of Israel's story. Let me elaborate.

God's sovereign call and election of Israel in Abraham was the intended reversal of humanity's rebellion in Adam and Eve. Exiled from the garden of God's presence, humanity was divided into nations at Babel, scattered to the ends of the earth (Genesis 11). But God chose Abraham to make him "into a great nation" (Genesis 12:1-3), as the instrument of redemption and reconciliation of the nations, that "all the peoples of the earth will be blessed through you". It addressed the questions of origin, election, identity, and purpose. Jesus saw himself as Abraham's seed fulfilling *that* intended identity and purpose for Israel (Galatians 3:14-16). But I must return to the story.

The decedents of Abraham, Isaac, and Jacob were enslaved in Egypt for four hundred years under foreign spiritual and political power.

God came as Warrior-King to save and deliver her through a mighty Exodus, by great signs and wonders, defeating the Egyptian powers (Exodus 15). Arguably, the Exodus, with the Passover deliverance and Sinai covenant, is the Mount Everest in the Jewish mind, from which they view world reality. Israel was God's covenant people, intended to be a holy nation of priests, kings, and prophets to the scattered nations (Exodus 19:6); to bring God's light of salvation to them (Isaiah 49:6); to represent and pray for them before God in his holy tabernacle and later Temple (Isaiah 56:7).

But Israel failed her wilderness testing, her training for reigning. She struggled to possess the Promised Land. David then established the theocracy, God's Kingdom in Israel. He became the model of the future Son of David, God's Messianic Son, whose royal throne and theocratic Kingdom will never end (2 Samuel 7:12-16).

However, despite centuries of repeated warnings by the prophets, ongoing idolatry resulted in judgement. God rejected Israel and sent her into exile, handing her over to be ruled by foreign gods. But the prophets said that, despite Israel's unfaithfulness, God's covenant faithfulness meant that he would come again as Redeemer-King to save Israel in a New Exodus. God will restore her into his Messianic Kingdom with a new covenant, to bring salvation to the nations. Then all things will be made new – "new heavens and a new earth" (Isaiah 65:17, 66:22) – in his everlasting Kingdom.

These stories further answered the questions of "who are we, why are we here, what went wrong, what is the solution, and what will become of us?" Jesus reinterpreted the stories and answered the questions in his mission and message of God's Kingdom come. Despite the return from exile in 538–432 BC, Jesus saw Israel still exiled, enslaved to foreign spiritual-political powers, that is, the Romans and the corrupt Temple system – the idolatrous Jewish politics of holiness.

Jesus believed God was coming as Warrior-King *in his mission and message* to redeem Israel in fulfilment of the prophets. Jesus believed God was calling Israel to return (repent) from exile by entering the Kingdom that he proclaimed and taught. Jesus believed he was the new Moses leading the New Exodus into the promised Kingdom of God, for the deliverance of Israel and the salvation of the nations. *That* was Israel's only hope of promised restoration in God's new covenant through Jesus' inauguration of the Kingdom. Thus, he saw himself as embodying and fulfilling Israel's calling and destiny.

Israel's Worldview Symbols and Praxis

Four standard or primary symbols constituted the Jewish worldview: Torah, Temple, the People, and the Land. There were other derived symbols, but I use caps because the four were most revered as the,

- *Holy People*: God's sovereign choice of Israel, set apart for no reason other than love, pure grace (Deuteronomy 7:7-9).

- *Holy Torah*: God's revealed will, his covenant law of life to be lived in and through the love of God (Deuteronomy 6:4-9).

- *Holy Temple*: God's dwelling of heaven on earth, the place of his rule among his people, the centre of worship for Israel.

- *Holy Land*: God's Kingdom inheritance for Israel an example and witness to all nations for their reconciliation and blessing.

These national symbols represented the greater invisible reality of God's love, life, presence, and Kingdom. Symbols embody and point to life praxis, i.e., how Israel should act and live and have her being under God, in expressing her worldview.

Any apparent negative or anti-nationalistic tampering with such highly emotive symbols in Second Temple Judaism would provoke an immediate reaction from the Jewish establishment. But Jesus saw himself in the tradition of the Hebrew prophets, who symbolically acted out the message God gave them, mostly in judgement of Israel. Jews lived an alternative, even contrary, life praxis – compared to the *goyim* (Gentiles) – as a witness to God's truth. But this was in the context of Israel's covenantal unfaithfulness. Wilderness prophets, like Jesus' forerunner, John, were highly confrontational and fearless. They not only spoke truth to power, but dramatically acted it out in public so that no one could miss their message.

Jesus saw the problem, the reason for continued exile, as the idolatrous corruption of the visible symbols that replaced true worship of the invisible God. Israel turned these symbols, and others like Sabbath keeping, kosher food, dress code, Jewish festivals, circumcision, etc., into outward boundary markers of pride and separation of Jews from Gentiles.

In summary, they became idols of Jewish identity, measures of ethnic and religious purity, a means of pride in being the chosen people. They became instruments of nationalistic legalism in the politics of holiness, i.e., the belief that Israel's deliverance depended on strict Torah obedience and the enforcement thereof. The Temple had become a corrupt system of political-economic power at the centre of Jewish life. The land was supposed to be 'holy' as in 'set apart' for God and his Kingdom purposes for the Gentile nations. But it was, in truth, a source of Jewish idolatry. It had become a symbol of possession, pride, and power. Nationalists, like the Zealots, would kill for its liberation.

Jesus' Reinterpretation of the Symbols and Praxis

Jesus, in his life praxis and teaching, radically redeemed and reinterpreted these primary symbols and their corrupt praxis. And he did it boldly, with great courage and faith in God his Father.

- *Holy People*: Jesus saw and treated *his followers*, all who believe in him, as the renewed Israel of the New Exodus, the fulfilment of God's chosen people (Matthew 19:28, Luke 22:28-30).

- *Holy Torah*: Jesus saw Torah as reinterpreted and fulfilled in himself (Matthew 5:17). His teaching of God's Kingdom was the Messianic Torah that Moses spoke of (Deuteronomy 18:18-19), the promised new covenant way of life (Jeremiah 31:31-34).

- *Holy Temple*: Jesus saw his body as the Temple where God dwelt, ruled, and forgave sins (Mark 2:5-7). The Temple of his body would be destroyed and rebuilt – he would die and rise again (John 2:19-22). It was also prophetic of the destruction of the Temple and its system under God's judgement (Mark 13:1-2). His Kingdom community would be the new living Temple.

- *Holy Land*: Jesus saw the land as symbolic of Israel's destiny: the eschatological inheritance of the nations (Psalm 2:8), which God will give to Jesus and his followers, "the meek" who "will inherit *the earth*" (Matthew 5:5). He did not see the land as a property in the Middle East for which to kill and be killed.

Jesus' mission, message, ministry, death, and resurrection have forever changed the symbols into their intended meaning and reality, which changes our praxis, and the way we live. Therefore, there are no longer any 'holy' places and spaces, as in the holy land, Temple, cities, etc. They are all re-placed and re-spaced, literally, by Messiah and his renewed people of the new covenant. Like God, *they* are holy, *they* are set apart and indwelt by God to fulfil his purpose to make *all* creation holy.

So, for example, the coming of Messiah reinterprets the 'holy city' as the heavenly Jerusalem, the mother of the true people of God, as "the present city of Jerusalem is in slavery with her children" (Galatians 4:24-26). In fact, the last NT reference to earthly Jerusalem, in Revelation 11:8, says that it is "figuratively called Sodom and Egypt, where their Lord was crucified". These are the most provocative symbols to the Jewish mind, a city of moral degeneration and sinful enslavement. Far from holy, even to this day! This is in contrast with "*the* Holy City, the new Jerusalem coming out of heaven, prepared as a bride beautifully dressed for her husband" (21:2), when heaven comes to earth in Messiah's eternal Kingdom.

Jesus' worldview reinterpreted family as the reality of those who do God's will – his believing eschatological community (Mark 3:31-34). He reinterpreted the Sabbath as a principle of freedom to rest, not as a bondage of legalism, because "the Son of Man is Lord even of the Sabbath", bringing *God's* eschatological rest (Mark 2:24-27).

He relaxed certain ceremonial and purity laws. They were symbols fulfilled in the coming of God's Kingdom. Eating with clean or unclean hands was not the issue, but eating in the Kingdom of God was (Mark 7:1f; Matthew 8:11-12). It's not what goes into the mouth that makes one unclean, but what comes out of the heart, in words and deeds, that makes one unclean (Mark 7:14-21). It's not the outward circumcision of the flesh that seals the covenant, but rather the circumcision of the believing heart.

More examples can be cited. These and other themes will be unpacked in later chapters.

In conclusion, the impact of Jesus' brilliant and brave prophetic reinterpretation of symbols for life practice as God intended for Israel and humanity, is seen in the NT trajectory that spiritualises and universalises *all* symbols for the salvation of *all* nations, for the renewal of *all* creation.

QUESTIONS FOR REFLECTION AND DISCUSSION

1. Sit back and reflect on one or two essential things that have spoken to you in this chapter. Write them down and talk to God about it.

2. In your own words, how would you explain Mark's version of Jesus' generic announcement of the Kingdom – that which embodied his mission and message?

3. Describe the difference(s) between the general Jewish expectation of the Kingdom of God and what Jesus meant by it?

4. Regarding his mission and message, why did Jesus not use "Son of God" and "Son of David" of himself? Why did he choose "Son of Man" and "servant" as his self-designations?

5. How did Jesus reinterpret the Jewish worldview of his day?

6. Reflect on how Jesus' worldview challenges and transforms your worldview. What does that mean, practically, for living your life? What do you need to change?

CONTEXT & COMMUNITY

We now detail the religious, socio-political, and economic context of Second Temple Judaism, where Jesus found himself. And how he, and other groups within Israel, responded to the crisis of the day.

It's part of Jesus' contextual analysis and relevance to "interpret the signs of the times", which, in his view, the Pharisees and Sadducees could not do. He asked, "How is it that you don't know how to interpret this present time?" (Luke 12:56; Matthew 16:1-4). His reading of "this present time" contributed to his self-understanding and role in God's Kingdom – the mission, message, and ministry that he believed God had called him to. Jesus did not live in a spiritual bubble. He was profoundly engaged in the concrete realities of his context.

The brutal Roman occupation was a challenging time for Israel. It led to heightened messianic expectation for God's deliverance. Jesus' self-designation, "Son of Man", had huge significance in that context. We will also give an overview summary of the various responses in Second Temple Judaism to the crisis they were facing as a nation under Roman oppression. Judaism was not a monolithic religion as in everyone believing all the same things. There were identifiable groups that responded differently to the context. We will discuss them.

We will then look at Jesus' particular response. As a Jewish apocalyptic prophet, he started an end-time Kingdom movement in Israel grounded in a mobile learning community through which he lived, expressed, and advanced the call of the Kingdom he proclaimed. We will examine Jesus' framework of Kingdom discipleship as 'the answer' to Israel and the crisis they were going through.

HISTORICAL CONTEXT AND MESSIANIC EXPECTATION

What follows is an overview of the salient details of the context of Second Temple Judaism. This fills out the historical timeline in my introduction (pp.30-32), the context that gave rise to heightened messianic expectation. And it helps us to understand the significance of Jesus' self-designation, "Son of Man", taken from Daniel's vision and prophecy. What did it mean and why did Jesus choose it?

The Roman and Jewish Context

The successful Maccabean revolt in 167-160 BC against the Syrian King Antiochus IV Epiphanes ("God manifest" in Greek), gave Judaism the heroic paradigm of violent resistance and martyrdom to liberate the city and Temple of Jerusalem, and the land of Judea and Israel.

Mattathias, from the house of Hasmon, began the revolt in 167. After his death in battle in 165, his son Judas, called Maccabeus, cleansed and rededicated the Temple on 25 *Kislev* (14 December 164) – commemorated annually as *Hannukah*, the Jewish Festival of Lights. This led into the Hasmonean dynasty and period (153-37) where Mattathias' two sons (Judas, then Simon), grandson (John Hycranus), and other Hasmoneans, ruled Judea. This period was marked by the end of the Zadokite High Priesthood – the line of Levi, Aaron, and Zadok (Exodus 28:1; 1 Chronicles 29:22; 2 Chronicles 31:10) – where a) the High Priest became a political appointee, and then, b) High Priest and king were joined as one in/by the Hasmonean rulers. That is why the Essenes, and the Pharisees to a lesser degree, viewed the High Priest as illegitimate, which Jesus evidently agreed with.

The Roman occupation of Israel and Judea began in 63 BC. They called the region Palestine, from the Philistines who had lived there. Palestine was ruled through puppet Jewish kings, like Herod the Great (an Idumean, marking the end of the Hasmonean kings), in collusion with regional Roman governors like Pontius Pilate at the time of Jesus.

Herod ruled from 37 BC to his death in 4 BC. His ambitious and extravagant project to rebuild/renovate the Second Temple was probably motivated by his desire to be seen as a messianic figure. It took 46 years to build (20 BC to AD 25) and was one of the wonders of the world at that time. He was, however, a brutal king, like the Roman rulers. He feared any rival Jewish king, as seen in his massacre of "all the boys in Bethlem and its vicinity who were two years old and under", because of Jesus' birth (Matthew 2:16). His three sons, who ruled territories after him, were no better.

Herod's son, Antipas, ruled (4 BC–AD 39) the Galilee where Jesus grew up, the hotbed of Jewish nationalist resistance against Roman oppression. He beheaded John the baptizer for publicly saying, in my RAP, "the king has no clothes on!" The Pharisees warned Jesus (in Luke 13:31-33) at a certain point in his ministry, "Leave this place and go somewhere else, Herod wants to kill you." Jesus replied, "Go tell that fox, 'I will keep on driving out demons and healing people today and tomorrow, and on the third day I will reach my goal'... for surely no prophet can die outside Jerusalem!" By publicly referring to the Jewish king as "that fox", Jesus boldly called him out as an unprincipled deceptive and treacherous predator of his people.

Jesus, evidently, followed his forerunner (John the baptizer) in political engagement, speaking truth to power. The point of all these stories is to show the context of ruthless repression.

Rome ruled Palestine more directly through local governors from 5 BC onwards. They ruled with the long-established Jewish Sanhedrin in Jerusalem, the supreme council and tribunal for Jewish affairs. The Hasmoneans had re-established the Sanhedrin, making their political appointments. It was comprised of seventy men, mainly from the party of the Sadducees, then elders, chief priest, scribes, and Pharisees (I discuss the groups below). The High Priest (a Sadducee) led the Sanhedrin, which had autonomy in religious, civil, and criminal affairs. But it operated under Roman rule, especially regarding taxes, law enforcement, and administration. Ordinary Jews had difficulty trusting these leaders because they not only supported the corrupt Temple system, also led by the High Priest, but they passively and often overtly enabled the Roman occupation.

The Exploitation and Violent Repression

Pilate, the Roman governor who ruled at the time of Jesus, was as cruel as Herod Antipas in Galilee. Luke (13:1) reports that he executed some Galilean pilgrims at the feast in Jerusalem while in the act of offering sacrifices, mixing their blood with their sacrifices. Josephus cites other violent incidences under Pilate's rule (1987:480, 608-9; *Antiquities* 18:3.55-62, *Wars* 2.9.169-77). Governors before and after Pilate were as violent in their repression of anything that smacked of Jewish subversion and possible revolt.

The taxes were exploitative, keeping the Roman occupation and corrupt Temple system operating. Jewish tax collectors were among the most hated people in society. There was widespread economic greed, exploitation, and poverty, evidenced in Second Temple literature. We see it in Jesus' concern for the poor, with his emphasis on Kingdom liberation and justice for the oppressed as seen in his beatitudes, his teachings about possessions and materialism, and his parables about money. Up to a third of Jesus' parables are framed in, or directly address economy and money.

This all contributed to social stress, upheaval, and longing for deliverance. There were many attempts at resisting the oppression, including revolts by false messiahs. Jesus constantly warned of false prophets and messiahs who would deceive people and lead the nation astray (Matthew 7:15f; 24:11, 23-24). To illustrate the volatile context in which heightened messianic expectation arose, I have listed some of the known revolts that were violently repressed.

- The first revolt took place when Herod the Great died in 4 BC.

- In AD 6, Judas the Galilean led a tax revolt, referred to in Acts 5:37. Rome retaliated by destroying Sepphoris and rebuilding it into a Roman town. Keener says, "Judas' model led to the revolutionaries who later came to be called the Zealots. Judas' sons also revolted in the war of 66-70; they were crucified" (2014:333). Sepphoris was four miles from Nazareth. Jesus would have been eleven or twelve years old when the revolt and destruction took place. What effect did it have on him?

- In AD 30, Jesus was crucified as "The King of the Jews", instead of the violent insurrectionist, Barabbas, whom Pilate set free.

- In 44, a Jewish revolutionary and magician-prophet named Theudas was killed (Acts 5:36).

- In 52–60, during Roman governor Felix's rule, another revolt was put down, "the Egyptian who started a revolt and led four thousand terrorists out into the wilderness" (Acts 21:38). Most messianic prophets went into the desert to draw followers in expectation of a new exodus under a new Moses.

- In 66–70, John Gischala and Simon bar Giora (led the Zealots), and Menahem ben Judah (who led their splinter group, the

Sicarii), rebelled against the Romans, resulting in the first Jewish-Roman war that destroyed Jerusalem and the Temple.
- After 70, post Second Temple period, Simon ben Koseba led the second war against the Romans (132–135), establishing a three-year-long independent state. The most revered rabbi of the time, Rabbi Akiva ben Yosef, hailed Simon as the Messiah. He famously named him "Bar Kokhba", meaning "Son of the Star", because of its messianic allusions.

Messianic Expectation and Daniel's Prophetic Timing

This desperate context turned Jews to the prophetic scriptures for answers, which heightened the messianic expectation. The Jewish worldview saw history in a theological way, a kind of prophetic eschatology of history that interpreted events as part of God's sovereign purposes and revelation of his plans. God works in and through history to realise 'The End', his pre-determined goal. God reveals those plans and workings, his "mysteries" (Daniel 2:28), to his prophets: "Surely the Sovereign LORD does nothing without revealing his plan to his servants the prophets" (Amos 3:7-8). And through them to his people: "The secret things belong to the LORD our God, but the things revealed belong to us and our children forever, that we may follow all the words of this law" (Deuteronomy 29:29).

Daniel is an example. He cites Jeremiah's prophesy that the exile would last seventy years (Daniel 9:2 cf. Jeremiah 25:11-12). Then, by confessing the sins of his nation, he intercedes for the end of the exile (Daniel 9:3-19). God then sends the angel Gabriel to reveal the timing that will bring (Jewish) history to its climax. God's goal is stated in 9:24: "to finish transgression, to put an end to sin, to atone for wickedness, to bring in everlasting righteousness, to seal up vision and prophecy and to anoint the Most Holy Place". Gabriel gives the timing to this end in "sevens", meaning seven years, explained in 9:24-27. Let me unpack this cryptic passage, as it was highly significant for Jews in Second Temple Judaism (Keener 2009:533, note 199). *How did Jesus interpret this text in light of Daniel's prophecies?*

Imagine having a countdown to the culmination of history? Gabriel said it would take "seventy-sevens" through to the goal in 9:24, i.e., there will be 490 years (70 x 7) to reach the end. Scholars debate if the years are symbolic or actual, e.g., "seventy-sevens" can symbolise a Jubilee of Jubilees. However, in the context of chapter 9 and the unfolding prophecies in chapters 10 to 12, the numbers consistently refer to years, months, and days. Chapter 9:25 gives the countdown: from the decree "to return and rebuild Jerusalem" there will be 483 years, "seven sevens and sixty-two sevens" (49 + 434), until the coming of Messiah, "the Anointed One, the ruler".

What decree is being referred to? There were three decrees to return from exile. The first was by Cyrus in 537 BC, for exiles to return and "rebuild the temple" (Ezra 1:1-4). The second was by Darius in 518 BC, to (further) "build the temple" (Ezra 6:1-12). The third, by Artaxerxes in 457 BC, was to restore and rebuild Jerusalem, *the city* (Ezra 7:1-28) – the reference in Daniel 9:25. Daniel's prophetic years, with these decrees, were studied in Second Temple Judaism. The Jews were doing their maths! Messianic expectation was at a fever pitch *because of Daniel's predicted timing* in the national crisis.

If we take Daniel's 483 years to Messiah's coming, from a) the first decree in 537, we get to 54 BC; b) the second in 518, we get to 35 BC; and c) the third in 457, we get to AD 26 (Archer 1985:26, 119-121). That was the year Jesus went to John to be baptised in water and was revealed to Israel as the Spirit-baptised Messiah, "the Anointed One" (John 1:31-34). We do not know whether Jesus was conscious of this exact timing and accordingly asked John to baptise him.

We do know that he knew the text and understood God's end goal to finish transgression, atone for sin, bring in everlasting righteousness, and seal up vision and prophecy. We also know, with historic *certainty* from the gospels, that he identified himself with Daniel 9:24-27 *in the context of the "son of man"* in 7:13.

Daniel's Empires and Son of Man

When a nation crosses boundaries God set for them at the Babel scattering (Deuteronomy 32:8), taking over other nations, it becomes an empire. Empires set themselves up in direct competition and conflict with God's Kingdom – empire against Empire.

Daniel had a series of revelations of four empires (2:27-45, 7:1-8, 8:1f): Babylonian (2:37-38, from 626 to 539), Medo-Persian (8:20, from 539 to 330), Greek (8:21, from 330 to 63), and Roman (from 63 onwards, from Jewish-Palestine perspective). The last empire was the most brutal (7:7,19 cf. 2:40). *That* beast, through one of its Roman "horns" (a ruler), waged war against God's people, "defeating them, *until* the Ancient of Days came and pronounced judgement" in their favour. Then "*they* possessed the Kingdom" (7:21-22).

Daniel described that event earlier (7:9-14) when he saw thrones in heaven and "the Ancient of Days took his seat" in the heavenly court. The "books were open" to pass judgement. Then he saw "one like a son of man coming with the clouds of heaven... *He* was given authority, glory and sovereign power; all nations and peoples of every language worshiped him. *His* dominion is an everlasting dominion that will not pass away". *Who is this "one like a son of man"?* He is a mysterious human-heavenly figure that needs explaining!

Daniel 2 to 7 was written in Aramaic and chapters 1, 8 to 12 in Hebrew. Aramaic *bar enash* (7:13), "son of man", is Hebrew *ben adam*. It means "human being", as in Psalm 8:4 and Ezekiel 2:1,3,8. Thus, as a human figure in the heavenly court, receiving everlasting dominion, he represents the new humanity that will rule the earth (Genesis 1:28, Psalm 8:4-8), enjoying dominion over the beasts, both literal (lions, Daniel 6) and metaphorical (empires, Daniel 7). The *ruling* "son of man" in David's Psalm 8 has links with the "son of David", *Yhwh's* Messianic Son in 2 Samuel 7:13-14 and Psalm 2:7. He will sit at *Yhwh's* right hand, *ruling* over kings and nations (Psalm 110:1-6).

Rabbi Akiva (AD 50–135) said Daniel 7 referred to one throne for God and one for David, his messianic son (Sanhedrin 38b). Joshua ben Levi (AD 225) taught that if Israel deserved it, the Messiah would come with the clouds of heaven after Daniel 7:13-14, but if not, he would come riding on a donkey after Zechariah 9:9 (Sanhedrin 98a).

Thus, Daniel's "son of man" represents and embodies God's people: true Israel *and* renewed humanity (Wright 1996:521-9). The angel's interpretation confirms it: the four beasts are four kings (7:16-17) that represent four kingdoms (7:23). The "son of man" is, therefore, the fifth King who represents God's holy people (7:18,22,27). He not only receives the Kingdom on behalf of "the saints" (ESV) but suffers with and for them under Rome, the fourth beast (7:21,25). That is, "*until* the Ancient of Days came and judgment was given for the saints of the Most High, and *the time came* when the saints possessed the kingdom" (7:22 ESV). Note the timing: when the son of man and the saints he represents is vindicated out of great suffering, he enters God's presence and is given the everlasting Kingdom, enthroned beside the Ancient of Days (7:13-14), as in Psalm 110:1.

However, Daniel sees *"one like"* a human being who enters God's presence *"with the clouds of heaven"*. Heiser (2015:249-53) shows that it referred to deity in the Ancient Near East, e.g., Ugaritic texts call the god of Baal "the one who rides the clouds". In Hebrew texts, only God (*Yhwh*) rides on the clouds saving and judging (Deuteronomy 33:26; Psalm 68:32-33, 104:1-4; Isaiah 19:1). Thus, Daniel's son of man is also a divine figure. All nations *serve/worship* (Aramaic *pelach*) him in Daniel 7:14,27. *Pelach* is to be rendered exclusively to God, not to false gods or human beings (3:12,14,17,18,28; 6:16,20). The worship of the "son of man" confirms the idea in Jewish monotheism of two divine powers or *Yhwh* figures in heaven.

This is borne out in the Aramaic use of *illayah* for "Most High" in 3:26,32; 4:14,21,29,31; 5:18,21; 7:25. This is in contrast to the phrase "saints of the Most High" in 7:18,22,25,27, where *elyonin* is used for "Most High". English translations do not indicate the change in words. Scholars (Caragounis 1986:75, Gentry 2003:73, Hamilton 2014:147-153) point out that *illayah* is Daniel's standard Aramaic adjective for Israel's God, *Yhwh*, "the King of Heaven" (4:37). *Elyonin* is Hebrew "majesty", *elyon*, with the Aramaic plural *'in'*, used as a title of honour, literally, "Highest Majesty". Daniel uses *elyonin* four times only *after* the son of man's enthronement with the Kingdom (7:13-14). He is the Highest One "of the saints". Daniel uses both terms side by side in 7:25, "He shall speak words against the Most High (*illayah*), and shall wear out the saints of the Most High (*elyonin*)" (ESV). Daniel's clear distinguishing between the divine figures associates *elyonin* with the saints. And the similarity of statements in 7:14 and 7:27 confirms that *elyonin* is the son of man, who receives the Kingdom with, and on behalf of, his holy people, and rules with them forever.

Daniel's "son of man" occurs 14 times in 1 Enoch, a 2nd century BC apocalyptic text (Charlesworth 1983a:7). "Dependence on Daniel is patent from the first reference" (Montgomery 1972:320). Enoch used "Son of Man" (caps) for a Messiah, "God's Anointed", and "light of the Gentiles", with divine attributes from before creation, bringing righteousness, defeating kings, acting in final judgement, sitting on a throne of glory (1 Enoch 46:1-4, 48:2-7, 62:1-16, 69:26-29, 71:6).

Hence, *this son of man is the eschatological Saviour who embodies the true saints, the new humanity that will reign with him forever.*

Jesus' Self-designation as The Son of Man

Jesus probably understood Daniel's (and Enoch's) "son of man" along those lines. It had become part of the messianic expectation in Second Temple Judaism. But Jesus, uniquely, took *this* messianic title to himself. It occurs 86 times in the NT. The gospels have 82 usages, *only* on the lips of Jesus, in contrast to relative silence in Second Temple literature (except for Enoch). Jesus believed and knew that he was the one of whom Daniel spoke. He built his identity and mission on it.

A study of Jesus' references to the "Son of Man" shows, among other things, that he used it, a) to validate his exercise of the authority of God's Kingdom (to drive out demons, forgive sins and heal, e.g., Mark 2:10); b) with reference to his suffering and death with/for God's people; c) his atoning for sin and bringing everlasting righteousness; d) to be vindicated in resurrection and ascension (Mark 9:31 cf. Daniel 12:1-2), whereby he is given all authority in heaven and earth – *literally* fulfilled in Matthew 28:18 – by taking his throne at God's right hand, as David saw in Psalm 110:1f. And e) to return on the clouds of heaven to establish the Kingdom on earth (Mark 13:26-27, 15:62).

Placing this in the context of Daniel's visions: the clash of empires began (2:24-49) when "the God of Heaven sets up a Kingdom that will never be destroyed... a rock... not made by human hands" will strike the final empire (2:23, Rome). The "rock (then) became a huge mountain and filled the whole earth", i.e., God's Empire took over (2:35, 44-45). The "rock" (Aramaic *eben*) is "the son" (Hebrew *ben*) of man in 7:13, a pun on words that interpreters in the NT, including Jesus, "observed and exploited", Wright says (1996:497-501).

In short, the rock in Daniel 2 is the son of man in Daniel 7, who is the Anointed One (Messiah) in Daniel 9, specifically 9:20-27.

Daniel's "Anointed One", 9:24-27

I cannot exegete this cryptic text here. I merely outline the historical messianic interpretation (see Montgomery 1972). The 'anti-Christ' Dispensationalist (re)interpretation is a novelty that has confused modern Christians with their pre-tribulation rapture theory.

As explained earlier, Messiah will come 483 years after the decree to rebuild Jerusalem. When he comes, he will confirm the covenant with Israel for one week (9:27, the seven-year period that makes up 490 years), i.e., he will bring the Kingdom to Israel. But he will be "cut off" (9:26, in retrospect, crucified) in the middle of that week (i.e., after three-and-a-half years of ministry, echoing 7:25). *That* "will put an end to sacrifice and offering" (9:27), i.e., the Temple system, because atonement will be made through his sacrifice (9:24, retrospectively understood).

There is, however, a "ruler who will come" (9:26, an anti-messiah) that will destroy the city and Temple with an "abomination that causes desolation" (9:27). Troubles and wars will continue "until the end" (9:26). That abomination of desolation happened in 167-165 BC under Antiochus Epiphanes and again in AD 66-70 under Titus (interpreted retrospectively). Troubles and wars continue to this day.

There is, therefore, a mystery. In Messiah Jesus' coming (3½ year ministry) and then being "cut off", the five-fold goal of 9:24 has been reached – *in principle* and *in power*. A 3½ year period of the last "week" remains, "a time, times, and half a time" in 7:25, 12:7, and 42 months or 1260 days in Revelation 11:1-3. This outstanding period indicates a short period of great tribulation, as seen in AD 66–70 (interpreted retrospectively). That points to a final great tribulation under the anti-christ before the end when the Christ (Jesus) returns to save the righteous and judge the wicked. *Then* the end goal of Daniel's rock (2:34-35), son of man (7:13), the Anointed One (9:24-25), will be realised *in fullness and finality*.

RESPONSES TO THE CRISIS IN SECOND TEMPLE JUDAISM

The Jews were one people with one faith and one confession, the *Shema Yisrael*. Yet they were divided along lines of socio-political and religious groups, parties, and schools of thought. Each had their response to the crisis of Roman occupation as per their interpretation of the Hebrew texts and their reading of "the signs of the times". These responses generated group identity and belonging, each with their disciples and adherents. They offered a story, answers, and life praxis – a worldview – based on their ideology and teachings, i.e., their *halakha* or way of living God's word and will in the context.

Jews did not have categories like conservative or liberal, right-wing or left-wing. We cannot read modern socio-political concepts back into history. We can, however, identify and describe the groups and parties on a rough continuum from the most nationalistic through to the 'sell-out' supporters of the Romans. What follows are brief descriptions to illustrate the varying responses in contrast to Jesus' response, his *halakha* through his Kingdom mission, movement, and community of disciples. I have drawn on, among other works, Meier's (2001), *Companions and Competitors* – a comprehensive historical study of these groups and the way of Jesus.

Zealots and related groups

During Jesus' lifetime, Zealots were not the group Josephus called Zealots. They only became an organised ultra-nationalist group in the build-up to the first Jewish war of AD 66–70.

The word *zelotes* initially referred to Jews who were intensely "zealous" for Torah purity, as in "Simon the Zealot", one of Jesus' disciples (Mark 3:18). They insisted on the practice of Mosaic law by fellow Jews as a means of separation from idolatrous Gentiles. They would harass Jews, even with violence, to force them into strict separation, hoping that their *halakha* – way of Torah purity – would bring the Messiah. Though nationalistic, not all (early) *zelotes* used violence or their *sicarii* (dagger) to kill, in God's name, 'backslidden' Jews or 'infidel' Romans.

'The Zealots', as they later became known and as we commonly know them today, emerged as an identifiable party with growing nationalist support before the first Jewish war. In modern terms, they would have been seen as 'freedom fighters' from the Jewish perspective, or 'terrorists' from the Roman perspective. They fought with their splinter group, called Sicarii, and similar brigands (bandits). These rebel groups had a theology of holy war as the means to bring God's Kingdom. They perished in Jerusalem (AD 70) and later (73) on Mount Masada near the Dead Sea. Josephus (1987:769, *Wars* 7.9.389-401) described how 960 men, women, and children took their own lives before Roman soldiers entered the fortress – an empty victory for the Romans. Masada is, to this day, a revered excavated monument to Jewish nationalism.

Pharisees – including the Scribes

The Pharisees (*Perushim*) were a nationalist sect in Second Temple Judaism. Unlike most other groups, they survived the destruction of AD 70, establishing Pharisaic-Orthodox Judaism via the synagogues, later called Rabbinical Judaism. They were the party of the synagogue and the rabbis. It's worth noting: the gospels are the earliest historical sources for Jews to study the Pharisees. Josephus and the comments in the Mishnah and Talmud are later sources.

Their roots go back to the 3rd/2nd centuries BC, in the emergence of the *Hasidim,* God's "holy/loyal ones", who supported the Maccabean revolt of 167-160 BC. The Pharisees were the spiritual decedents of the *Hasidim*. Not long after the revolt tensions arose between the Maccabean-Hasmonean rulers and the Pharisees because the former a) ended the High Priest Zadokite line, b) their kings were not in the Davidic line, and c) they united High Priest and king.

So, Alexander Jannaeus (104-76), the Hasmonean king-High Priest, aligned himself with the Sadducees to stay in power and hung 800 Pharisees on crosses in Jerusalem. He had the throats of their wives and children cut before their eyes as he watched while drinking and lying with his concubines (Josephus 1987:550-1, *Wars* 1.4.96-8). On his death, he gave the rule/kingdom to his wife Salome Alexandra (76-67). She saw the firm conviction of the Pharisees as a religious authority and thus formally recognised them, putting them in the Sanhedrin. They then became dominant in Jewish life.

The Pharisees responded to the contextual crisis with a *halakha* of Torah obedience, to all 613 commandments. They believed Israel's exile was due to her failure to keep the Mosaic law. So, they taught strict obedience in *all aspects of life* as a national duty, for Messiah to deliver them. Some said that if all Israel obeyed Torah for one day, Messiah would come! Jewish scholar, Neusner (1990:v-ix) argues that they were driven by the ideal of priestly holiness in fulfilment of the Leviticus Holiness Code, to be holy as God is holy. But that led to the politics of holiness. The Pharisees policed the rules of Sabbath-keeping (39 prohibited acts), ceremonial cleansing, purity laws, eating practices, dress code, circumcision, tithing, marriage and divorce, etc. They, furthermore, took regulations pertaining to the temple precinct and made them applicable to the whole land. Hence their legalism which led to regular clashes with Jesus. Jesus condemned them for laying heavy burdens on people (Matthew 23:1-4).

The Pharisees are known in many gospel texts for a), their legalistic righteousness imposed on the nation as the way to eschatological salvation, b) with their claim to the right interpretation of Torah in all aspects of life, c) backed by "the tradition of the elders" (Mark 7:3, the oral tradition), and d) their opposition to and conflict with Jesus and his *halakha* – way of the Kingdom that he offered Israel.

Jesus reserved his most severe rebukes for the Pharisees (e.g., Matthew 23), which included the Scribes. Scribes were mentioned mostly alongside the Pharisees in the gospels. However, they were originally writers who recorded and copied documents. Over time, they were known as studied writers, and learned Mosaic law (Torah) teachers, and/or officials who had authority and prestige in Jewish society. The synoptic gospels call them "teachers/experts of the law" (Matthew 22:35), but they taught without authority (Mark 1:22, 2:16). Being identified with the Pharisees, they too were opposed to Jesus and conspired to kill him (3:22, 8:31, 10:33).

Sadducees

The Sadducees did not survive the destruction of Jerusalem and the Temple. As with the Pharisees, the sources *outside the NT* of the origins and nature of the Sadducees, as in Josephus and rabbinic literature, are post-AD 70. And due to their hostility to the Sadducees, these sources are inadequate for an accurate picture.

The Sadducees emerged as an identifiable political party and religious group in the 3rd/2nd century BC. Their roots seem to be a mix of priestly officials, Judean Hellenists (pro-Greco-Roman influence), rural landowners and urban aristocracy (seen as the rich). Under the Hasmonean rulers, and then the Romans and the Herods, they were predominant in the Jewish Sanhedrin and the corrupt Temple system. As 'the party of the Temple', the High Priest and many priests were Sadducees. Having no following among the populace, their presence and authority were centred in Jerusalem.

They were not political nationalists, expediently using the Roman and Temple system for power and wealth. They suffered a great loss when the Zealots/Sicarii burnt the public archives to destroy debt records, dissolving all repayment – one of the first things they did in AD 67 to "persuade the poorer sort to join their insurrection with safety against the wealthy" (Josephus 1987:625, *Wars* 2.17.427).

Sadducees were proud and rude to their peers, counting it a virtue to dispute with teachers, including Jesus (Matthew 16:1-12, 22:23f). As religious conservatives, they believed only Moses' five books (the Pentateuch) were inspired. Rejecting other texts and oral tradition, they denied belief in the soul, the afterlife, resurrection, and angels and demons (Acts 23:8). For them, God was not actively involved in the world, so they emphasised complete free will: good or evil are in choices that either prosper or ruin the person. Not having messianic expectations, their offering to Israel was simply Temple worship. Their supposed holy way (*halakha*) was to live well in the context.

Essenes

Essenes were a Jewish religious group that arose in the 3rd/2nd century BC and flourished till AD 70. The NT does not mention them and/or their community at Qumran. We only know about them through the writings of Philo, Pliny, and Josephus. For Josephus (1987:605-7, *Wars* 2.8.119–61), the Essenes were the third of the Jewish "philosophies" (schools of thought or sects of Judaism). The other two sects were the Pharisees and Sadducees, with the Zealots later seen as the fourth philosophy (Josephus 1987:477, *Antiquities* 18:1.11-25).

The Essenes were not nationalistic because they had a very narrow ideological sense of being the only true Israel of God. Initially present in Jerusalem, towns, and villages, they withdrew into the Judean desert, creating an apocalyptic end-time 'monastic' community, to use modern terms. The excavations at Qumran near the Dead Sea have led to the Essenes being spoken of as the Qumran community.

Their answer to the crisis of Second Temple Judaism was to withdraw from idolatrous society and the corrupt Temple system, to be pure in anticipation of the Messiah's coming. It was the option of spiritual escape. They had a demanding legalistic order, with ceremonial purity, celibacy, common economic ownership, and no slaves. They produced their food and studied and copied sacred texts. Messiah would deliver and save only them, "the sons of light", while all others were seen as the hated "the sons of darkness".

Meier (2001:489-91) shows that the theories of some modern scholars who link Jesus and/or John the Baptist to Qumran, are mere speculation. Though they would have been aware of the Essenes, not John, nor Jesus, was their messianic "Teacher of Righteousness". Neither the "Wicked Priest" nor the "Man of Lies" that opposed them. There are points of similarity in their teaching with Jesus and John, and points of significant difference, but there is no historical evidence to claim the levels of engagement these scholars do.

The Essenes hid their library in caves before the Romans destroyed Qumran in AD 68. They are the Dead Sea Scrolls discovered in 1947.

Herodians

Meier (2001:560-5) shows the difficulty in defining and describing this group with historical accuracy. In brief, they were servants, members, and officials of King Herod's household. But broadly, 'Herodians' probably referred to supporters of Herod's regime, both Herod the Great and his sons who ruled after him. They worked closely with the Roman governors. In other words, they supported the Roman rule of the Herod dynasty.

Thus, the Herodian response to the context recognised the Jewish Herodian King-Messiah, in collaboration with Rome, to experience peace and prosperity (*Pax Romana*) in Palestine. They offered Israel the option of supporting and maintaining the status quo. But Jews generally saw Herodians as sell-outs to the Roman occupation. Jewish nationalists would have hated them.

The Herodians are referred to in Mark 3:6 and 12:13 (cf. Matthew 22:16). These texts give insight into their nature because, ironically, they conspired with the Pharisees to question Jesus and to plot how they might kill him, e.g., trying to 'trap' Jesus by asking if it was right to pay taxes to Caesar (Mark 12:13-17, discussed later in the chapter, Suffering & Crucifixion). Therefore, they appeared to work with the nationalist Pharisees for a common purpose, but for different reasons: they opposed Jesus' subversive influence on the people with his unsettling of the status quo – Herod-Roman rule.

Anawim and other groupings

Then there was the general populace. They too can be described in subcategories. The Hebrew *anawim* (pronounced ann-a-weem) is a broad term for the poor, marginalised, vulnerable, socio-economically oppressed, and needy people. The less privileged majority lived relatively side-lined, on the underside of power. They are the kinds of people Jesus described in beatitudes (Matthew 5:3-11): the poor, grieving, meek, humble, hungering for justice, merciful, trying to make peace, to make ends meet, i.e., those who struggle and suffer. The people who were open to the Kingdom Jesus offered. Especially with his messianic message of hope ("good news to the poor... freedom for the prisoners... to set the oppressed free", Luke 4:18), where society in God's Kingdom will be inverted because justice will reign.

Anawim was originally, from the OT background, more strictly understood as "the poor ones", as in God's faithful remnant who remained loyal to God through suffering. Even in this narrow sense, it can refer to those people in "the crowds" or "multitudes", especially from rural towns and villages, who flocked to Jesus, to hear him speak and be healed of their sicknesses.

Within this broader populace, we should cite a few groups or categories of Jewish people mentioned in the gospels.

- *Tax collectors*: of the most despised and hated people in Second Temple Judaism because they not only collected taxes to sustain the Roman occupation, but they exploited their fellow Jews to make a profit, e.g., Zacchaeus (Luke 19:1f). They could not serve as witnesses in court and were expelled from the synagogue.

- *Drunkards and prostitutes*: also despised and rejected by the establishment. Jesus socialised with these people, giving them a radical welcome in his Kingdom movement. So much so that he had a reputation as a friend of tax collectors, sinners, drunkards, and prostitutes (Luke 5:30, 7:34; Matthew 21:31). These kinds of people entered the Kingdom that Jesus proclaimed.

- *Sinners*: were non-Torah observant Jews, people who refused to follow the Mosaic law as interpreted by the teachers of the law. They were seen and despised as notoriously evil in the politics of holiness. It was a general term that referred to tax collectors, drunkards, adulterers, robbers, i.e., overtly immoral people.

- *Samaritans*: were a mixed-blood race from the intermarriage of

Israelites left behind when the northern kingdom was exiled. Assyrians brought Gentiles into the land leading to intermarriage with locals (2 Kings 17:24). They developed their own identity and beliefs as Samaritans. There was hostility, even enmity, between Jews and Samaritans in Jesus' day. That made the point of Jesus' parable of "the good Samaritan" especially powerful: to love your enemy (Luke 10:25-37). Jesus also engaged Samaritans with the Kingdom, as seen in John 4.

JESUS' KINGDOM RESPONSE TO THE CONTEXT

We have given an extensive overview of the context of Second Temple Judaism and the various groups in Palestine, each with its response to the crisis. John the Baptist and Jesus of Nazareth stepped publicly into this context in AD 24/25 and 26/27. They did not identify with or join any of the above groups but, instead, offered Israel the way of God's eschatological Kingdom. It was their response to the crisis of the day. John's ministry prepared the way for Jesus, who inaugurated his Kingdom movement. Jesus believed it was God's *halakha,* God's way of salvation for Israel and the nations. Let us unpack his Kingdom response in answer to the *kairos*, the time of pending disaster and the divine opportunity that Israel found herself in.

In the previous chapter, we examined Jesus' Kingdom *mission* by explaining his generic *message* in Mark 1:14-15 (NRSV), "The time is fulfilled, the kingdom of God has come near; repent, and believe in the good news!" Mark immediately has Jesus calling people to follow him. This is key. His generic message was accompanied by a generic call into *Kingdom community,* for Kingdom apprenticeship. In announcing the Kingdom, he called people to "repent and believe" by following him and joining his disciples. He intended to live and advance the Kingdom in and through his community movement as an alternate incarnate witness to all other groups and people in Palestine.

Mark says (1:16-20) that as Jesus walked beside the Sea of Galilee, he called fishermen, "Come, follow me, and I will make you fishers of people". Imagine seasoned fishermen hearing a young 30-year-old rabbi walking past and calling them to leave their boats and follow him. With the promise of fishing people for God's Kingdom.

The Jewish establishment – the powerful groups and the powerless populace – would've initially seen Jesus as a self-appointed precocious rabbi trying get people to follow him. No self-respecting rabbi in that day would call people to follow them. Jews chose who they wanted to follow and learn from out of respect for the rabbi and his teaching. In any case, most rabbis were much older teachers, elders, and sages. How desperate of this young man from Nazareth, who learnt from the wild apocalyptic prophet in the desert, John the Baptist. The remarkable thing is that, as Mark reports, the fishermen left their nets and followed this unknown rabbi from Nazareth!

Therefore, what did Jesus intend by calling disciples into a learning community? To launch his Kingdom movement that inaugurated the *future* Kingdom of God as a *present spiritual reality:* God's power of wholistic salvation, which included socio-political-economic transformation. By following Jesus, all who believe enter and experience *that* reality, spiritually born again in the Kingdom "come near".

The Core Values of Jesus' Kingdom Group

In contrast to the other sects and schools of thought, Jesus' movement would have been seen as a form of end-time *Messianic* Judaism because of the message he proclaimed. We need to examine the culture and purpose of his Kingdom community with its core values and offer to Israel compared to the other groups.

I see three core elements in Jesus' generic call in Mark 1:17-18:

- *Follow:* "Come and follow me".
- *Form:* "I will make you". I change "make" to "form", not only to have three F's for easy memorisation, but because "form" is the richer intended meaning of formation and equipping to fish people for the Kingdom of God.
- *Fish:* "Into fishers of people".

These three values are the historical Jesus' framework of Kingdom discipleship. In short, we follow Jesus, in community, for the world.

Following Jesus – The Person

When Jesus announced the Kingdom that "has come near", he called people to follow *him* to experience and live the Kingdom. He called them to follow him as he followed *Yhwh*, his *Abba,* the King of Israel. Jesus' *halakha,* in contrast to all other groups, was his way of following God in his interpretation of The Law and The Prophets in the context of the times. He believed he was doing God's will on earth as in heaven – the way of God's Kingdom revealed and imparted in his teachings and actions – "I am the way and the truth and the life" (John 14:6). The earliest (self)designation for Jesus' disciples was the followers of "the Way" (Acts 9:1-2, 19:9, 22:4). The civil authorities in Antioch called them "Christians" (11:26) to distinguish them from other Jews in the city. "Christian" meant "Messianic" – "of the party or tribe of Christ (*Christos*)" – the "another king" whom they proclaimed (17:7).

The verb "to follow" (*akoloutheo*, going after, walking behind) occurs 90 times in the NT. The gospels have 79 of them (25 in Matthew, 18 in Mark, 17 in Luke, and 19 in John). In almost every case Jesus is the one being followed, the exceptions being Mark 14:13; Matthew 9:19; John 11:31. Followers in the gospels are, by definition, disciples. Greek *mathetes* (and Hebrew *talmidim*) means "disciplined learners" – hence students, or apprentices. The word occurs 233 times in the gospels: 72 times in Matthew, 46 times in Mark, 37 times in Luke, and 78 times in John. This huge occurrence highlights the extraordinary focus on following the historical Jesus *as his apprentice* by the gospel writers, and by Jesus himself.

Jesus' call echoed the book of Deuteronomy, *Yhwh's* call on Israel to follow him in the Exodus out of Egypt, through the wilderness, to her inheritance, the Promised Land. Israel was to "walk behind" *Yhwh* (Hebrew *halakh ahare*, used of Elisha following Elijah, 1 Kings 19:20) in "the way" (*derekh*) of *Yhwh*, i.e., in God's covenant/Torah. Hence, "follow" is used 27 times in Deuteronomy (NIV): to follow *Yhwh* (3 times), to follow his way/decrees/laws (20 times), and *not* to follow other gods (4 times). In short, to follow *Yhwh* was to obey his Word and Spirit in the way of formation to full freedom in his Kingdom.

Jesus saw himself as *Israel's representative*: by following *Yhwh* in absolute obedience, he fulfils Israel's call and destiny. At the same time, he sees himself as *Yhwh's representative*: by following Jesus, Israel follows *Yhwh* in a New Exodus into a new Kingdom covenant.

That is why he said "to the Jews who had believed him, 'If you hold to my teaching, you are really my disciples. Then you will know the truth, and the truth will set you free'" (John 8:31-32). That is why he called people to follow *him* in apprenticeship to his Kingdom word and life for the salvation of Israel and the nations. That is why he personalised it in "follow me", telling his fellow Jews, "You study the Scriptures diligently because you think that in them you have eternal life. These are the very Scriptures that testify about me, yet you refuse to come to me to have life" (John 5:39-40).

Jewish theologian, Jacob Neusner (2000:62-3, in *A Rabbi talks with Jesus*), is right in observing "how deeply personal is the focus of Jesus' teaching... Jesus is the only model". Neusner concludes that Jesus sets himself above Torah and "eternal Israel", which is why he cannot follow the rabbi from Nazareth. He says that Christians are people of the Person, but Jews are people of the Book. However, Jesus was indeed saying, in effect, "imitate God by imitating me, and you will become holy as God is holy", echoing and fulfilling Leviticus 19:2.

Forming (in) Community – The Power

Jesus' "I will make you" echoes *Yhwh's* formation of Israel in covenant community, through her wilderness journey, to fulfil her destiny in the Promised Land. When Jesus said, "Come, follow me", he meant "join my Kingdom movement and be formed in and through my new covenant family to fulfil God's purposes". We do not, and cannot, follow Jesus in isolation, "just Jesus and me!" *That* is the postmodern neurosis – many people, including Christians, long to go to heaven without going to church! We follow Jesus *as community*, in concrete belonging and participation in Jesus' local church.

To follow Jesus in his day was to meet and share Kingdom life with his friends. Friends who became brothers and sisters. We can choose our friends but not brothers and sisters. They are born into the family by God's design, to grow and mature us for life. For example, after calling fishermen to follow him, Jesus called Levi the tax collector to follow him (Mark 2:13-17). Levi had to put up with the smell of fishermen while they had to associate with one of the most hated people in Israel. Levi threw a party for his new rabbi, where many tax collectors and "sinners" (of all kinds) ate with Jesus and his disciples. Then Jesus called Simon the Zealot to follow him (3:18). How did he get along with Levi, his religious-ideological-opposite-enemy, an ex-tax collector apostle (Levi was Matthew, who wrote the gospel)? What did he think of Jesus having such sinners (tax collectors, drunkards, and prostitutes) as friends? And what of the other disciples? Yet they all followed and were formed in Jesus' diverse community.

Luke 8:1-3 reported that women were part of Jesus' mobile Kingdom community, learning Torah and helping to fund his group. He names Mary of Magdala, "from whom seven demons had come out", and "Joanna, the wife of Chuza, the manager of Herod's household". Besides being female, it was unheard of that a rabbi would have women in his learning school. Joanna was from Herod's household (technically, a Herodian), and shared her husband-manager's money with Jesus and his community. Joseph of Arimathea, a wealthy member of the Jewish ruling council, became a follower of Jesus (Mark 15:43; Matthew 27:57). Nicodemus, a prominent Pharisee, and member of the Sanhedrin followed Jesus (John 3:1f). Evidently, some people from groups mentioned above joined Jesus' end-time Kingdom movement, coming under his power.

Jesus crossed all ideological, gender, class, and racial divides, ministering to Samaritans, Roman officers, and Gentiles, bridging the boundaries of his day in a community of reconciliation. In a study of the twelve apostles and Jesus' broader discipling group, Meier (2001) shows that it was a radically diverse mix of personality, background, social class, religious persuasion, political ideology, morality, and gender. Jesus' faith-family was the impossible community of diverse opposites reconciled in his Kingdom. He was the glue that held people together who otherwise lived disparate lives in different groups under divisive powers. His community witnessed to Palestinian society that God's end-time Kingdom "has come near". The spiritual and political powers knew their end had come because God was King.

This is the context in which Jesus said, "love one another, as I have loved you. By *this* love everyone will know that you are my disciples" (John 13:34-35). *This* was his family of formation, which he highly valued, even above his blood family (Mark 3:31-35). This Kingdom family was the place of reconciliation, healing, and transformation to be equipped with the power to fish people into God's Kingdom.

Fishing the World – The Purpose

His community-movement was essentially missional, to bring God's

Kingdom to Israel and the nations. Because they were fishermen, he said he would form them to fish people, to catch people, as it were, for the Kingdom. He later used that same picture-parable to explain the Kingdom (Matthew 13:47-50).

Thus, "fishing people" was first contextual; that is, he called fishermen to follow him. If they were carpenters, he would make them Kingdom carpenters! When calling farmers, he would form them to farm people for the Kingdom; and businesspeople to do business for the Kingdom; and mothers to be mothers for God's Kingdom. Jesus intended to call people in whatever they were doing in life, reframing whatever occupied their daily time, to use it to live and extend God's Kingdom. Hence, their daily occupation became their daily Kingdom vocation, advancing God's Rule and Reign.

God's purpose for Israel was to make her a holy nation of kings, priests, and prophets (Exodus 19:6 cf. Numbers 11:29), to bring God's Kingdom to the nations and to bring the nations to God. This was God's intention for Israel in the Promised Land. But she failed in her missional calling, turned inward to idolatry, and was consequently exiled. Jesus believed he was reinstating God's original purpose.

Therefore, in calling and forming his followers to be "fishers of people", he was consciously alluding to and fulfilling the prophets. They said God would send fishermen to fish Israel out of exile, putting hooks in her mouth, restoring her into God's Kingdom (Jeremiah 16:14-16; Ezekiel 12:13, 29:4; Amos 4:2). Jesus saw his followers as these eschatological messengers, end-time *evangelists* who proclaim the *evangelion*, the gospel of the Kingdom that says, "Your God reigns" (Isaiah 52:7). Enter the Kingdom – the ultimate goal.

The Paradigm in Summary

Jesus' historical core community became his Kingdom paradigm for all his followers, for all time, as represented in the diagram below. Jesus' intention for the twelve was to be exemplars of Kingdom discipleship, living out his apprenticeship framework in spiritual formation to his person, faith, and life praxis. This is borne out in Mark's statement, that Jesus "appointed twelve, whom he also named apostles, to be with him, and to send them out to proclaim the message and have authority to drive out demons" (3:14-15).

Like Jesus' apostles, we too are called and appointed as *followers*, to be with Jesus in *formation*, to be sent out to *fish* people into God's Kingdom, as we preach and enact its message. These three core values centre us under Jesus' Kingship in his Kingdom, making us fit for life and rule in God's Rule and Reign. We apply and live these values as *fits our context*, i.e., the way we live Jesus' apprenticeship framework must be relevant to and workable in our specific life context. We cannot be like David in Saul's armour trying to live and fight our battles.

Figure 2. Jesus' Framework of Discipleship

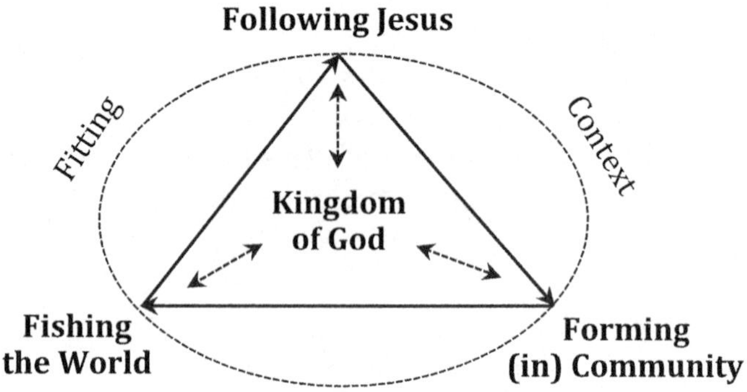

```
                  Following Jesus
                        ▲
            Fitting   /   \   Context
                    /       \
                  /  Kingdom  \
                 /   of God    \
                /               \
         Fishing ─────────── Forming
         the World          (in) Community
```

Levels and Circles of Jesus' Followers

Meier (2001:19-21) shows that "the noun 'follower' is an umbrella term to cover all the various relationships to Jesus" in the gospels. There were varying levels and circles of 'followership' in relational proximity and engagement with Jesus and his Kingdom movement. Imagine throwing a rock into a pond with the ripples going outwards in ever-increasing circles. We can identify the following circles and levels of following Jesus, starting from the centre, Jesus. He is "the rock" not cut with human hands, which becomes a huge mountain filling the whole earth, to change the metaphor to Daniel 2:35.

The twelve. After being well into his ministry, and having a good number of followers, one night Jesus prayed through to the morning, then "called his disciples to him and chose twelve of them, whom he designated apostles" (Luke 6:12-16). The twelve were his closest group, with three of them being his inner circle – Peter, James, and John – especially close to Jesus (Mark 5:37). The twelve symbolised the twelve tribes of Israel – the new Israel – the twelve 'patriarchs' of his Kingdom followers. They will sit on thrones judging the twelve tribes of Israel at the renewal of all things (Matthew 19:28).

The mobile community. Then there was Jesus' mobile community that grew and shrunk as he went through the towns and villages of Palestine. It had a stable core of the twelve *and* other men and women who travelled with him (Luke 8:1-3), probably ranging between eighteen and thirty disciples. They were his immediate Kingdom family doing the will of God on earth as in heaven (Mark 3:31-34).

The seventy. Seventy-two in some manuscripts. Jesus evidently had a recognised tier of discipleship trust in the seventy that he sent out (Luke 10:1f) after the twelve (9:1f). They were the eschatological "fishermen" the prophets spoke of, mentioned earlier, going to every town and village, proclaiming and demonstrating the Kingdom as Jesus did. Having been trained and equipped by Jesus, they did signs and wonders in his name. Jesus saw spiritual powers dislodged and defeated by the advance of the Kingdom (10:17-19).

Seventy was the number of the table of nations (Genesis 10) and the number of Jacob's descendants that went into Egypt (Genesis 46:27). If the twelve represented the new Israel of the new covenant, the seventy was the new Israel in mission to all nations. Thus, Jesus used intentional symbolic meaning: the whole nation of Israel for all the nations of the world. Luke takes it further in Acts 1:15. There were one hundred and twenty disciples in Jerusalem waiting for the Spirit's outpouring. That was the precise number required in a town or village in ancient Israel for a Sanhedrin, a local ruling body, to be constituted. So, before Pentecost, after Jesus' ministry, death, and resurrection, the newly constituted people of God were all in place: the twelve – the new Israel; the seventy – all the new Israel in mission to all the nations; and the one hundred and twenty – the self-governing people of God waiting for the Spirit's empowering of Jesus' heavenly coronation and rule at God's right hand.

Many supporters in towns and villages. This follows naturally from the previous point. People became believers in Jesus through his direct ministry in the towns and villages (Mark 1:38-39) *and* the multiplication of his ministry when he sent out the twelve and then the seventy-two. They did not have to join his mobile community to be followers. They followed and practised his message, meeting with other believers in their locality, while remaining in their homes and doing their daily work. We see this in Martha, Mary, and Lazarus, who were friends of Jesus and hosted him in their village of Bethany on his trips to Jerusalem (Luke 10:38). This would have been the case in other towns and villages in Israel.

The crowds. Lastly, there is reference to "the crowds", "the multitudes", that flocked to hear Jesus and to be healed of their diseases. For example, "a large crowd from Galilee followed. When they heard about all he was doing, many people came to him from Judea, Jerusalem, Idumea, and the regions across the Jordan and around Tyre and Sidon" (Mark 3:7-8). These were both Jewish and Gentile mixed areas. He fed the 5000 (6:30-44), then the 4000 (8:1-9) – the latter in a mixed Gentile area. These crowds followed Jesus in varying degrees of belief and engagement, each for their reasons – essentially selfish, as Jesus pointed out in John 6:25-27.

The gospels record the growth of Jesus' ministry to the peak of public popularity. Then, as opposition and confrontation with the leading authorities increased, his followers whittled away. It ended with most of his twelve abandoning him (temporarily) when he was betrayed and crucified. But the gospels equally show the dramatic impact of Jesus and his Kingdom movement in Second Temple Judaism, and his response to the national crisis. That is why the political and spiritual powers opposed him and finally killed him.

QUESTIONS FOR REFLECTION AND DISCUSSION

1. Once again, on reflection, what two or three things have impacted you in this chapter?

2. Why is it so important to understand the context of Second Temple Judaism and the nature of the national crisis the Jews were facing?

3. Placing Jesus in that context, how different was he? How would you describe his response to a) the times and context in Palestine, and b) the various groups, sects, and categories of people?

4. Why did he choose "Son of Man" as his common self-designation? What was its significance in terms of its origin in Daniel as applied to Jesus' context?

5. Summarize in your own words Jesus' generic call to all people for all time. What do you think of the core values of his generic call to discipleship in his Kingdom?

6. Do you follow Jesus? Are you an apprentice in his Kingdom movement? How intentional is your "disciplined learning" of him?

MINISTRY & MIRACLES

We saw an overview of the volatile context of Roman oppression, with heightened messianic expectation and various responses in Second Temple Judaism. This was the context in which Jesus was raised. He began his ministry of the end-time Kingdom of God, believing it was God's answer for Israel. The time had come. God was on the march bringing Israel's history to fulfilment. God was becoming King for Israel's deliverance and salvation.

Jesus announced and proclaimed God's Kingdom and ministered and enacted it in the power of the Holy Spirit. He taught and explained the Kingdom and imparted and demonstrated it through touching people, doing healings and miracles, and delivering people from demonic oppression.

In worldview terms, discussed in Jesus' mission and message, his ministry and miracles were his *praxis* of the Kingdom as witness to all of Israel. By doing healings and miracles Jesus practised the *story* of the Kingdom and answered the *life questions* people were asking – as in what went wrong and what is the God-given solution?

His ministry and miracles constitute a significant feature of the historical Jesus. Few scholars give it the attention and prominence it deserves. Jesus was well known as a miracle worker. It greatly impacted his Kingdom message, making it tangible, accessible, and life changing, especially for the recipients of healings and miracles. Jesus' ministry demonstrated and confirmed that God's Kingdom "has come near" (Mark 1:15), and, more so, "has come upon you" (Luke 11:20).

I begin by introducing miracles and their controversial nature, at least for the modern mind that discounts anything supernatural. It raises many questions. Much philosophic debate has been on the healings and miracles reported in the gospels.

The practice in historical Jesus studies is to start with Mark, the earliest gospel. So, we examine Mark's account of Jesus' ministry and miracles. Then we briefly outline how Matthew, Luke, and John frame and explain Jesus' Kingdom ministry and miracles. In this regard, a full examination of each of the gospel writer would fill a sizable book or two! Jesus was clearly a miracle-working prophet to Israel.

Books such as these, authoritative sources, that the reader can consult in this field of study. See Graham Twelftree's books in my bibliography of references, especially *A Historical and Theological Study: Jesus the Miracle Worker* (1999). He has specialised in researching Jesus' healings, demonic expulsions, and nature miracles. Keener (2011) has written two bench-mark volumes on *Miracles: The Credibility of the New Testament Accounts*. I also draw on Meier's (1994) *The Marginal Jew, Volume II: Mentor, Message, and Miracles*.

THE QUESTION OF HEALINGS AND MIRACLES

Jesus' ministry in the gospels raises many questions for historians.

What is the nature of Jesus' healings and miracles? How do we evaluate them with the modern mind? How do we know if they happened? Or if they were mythical stories the early church told, at worst invented, to 'prove' Jesus was 'the Messiah'?

How do we classify the healings, and exorcisms, and miracles? Especially the nature miracles, like Jesus walking on water. Are they comparable with other Jewish and pagan miracle workers in the Second Temple period? Is there a difference between miracles and magic? How did Jesus understand his healings and miracles? Why did he do them? Were they theologically interpreted? If so, how?

These are the kinds of questions, and more, with which historians wrestle. The scholars mentioned above offer well-researched and reasoned answers. I give a brief perspective by way of introduction to our examination of Jesus' ministry and miracles in the gospels.

The faulty method of many scholars is to evaluate the authenticity of the miracles through their modern worldview, leading to misguided conclusions. The issue is how the gospel writers understood the miracles, with the implications for their portrait of Jesus, how healings and miracles functioned in Jesus' ministry. And what the writers understood the miracles meant for their readers in their day, in the worldview of Second Temple Judaism.

The early gospel readers would not have had a problem with the healings, exorcisms, and miracles. They assumed an unseen spiritual reality, accepting and expecting God's intervention in human affairs. They believed in miracles, spiritual revelation, angelic encounters, personal evil, and demonic engagement with people. The rational material worldview of modernism dismisses the experiential spiritual worldview of the Bible as primitive and naïve. They state that only what can be scientifically verified or proven is real: God and spiritual reality are matters of "faith and religion", not real knowledge or truth.

Philosopher David Hume (1711–76) was the decisive sceptical influence. He argued that so-called miracles violate the fixed laws of nature (Newtonian science). There are no 'supernatural' happenings not subject to natural laws. Hence, the dichotomy between the so-called supernatural and the natural. Hume also claimed that eye-witness accounts of events are notoriously untrustworthy. Thus, earlier scholars discounted Jesus' miracles due to their modernist assumptions and because the miracles were "novelistic flourishes or legendary accreditations" (Keener 2011:15), i.e., the miracle stories were 'accredited', became 'legitimized legends' over time.

But Keener's exhaustive study (2011, over 1000 pages) of eye-witness miracles from Jesus through the entire history of the church to our day (in every major epoch, in every major Christian tradition, in a wide variety of cultures and nations), shows that people report miracles that are contemporary with themselves, i.e., when they happen. Keener shows that most people in most societies in history, including contemporary Western societies, believe miracles occur. That makes the scholarly modernist elite in the West, who have a materialist worldview, a minority within a minority. The historical criteria of analogy and multiple attestation argue for Jesus' miracles. Keener (2011:107-208) shows that "Hume's argument proceeds mostly by modern definition rather than induction and is logically unworkable even on his own philosophic premises". See also Brown's (1984:79-102) critique of Hume's anti-supernaturalism.

The question in Jesus' time was not whether healings and miracles happened, but rather, what was their nature, source, and purpose? The biblical worldview distinguishes between "miracle" and "magic". They are two distinct categories opposed to each other, reflecting a different source, power, and purpose. "Miracle" indicates works of wonder by God's Spirit-power for people's wellbeing. "Magic" means apparent miracles done by evil powers to deceive people through "signs and wonders" (2 Thessalonians 2:9-10). Pharoah's magicians tried to copy and counter Moses' miracles that were done by "the finger of God" (God's Spirit, Exodus 7:11-12, 8:19 cf. Luke 11:20).

There were two known Jewish miracle workers at the time of Jesus, *Honi HaMe'agel* (Honi the Circle Drawer, 1st century BC) and *Hanina Ben Dosa* (1st century AD), mentioned in Josephus and the Talmud. But their miracles lacked eschatological context, as in no teaching of and witness to God's end-time Kingdom (Keener 2009:40-1). There were also pagan miracle workers. Comparing all these with Jesus and the gospel accounts raises the question of miracle or magic.

In conclusion, within the worldview of the day, together with the scholars mentioned above we take the gospel accounts of healings, demonic expulsions, and nature miracles, as historically reliable. Jesus' "signs and wonders", commonly called (Hebrews 2:3-4), were framed in an eschatological context and interpretation, pointing to the reality that God's end-time Kingdom "has come near" (Mark 1:15). "Signs" point to a greater reality, the King and his Kingdom. "Wonders" are works of power that amaze people, indicating and confirming that the Kingdom is actively setting people free. Thus, the purpose of Jesus' signs and wonders was to lead people to "repent and believe the good news" of God's Kingdom (Mark 1:15). That is how Jesus and the gospel writers, including the first readers, understood them.

MARK'S ACCOUNT OF JESUS' MINISTRY AND MIRACLES

Mark's account of Jesus' ministry and miracles is framed in Jesus as the Son of God (1:1), who is the Son of Man (2:10) and Servant of *Yhwh* (10:45 cf. Isaiah 53:10-12). The Son of Man's authority to heal and do miracles leads to growing clash of authorities and spiritual powers.

Mark begins his story with Jesus having a clear set of priorities:

- Jesus *announced the Kingdom*, calling people to "repent and believe" his good news to enter the Kingdom (1:14-15).

- Then he called a *community of the Kingdom* into being, followers who repented and believed (1:16-20).

- Then began his *ministry of the Kingdom* by expelling demons in the synagogue (1:21-28) and continued his signs and wonders at an intense pace (1:29f).

In this way Mark sets the agenda of Jesus' ministry and miracles that clash with evil powers in public confrontation. Put another way, when Jesus announced the Kingdom, he demonstrated and imparted it to needy people. It called for and resulted in "repent and believe", to return to God by turning to Jesus, with a change of thinking to open one's mind to God's wildest Kingdom possibilities. This is repeatedly illustrated in the stories of Jesus' ministry and miracles.

John Mark reportedly wrote his biography of Jesus from the stories that Peter the apostle told. Papias (AD 60-130), an early church father, said John Mark was Peter's scribe. He recorded Peter's eyewitness accounts of Jesus' ministry and miracles. This explains why Mark's gospel is a fast-moving action-packed string of stories based on historical events in Jesus' life, as Peter (and the other apostles) experienced, remembered, and retold them.

Mark repeatedly uses three keywords in his action-story of Jesus:

- *"Authority"*: Jesus' authority is asserted over the authority of evil in all its forms (e.g. 1:22,27).

- *"Immediately"*: The immediacy of events in Jesus' ministry that follow one another with increasing clash of powers (e.g. 1:42).

- *"Amazed/astonished"*: The regular reaction and response to Jesus' authority in his ministry and miracles (e.g. 1:27).

They appear repeatedly in Jesus' teaching, ministry, and miracles. The *words* (authority) of the Kingdom create the *works* (immediacy) of the Kingdom that are the *wonders* (astonishment) of the Kingdom. Jesus experienced the Kingdom as a spiritual reality, a power zone or "field of force… in which the power of the Kingdom is concretely present" (Meier 1994:161). Mark chose and framed Peter's stories of Jesus to suit his theological purpose, demonstrating that God's end-time Kingdom was powerfully present in Jesus for people's salvation.

As Mark's gospel unfolds, we see Jesus asserting his authority over Satan's kingdom in six dimensions of human need. He defeated evil by setting people free through: 1) ruling over demons, 2) ruling over sickness, 3) forgiving sins, 4) ruling over nature, 5) ruling over death, and 6) ruling over human hunger. To illustrate how this happened, I retell six stories as Mark reports them, highlighting the nuances of interpretation and understanding.

This echoes Peter's summary of Jesus' ministry in Acts 10:38, "We know how God anointed Jesus of Nazareth with the Holy Spirit and power, and how he went around doing good and healing all who were under the power of the devil, because God was with him". The word "power" is *dynamis,* from which we get the English word dynamite. It was power against power! Jesus went around blowing up the works of evil, freeing people from the devil's power. The phrase, "because God was with him", affirms Jesus' humanity. He did miracles as a human being by faith in God and the Holy Spirit's power, and not as God, as a "divine man" (*theios aner*).

John summarised it so well, "The reason the Son of God appeared was to destroy the devil's work" (1 John 3:8b).

Jesus rules over evil spirits (Mark 1:21-28)

Mark chose his first story: a raw public confrontation with evil, shortly after *ha satan* had confronted Jesus in his desert fasting and prayer. This, however, was a clash with Satan's representatives, the evil spirits that had demonised a man for years. He attended a synagogue where Jesus taught, and the demons could not resist Jesus' authority.

Imagine being a synagogue/church member for many years while inhabited by evil spirits. They had hidden so well in the man that either, a) no one knew about them, or b) no one could help the man, or c) he was so ashamed of his tormenting demonisation that he kept it secret, or d) he was conditioned into accepting it for life.

When the King is present, his Kingdom disrupts 'the service', confronting our kingdoms, and that of the devil. What was hidden for years was pushed into the open by the authority of Jesus' teaching: "The people were amazed at his teaching, because he taught them as one who had authority, not as the teachers of the law" (1:22). He taught as one speaking directly from God, not appealing to traditions and other interpretations. "*Just then* a man... who was possessed by an impure spirit cried out" (1:23). The demon(s) could no longer hide in the man's body. They were unmasked and screamed in terror.

In Mark's gospel, evil spirits were the first to know and confess who Jesus was, "The Holy One of God" (1:24). This was long before his disciples, other Jews, and Jewish leaders acknowledged Jesus as the Messiah. The demons shouted, "What do you want with us, Jesus of

Nazareth? Have you come to destroy us? I know who you are..." (1:24). The interchange between "us" and "I", the plural and singular, is common in most accounts of demonic expulsions. The "strongman" speaks on behalf of the other spirits banded together to afflict, oppress, or torment, or even possess the person.

Satan and his demons know their time is limited, and that God will judge them. They felt the tremors of that Judgement Day in God's Holy One, in his words weighted with Kingdom authority. In Matthew 8:29 the demons screamed, "Have you come here to torture us *before the appointed time?*" That future time was before them, already present in Jesus. Their end had come – the end of inhabiting that tormented man. The end of their rule and reign. God's promised Kingdom, come in Jesus, was their torture and torment, a foretaste of their end.

Jesus said that demons were driven out into "a dry place" (Luke 8:31), while they sought another person to entice, entangle, and inhabit. Eventually they will be sent into "the Abyss" (Luke 11:24).

Jesus responded sternly, "Be quiet! Come out of him!" (Mark 1:25). The rebuke was, in effect, "Shut up and leave this man!" The was the command of the King, not a magical incantation common to other Jewish exorcists who invoked names to subdue and have authority over evil spirits (e.g. Acts 19:13-16). If the demons tried to subdue him by naming Jesus "the Holy One of God", it backfired! Jesus' rebuke was not reliant on particular words, but on God's authority and power.

"The impure spirit shook the man violently and came out of him with a shriek" (Mark 1:26). Exiting demons were known to resist, negotiate, and cause a commotion (see 5:10-13; this story shows their insatiable desire to inhabit bodies, even pigs as a last resort).

"The people were all *amazed*" (1:27). First they were amazed at his authority in teaching; now they were amazed at his authority in driving out demons. "He even gives orders to impure spirits and they obey him" (1:27). Their thinking was shaken. It was a sign to turn to God and open themselves to God's Kingdom possibilities in Jesus of Nazareth. They were challenged to "repent and believe", to entrust themselves to what God was doing.

Because of this dramatic deliverance, "news about him spread quickly over the whole region of Galilee" (1:28). The expulsion of demons was a regular feature of Jesus' ministry (1:32-34), marking him as different from all other supposed exorcists.

Jesus rules over sickness of all kinds (Mark 1:29-34)

Mark's first story is about the confrontation of two kingdoms: God's end-time Kingdom come in Jesus and the defeat of the works of Satan's kingdom. Satan and his demons are the real enemies that oppressed Israel and dominated the earth. This sets the scene for confrontation with other manifestations of evil as Mark's next story reveals: Jesus rules over sickness and disease of all kinds.

The fast-moving story: *"as soon as"* the worship service was over, Jesus and his disciples went to Simon and Andrew's house for lunch. Nothing was prepared because Simon's mother-in-law was sick with a high temperature – only women made the food! However, the men were concerned for her and *"immediately* told Jesus about her" (1:30). They changed their thinking from "where's the food?", opening up to God's possibilities in Jesus, "please help her, she's sick".

Both Mark (1:31) and Matthew (8:15) report that Jesus touched her, implying an impartation of healing. Luke says Jesus *"rebuked* the fever, and it left her" (4:39). "Rebuke" (*epitimao*) was the common word used to expel demons (Mark 3:12, 9:25), implying that Jesus treated the fever as an expression of Satan's kingdom and addressed it as such. Jesus drove it out and set her free. Then Mark adds, "and she began to wait on them" – the men could now eat – hallelujah!

Theologically (biblical worldview), disease and sickness entered humanity through "The Fall" in Eden. Our bodies became mortal through "original sin", Adam and Eve's disobedience. If they had never sinned, they would be alive today, their bodies ablaze with God's glory. The human body was created in God's image (Genesis 1:26-27). Death, mortality, and corruption entered creation via sin (Romans 5:12). The result is sickness and broken creation under the rule of "the god of this age" (2 Corinthians 4:4). In this sense, all disease and brokenness are a foretaste of death, ultimately the work of the devil.

Hence, Jesus rebuked sickness, exercising the authority of God's Kingdom. He died and rose again to defeat the power of sin and death, reversing mortality in bodily resurrection. Eternal life – life in God's Kingdom – is *embodied* life, not *disembodied* spirit-soul-consciousness "in heaven". Because of Jesus' resurrection, our bodies will be resurrected, free from sin, sickness, demons, and death.

Therefore, healing is a power surge of the future resurrection, reversing present brokenness. Healing is a foretaste and anticipation of resurrected wholeness. It is God's Kingdom, "the powers of the coming age" (Hebrews 6:5), coming on us in the whole of who we are. Healing is *not just physical*. It is God's wholeness for the whole person: spiritual, psycho-emotional, physical, and relational healing. See the six dimensions of healing in my *Doing Healing* (2018:215-297).

The story ends with how "the whole town gathered" at the house, bringing "all the sick and demonised", and *Jesus healed them* (Mark 1:32-34). In other words, in the coming of the Kingdom, Jesus has authority over sickness and disease. Mark *immediately* confirms this with his next story of Jesus doing the unthinkable: touching a leper who asked for help (1:40-45). He "repented and believed", going against the religious prohibitions on lepers, running to Jesus and begging for help. Jesus healed the leper by touch (impartation of power) *and* by command (exercise of authority) of the Kingdom.

Jesus rules over sin (Mark 2:1-12)

"A few days later" when people heard that Jesus was in the same house, they gathered in large numbers again. Some men brought their paralysed friend to Jesus but could not get him into the house due to the crowd. So, they "repented and believed". Changing their thinking, and opening themselves to God's possibilities, they went up onto the roof. They dug a hole large enough to lower their paralysed friend before Jesus. Imagine the determination and effort. And the disruption to Jesus' teaching.

On seeing the faith of his friends, Jesus said to the paralysed man, "your sins are forgiven" (2:5). Hugely controversial. The teachers of Torah (theologians), who were there to hear Jesus, thought, "Why does this fellow talk like that? He's blaspheming! Who can forgive sins but God alone?" (2:7). Prophets could do many supernatural things, but never forgive sins. That was God's domain (Isaiah 43:25), through the Temple system where priests pronounced forgiveness on God's behalf, once the required sacrifices had been offered. Considering this, one can understand their offence, accusing Jesus of blasphemy.

However, Jesus "immediately knew in his spirit what they were thinking" and asked them, "Why are you thinking these things? Which is easier: to say to this paralyzed man, 'Your sins are forgiven,' or to say, 'Get up, take your mat and walk'?" (Mark 2:8-9). The answer was obvious. It is easier to say, "Your sins are forgiven", because it's an invisible gift of God; no one sees if it happens. But commanding a paralysed man to "get up and walk" is a visible public test. Everyone knew that. They were watching. Jesus put his credibility on the line. He would stand or fall on whether the paralysed man would walk.

Then Jesus said, "But I want you to know that the Son of Man has authority on earth to forgive sins." Thus, he told the man, "I tell you, get up, take your mat and go home" (2:10-11). Then the man "got up, took his mat and walked out in full view of them all" (2:12). Wow! This challenged and changed mindsets. It opened people to God's Kingdom presence and power! Everyone was "amazed... and they praised God, saying, 'We have never seen anything like this!'" (2:12).

Jesus' explanation and rationale in verse 10 was key. He wanted them to know that he was "the Son of Man", that the Son of Man had the authority of God's Kingdom to forgive sins – besides driving out demons and healing sicknesses. The Torah teachers, and others who knew the scriptures, would have immediately called to mind Daniel 7:13-25. The Ancient of Days gave the Son of Man the "authority and sovereign power" of the eternal Kingdom of God.

Jesus did not overtly imply that he was God. He claimed to be the human messianic "Son of Man" that Daniel predicted. Jesus exercised *that* authority, in faith, to forgive sins. In so doing, he also enacted the promised new Temple and priesthood, not fixed and functioning in concrete, but moving through Israel, offering God's forgiveness to all who "repent and believe". That authority would ultimately be vindicated through his atoning death as God's once-for-all sacrifice for sin. *Yeshua* will "save his people from their sins" (Matthew 1:21).

Jesus rules over nature (Mark 4:35-41 and 6:45-52)

Mark reports a nature miracle: Jesus calming the storm. It has all the hallmarks of personal experience (Peter's eyewitness account): the precise time and place; the (unnecessary) reference to the "other boats" (4:36); the detail that the boat "was nearly swamped" (4:37) and Jesus was "in the stern sleeping on a cushion" (4:38); the disciples' panic and their rebuking Jesus in anger, "Rabbi, don't you care if we drown?"; and their bewilderment at the end, "Who is this?" (4:41).

After teaching all day on God's Kingdom, as the sun set, Jesus told his apostles, "Let us go over to the other side" of the Sea of Galilee. He was tired and fell asleep. Suddenly "a furious squall came up, and the waves broke over the boat, so that it was nearly swamped" (4:37). The Sea of Galilee was known for its sudden and fierce gusts of wind that drove waves into the boat. Many of them were seasoned fishermen who would have endured storms while fishing. It was not uncommon for fishermen to drown. If the boat "was nearly swamped", it was very serious. We see this in their fearful panic, waking Jesus with a terrified cry, "Rabbi, don't you care if we drown?"

Jewish readers would be reminded of the story of Jonah (1:5-6) with its similarities. However, whereas Jonah was running away from God's call and asked to be thrown into the sea to calm the storm, Jesus obeyed God's call and stood up to rebuke the storm and calm the sea with *shalom*: God's peace, order, and well-being.

In response to the angry challenge and rebuke of the disciples, Jesus rose to confront and rebuke the wind and waves authoritatively. His "rebuke" (*epitimao*) was a command, "Quiet! Be still!" (*phimoun*, literally, "be muzzled", as a dog's muzzle/snout is shut tight, Mark 4:39). Mark used both these words in his first story (1:25). In other words, Jesus treated the storm as he did the demons. He saw evil intent in the storm, to harm and destroy through disordered creation. So, he asserted God's Kingdom authority (as the Son of Man) over nature and the evil that worked through it. "Then the wind died down and it was completely calm" (4:39).

In Jewish tradition, God ruled the wind and the waves, as seen in scripture (Psalms 65:7, 89:9, 107:23-32), II Maccabees 9:8, and in rabbinic literature. What is true of the God of Israel now seemed true of Jesus of Nazareth. No wonder his disciples were bewildered beyond astonishment at Jesus, at his authority and power "even" over nature. Mark said, "they were *terrified* and asked each other, 'Who is this? *Even* the wind and the waves obey him!'" (4:41). Their human terror of the storm with evil intent was transformed into the holy terror of God's servant with Kingdom intent. They had seen demons obey him. Sickness and sin obeyed him. Now nature. What's next?

There was a subtext lesson to this story. The fact that Jesus slept through the storm and had to be awakened did not mean he was over-exhausted. Rather, he rested in faith, secure in God's rule over nature.

He had "repented and believed", which he expected his disciples to have done. They had to change their thinking from fear through what their five senses told them, to faith in God's possibilities in his Kingdom come. That is what Jesus hoped they had learnt in their apprenticeship to him in his Kingdom ministry and miracles. This was clear in his response to them after he stilled the storm: *"Why are you so afraid? Do you still have no faith?"* (4:40 cf. 16:14).

In my RAP, "I was having a good sleep. Why did you wake me? I expect you to have learnt by now to 'repent and believe', to do what I have been doing. You should have commanded the wind and waves as you've seen me command demons and sicknesses. Do you *not yet* have faith?" Greek, *oupo,* is "not yet" have faith, better than "still" have no faith (NIV). Jesus expected them by this time to have demonstrated more faith in God's Kingdom come in him. Here is the "not yet" *and* the "already" of the Kingdom – discussed in the next chapter.

Jesus rules over death (Mark 5:21-43)

After Jesus rules over the storm, Mark again shows Jesus ruling over demons – a "legion" that had completely tortured and demented a man with self-cutting. The result was, once again, "all the people were amazed" (5:1-20). In the very next story, Jesus overcame death by bringing a child back to life (5:21-43). "At *this* they were *completely astonished*" (5:42). The higher the stakes, the greater the warfare, and the more mind-blowing the astonishment. It was building to a climax.

A Synagogue leader named Jairus, came to Jesus and fell at his feet, pleading earnestly with him, "My little daughter is dying. Please come and put your hands on her so that she will be healed and live" (5:23). He had heard about Jesus and believed (Romans 10:17).

"So Jesus went with him", but was interrupted by a woman who had been haemorrhaging for twelve years. She "had spent all she had" on doctors but "grew worse" (5:26). Having also "heard about Jesus", she changed her thinking and turned to God's Kingdom active in Jesus of Nazareth. She pushed her way through the crowd believing, "if I just touch his clothes, I will be healed". *Immediately* her bleeding stopped. She felt in her body that she was freed from her suffering (5:28-29). Jesus "realised that power (*dynamis*) had gone out from him" and said, "your faith has healed you, go in *shalom*" (5:34). Go in God's peace, a foretaste of new creation order and wellbeing.

While Jesus was still speaking, people came from Jairus' house and told him, "Your daughter is dead. Why bother the teacher anymore?" (5:35). The delay of the haemorrhaging women had caused a tragedy! But Jesus overheard what was said and interrupted with, "Don't be afraid; just believe" (5:36). Imagine hearing your young daughter had died. Fear is the mortal enemy of faith. But faith overcomes fear. Jesus' RAP was, "repent and believe. Don't react to what you're hearing. Hold God's possibilities before you. Respond in faith to what he's doing in this dark hour. God is in control. Let's go to her!"

When they got to the house "Jesus saw a commotion, with people crying and wailing loudly" (5:38). In that culture, professional mourners were required to assemble, even immediately when someone died, because bodies decomposed rapidly in Palestine's heat. The daughter was twelve years old (5:42), "probably soon to be married... to die unmarried – especially just short of it – was lamented as a particularly great tragedy" (Keener 2014:141). Jesus' response, however, was challenging, "Why all this commotion and wailing? The child is not dead but asleep" (5:39). "But they laughed at him" (5:40).

First, Jesus didn't mean she was "just sleeping". He used a common euphemism for death, also used when Lazarus was raised to life (John 11:11-14). Luke (8:53-55) confirmed that the mourners knew she was dead, and that "her spirit returned" when Jesus said, "get up".

Second, from weeping and wailing to scornful laughing showed how artificial the mourning customs had become. Jesus "put them all out" to remove the hypocritical hysteria and unbelief, and to focus in faith on the child. Thus, he took only the parents and his three closest disciples to "where the child was" (Mark 5:40).

Then he took her by the hand and said, *"Talitha koum!"* Mark gives the Aramaic translation, "Little girl, get up!" (5:41). She was a "young daughter" in Jewish classification, twelve years old (5:42). But Jesus, taking her hand, addressed her as "little girl". He was deeply moved and endeared to her. He was tender, gentle, and compassionate. Note the touch *and* the command and *"immediately* the girl stood up" (5:42). Luke's rendering implies that Jesus' touch and words *rebuked death,* because "her spirit returned, and at once she stood up" (8:54-55). Luke also referred to Jesus' tender care, "then Jesus told them (Jairus and his wife) to give her something to eat".

The conclusion is clear, Jesus has authority over death. It was not a once-off happening. The gospels record three such events in Jesus' Kingdom ministry: The widow's son (Luke 7:11-17), Jairus' daughter (Mark 5:21-43; Luke 8:51-56), and Lazarus (John 11:1-44).

Jesus rules over human hunger (Mark 6:30-44 and 8:1-10)

With this story, we reach the peak of Jesus' ministry in how Mark structured his gospel. The story of the multiplication of food is, in fact, two similar events with different symbolic applications.

6:30-44 is the feeding of the 5000 on the Jewish side of Galilee. The twelve remaining basketfuls of bread and fish symbolise God's Kingdom provision for the twelve tribes of Israel (Leviticus 24:5-9).

8:1-10 is the feeding of the 4000 on the mixed Jewish-Gentile area of the Decapolis (7:31). The seven remaining basketfuls symbolise the completion of God's Kingdom provision for the nations.

It is followed by the turning point in Mark's gospel (8:27-38) when Jesus disclosed his identity as "*the* Messiah" (8:29, *the* Son of God, Matthew 16:16), who will suffer and be killed in the climactic triumph over the kingdom of evil. In other words, Jesus' crucifixion will be his greatest ministry and miracle, vindicated in the resurrection (8:31), as he gives his body, broken as the bread of heaven, for Israel and the nations. John clearly states that in the multiplication of bread (6:1f): Jesus teaches that his body is (given as) the bread of eternal life.

Thus, the two stories illustrate that Jesus rules over human hunger. They are nature miracles, not control of disordered creation used by evil, but instead meeting the deepest human need exploited by evil. It recalls Moses' miracle of the manna (made overt in John 6) that gave daily life and sustenance to Israel through her wilderness journey until she entered the Promised Land of milk and honey.

The miracle in Mark 6:30-44 occurred in an isolated area where crowds had flocked to see Jesus. In that culture, they counted the men. Mark says there were 5000 men (6:44; Luke 9:14). Counting women and children who would have been present, Jesus would have fed upwards of 8000 – an enormous number. The closest towns of Capernaum and Bethsaida had between 2000 and 3000 each (Lane 1974:232). The feeding of the 5000 is attested to in all four gospels, so as we retell Mark's story, I add details from the other gospels.

Jesus saw the vast crowd as sheep without a shepherd, so he had compassion on them and taught them for hours about God's Kingdom (Mark 6:34). He saw himself as the promised Good Shepherd of Ezekiel 34:11-16 (cf. John 10:1-10), feeding God's regathered flock by teaching, and then literally feeding them with fish and bread.

Late in the day, his disciples asked Jesus to send them all away to buy food in the nearby villages. Jesus said, "No! You feed them!" (Mark 6:37). John (6:6) adds that Jesus was testing them, "for he already had in mind what he was going to do". After all they had been through with Jesus, notably the calming of the storm, surely they would now "repent and believe" – turn from their old ways, change their thinking, and work in faith with God to meet the human need. With God nothing is impossible. The Kingdom is present. But, they failed, again.

Using 'preacher's licence': my RAP is that they called an elder's meeting, the Apostolic Council, to discuss Jesus' instruction, "you feed them". Doubting Thomas surveyed the crowd and estimated it would take an impossible amount of eight months of an average salary to feed them (6:37). Treasurer Judas quickly calculated with his long fingers to see how much was in the common purse, "Are we to go and *spend that much* on bread and give it to them to eat?" (6:37). Philip retorted, "Eight month's wages would never buy enough food for everyone to have a bite; we'd need much more!" (John 6:7). Peter said, "Sending them away to buy food in nearby towns and villages will not do because there won't be enough food for so many". John responded, "We can't send them away; they're hungry and weak". Someone added, "It's getting dark, they might lose their way!" (Mark 6:35).

These were the minutes of the meeting to answer, "you feed them". In fact, Philip had his laptop ready to present their feasibility study on why they could not feed the people. But on their way to Jesus, the Apostolic Council ran into Andrew, who had missed the meeting. They asked, "where were you?" Andrew replied (John 6:8-9), "I was out looking for food, because Jesus said we must feed them, and found *a boy* who bunked school to come to Jesus' Kingdom Conference. He gave me his lunch box with five fish sandwiches". You can imagine the looks of disbelief, especially on the face of Peter, Andrew's brother.

Andrew "repented and believed". He changed his thinking, opening himself to God's wildest possibilities, thus acting in faith on Jesus' instruction. He found food and brought it to Jesus. What would he do with it to feed the multitudes? Andrew's faith in God's Kingdom abundance rebuked his colleagues' fear of human scarcity. Jesus dismissed Philip's power-point presentation and received Andrew's "five barley loaves and two small fish" (John 6:9, barley loaf was the food of the poor). Let me return to Mark's historical account.

Jesus directed the disciples to seat the people in groups for easier food distribution (Mark 6:39). Taking the boy's five loaves and two small fish, he gave thanks, speaking the Hebrew blessing. Then he broke them and gave them to his disciples to distribute to the groups. So, *the miracle of multiplication happened through their hands*, and those of the people. "The Kingdom of God is *at hand*" (1:15 ESV). All four gospels say that all the people ate and were fully satisfied.

Then Jesus rubbed it in, as it were, instructing his disciples to use twelve baskets to pick up all the remaining pieces of bread and fish. Only then did they realise the astounding miracle of the multiplication of food to feed over 8000 people, with so much leftover! It was dramatic. John (6:14-15) reported that the people said, "Surely this is the Prophet who is to come into the world". They even "intended to come and make him king by force". Jesus knew it and withdrew.

God's Kingdom provision for human life is more than enough. It is excessively abundant for all in need, for all Israel and all nations.

JESUS' MINISTRY AND MIRACLES IN THE OTHER GOSPELS

Here I merely give an overview of how Matthew, Luke, and John frame and present Jesus' ministry and miracles. To repeat, their theological framing does not discount their historical integrity.

Matthew's Gospel

Matthew also saw Jesus as Daniel's Son of Man (9:6) and Isaiah's Servant of *Yhwh* (8:17, quoting Isaiah 53:4). Both references appear in the context of Jesus' ministry and miracles. Son of David (1:1) and Son of God (3:17, 14:33) are also used. However, because he wrote his gospel to Jews, Matthew's overall framing of Jesus is the new Moses leading a new Exodus into the Kingdom of Heaven. Moses spoke of this 'greater Moses', saying he would fulfil the Law and the Prophets, speaking words from God's mouth (Deuteronomy 18:18-19).

In our earlier discussion of Jesus' birth, we saw how Matthew begins his gospel with the clash of powers, the massacre of Jewish baby boys (2:1-12), echoing Pharoah's killing of Hebrew baby boys when Moses was born. Like Moses, Jesus survives the infanticide and goes to Egypt. His coming out of Egypt is equated with God's calling of Israel, "my son", in a new Exodus (2:13-17). This was confirmed in Jesus' water baptism and his forty days of desert testing as Israel's representative, symbolising the Exodus through the waters and his obedience for Israel's forty years in the wilderness.

This leads into Jesus' first teaching: "he went up on a mountain and sat down... and began to teach *his disciples*" (5:1f), the new Israel of the new covenant. This recalls and fulfils Moses' going up Mount Sinai to receive the covenant and then to sit and teach Israel (teachers of Torah sat "in the seat of Moses" to teach, 23:1).

Matthew's framing of Jesus as the new Moses is also evidenced in his intentional gospel *structure,* built on *five teaching blocks* that represent Moses' five books. Jesus is the messianic fulfilment of Torah. The teaching blocks each have an introductory narrative section.

- Chapters 3-4, narrative intro; 5-7, first teaching block, the Sermon on the Mount, is on the *Messianic Torah of Kingdom Life.*

- 8-9, narrative intro; 10, teaching the *Kingdom Mission.*

- 11-12, narrative intro; 13, teaching the *Kingdom Mystery.*

- 14-17, narrative intro; 18, teaching the *Kingdom Community.*

- 19-22, narrative intro; 23-25, the last teaching block is the *Judgements and Coming of the Kingdom.*

Chapters 1-2 are the prologue, Jesus' birth, and 26-28 is the conclusion, Jesus' death and resurrection. The first and last teaching blocks have three chapters each. This is a well-balanced structure.

Chapters 8-9 are of particular interest. Here Matthew has ten specific healing/miracle narratives that lead into chapter 10, Jesus' teaching on the Exodus-Mission into God's Kingdom. It recalls Moses' ten plagues/miracles that defeated the ten primary gods of Egypt, leading to the Exodus of Israel into *Yhwh's* covenantal Kingship.

The last of these ten healing miracles is followed by Matthew's account of Jesus' transfer of his ministry and miracles to the twelve apostles, whom he authorised and sent as "workers into the harvest field" (9:35-38, 10:1-5). Chapter 10 is, essentially, Jesus' teaching on the co-mission to go and proclaim, "The Kingdom of Heaven is near; heal the sick, raise the dead, cleanse the lepers, drive out demons, because freely you have received, so freely give" (10:7-8). The remainder of the chapter is his instruction on the praxis, on the how-to, with warnings of opposition and preparation for persecution.

Luke-Acts

Luke uses Mark and Matthew's messianic titles, but he frames his biography of Jesus as God's prophet anointed with God's Spirit. Luke 4:18 (Isaiah 61:1-2) summarised Jesus' mission and message (see pp.92-3), as well as his ministry and miracles.

Luke wrote a two-part book: his story of Jesus (his gospel) and that of his early followers (Acts of the Apostles). Both are addressed to Theophilus, Acts being a continuation of Luke's gospel (Luke 1:1-3 cf. Acts 1:1). Taken as a whole, Keener (2012:712-21) has shown that Luke-Acts is a succession narrative of Jesus and his followers, as in Elijah and Elisha. Luke framed Jesus as Elijah and his followers as Elisha, ministering God's Kingdom in signs and wonders.

Jesus begins his ministry by saying he's anointed by God's Spirit to do God's works (Luke 4:18), then he compares himself to Elijah and Elisha (4:24-27). As his ministry of miracles with his disciples unfolds, after an appropriate time of modelling, Jesus imparts his *dynamis* (power) and *exousia* (authority) to them, to go and do his Kingdom works. Luke is the only gospel writer who reports Jesus transferring his ministry to the twelve *and* the seventy-two (or seventy, see NIV note, 9:1f and 10:1f). This implies a larger group of disciples in training, a school of prophets to do what Jesus was doing. In this context of impartation from Jesus to his disciples, Keener's (2012:714-5) list of comparisons of Jesus' ministry and miracles in Luke (especially chapters 8 to 10) with that of Elijah, reinforces the succession narrative.

Luke then closes Jesus' (earthly) ministry with his ascension to heaven (24:50-52), clearly echoing Elijah's ascension (2 Kings 2:1-15). "While he (Jesus) was blessing them, he was taken up into heaven" (Luke 24:52). In 2 Kings 2:10, "Elijah said, 'if you see me when I am taken from you, it will be yours'" – referring to Elisha's request to "inherit a double portion of your spirit" in verse 9. Elisha picked up the mantle that fell from Elijah and went on to do twice as many miracles (in 2 Kings 2 to 13) as Elijah did (in 1 Kings 17 to 2 Kings 2).

The book of Acts opens with a repeat of this succession story: Jesus' disciples watched him "taken up before their very eyes" and are then "clothed with *dynamis* (power) from on high" (Luke 24:49; Acts 1:8-11 cf. 2:1-4). The ascended Christ poured out his Spirit at Pentecost, giving his mantle to his prophetic community, and they went out to continue his ministry, doing "greater" works/miracles (John 14:12). For Luke, the Acts of the Apostles are the acts of the ascended Jesus, by his outpoured Spirit, through his church, to advance his Kingdom ministry and miracles to the ends of the earth.

A closer look at Luke-Acts confirms the prophetic features and source of Jesus' ministry and miracles, *and* that of his disciples: the *Spirit*, *power*, and *prayer*. The other distinctive is that Jesus' ministry crosses all social barriers, as in *Elijah* and *Elisha* (Luke 4:25-27).

- By the eschatological Spirit (4:18): Jesus did miracles by "the finger of God" for God's Kingdom to "come upon you" (11:20). Likewise, his followers did ministry by being filled/anointed with the Spirit (Acts 1:5,8; 2:4).

- In the power of the Spirit: Luke uses *dynamis* eleven times in his gospel, e.g., "the *power* of the Lord was present for him to heal the sick" (5:17); and eight times in Acts, e.g., Stephen, "full of God's grace and *power*, performed great wonders and signs" (Acts 6:8). This text anticipates 10:38, Jesus' example.

- Through a prayer-filled life: Luke emphasises Jesus' profound prayerfulness throughout his ministry, e.g., Jesus often withdrew from ministry and healing to lonely places to pray (Luke 5:15-16). Likewise, the early church was born and continued in prayer, receiving the Spirit and power in prayer to do ministry and miracles (e.g., Acts 1:12-14, 2:1-4, 3:1, 4:23-31).

- Across all societal divides: Luke's interest is Jesus' ministry and miracles to outcast groups in Jewish society, Gentiles, Samaritans, sinners, the poor, women, children, the sick and demonised. Likewise, Jesus' prophetic community crosses racial-cultural, national-geographic, ideological-economic, and gender-generation barriers, "to the ends of the earth" (Acts 1:8).

John's Gospel

Like Mark's gospel, Jesus' miracles take centre stage in John. He structures his story of Jesus around miraculous "signs". In this and other ways, John's gospel is unique. Twelftree (1999) says,

> "No other Gospel gives such a high profile to the miracles of Jesus. Yet no other gospel has so few miracle stories. And no other Gospel portrays the miracles as so profound and larger than life or other worldly. No other Gospel has such distinctive language in relation to the miracle tradition" (p.339).

John says that Jesus did "many other miraculous signs... not recorded in this book. But these are written that you may believe that Jesus is the Messiah, the Son of God, and that by believing you may have life in his name" (20:30-31).

Thus, to summarise, the purpose of Jesus' miracles is, a) they are *semeion*, signs, that point to the identity and glory of Jesus as the Messiah, the Son of God; and b) they lead to faith in Jesus as the Messiah, if one chooses to believe. They are not an end in themselves for self-satisfaction or spiritual entertainment (6:26).

John's gospel has two halves: chapters 1-11, seven miraculous signs and seven discourses; chapters 12-21, Jesus' passion and vindication (death and resurrection), often seen as the eighth sign.

1. Changing water into wine (2:1-11), "the first of the signs" that points to the ultimate sign of "my hour has come", i.e., Jesus' passion on the cross (19:34-35). And the 1st discourse on the new birth (3:1-16).

2. The 2nd discourse on the water of life (4:1-42), followed by the 2nd sign of healing the royal official's son (4:46-54).

3. Healing the paralytic (5:1-18), followed by the 3rd discourse on the divine Son of God (5:19-47).

4. Feeding the multitude (6:1-15).

5. Followed by Jesus walking on the water (6:16-24), followed by the 4th discourse on the bread of life (6:22-66), and the 5th discourse on

the life-giving Spirit (7:1-52).

6. The 6th discourse of the light of the world (8:12-59), followed by the 6th sign, the healing of the man born blind (9:1-42).

7. The 7th discourse of the good shepherd (10:1-42), followed by the 7th sign, raising Lazarus from the tomb (11:1-45).

Some scholars join the feeding of the multitudes and the walking on water, saying that Jesus' death *and* resurrection are the seventh sign. It is clear, however, from John's gospel structure that Jesus' *death and resurrection* is the ultimate miraculous sign to which all others point – the completion and the source of *all* God's signs and wonders. That is where Jesus' identity, glory, and destiny as the King, the Son of God, is fully revealed for complete faith in him.

John's use of "works" is important. The Greek translation of the OT (Septuagint) uses *ergon,* "work", for *Yhwh's* work of salvation for his people. John uses the same word for the entire ministry of Jesus, and particularly for his miracles, thus indicating that, a) they are works of salvation, and b) God is the source of the miracles. Jesus said as much, after healing the paralytic, "My Father is always at his work to this very day, and I too am working" (5:17).

Then he explained, "Very truly I tell you, the Son can do nothing by himself; he can do only what he sees his Father doing, because whatever the Father does the Son also does. For the Father loves the Son and shows him all he does" (5:19-20). Jesus did nothing on his initiative. He only did what he saw his Father doing and said what he heard his Father saying (8:28). The *"words"* of the Father that Jesus spoke created the *"works"* of the Father that Jesus did (14:10), which were the *wonders* of the end-time Kingdom come in God's Son.

This all points to the profound intimacy between the Father and the Son by the indwelling Holy Spirit (1:32-33). *That* is the model and the means of the relationship Jesus' followers are called into – with the Father through the Son by the Spirit – as in Jesus' commission: "As the Father has sent me, *so send I you. Receive the Holy Spirit*" (20:21-22). Indeed, as Jesus said, "whoever believes in me will do the works I have been doing, and even greater things than these, because I am going to the Father" (14:12).

Therefore, Jesus' believers/apprentices speak his words and do his works and wonders.

CONCLUSION

There is no doubt that the Jesus of history was an eschatological Jewish prophet who worked healings and miracles like Elijah, the most respected prophet in Israel's history (besides Moses, Israel's greatest prophet-deliverer). Clearly, all the healings, demonic expulsions, and miracles that Jesus did were signs and wonders of the presence and power of God's future Kingdom already come in Jesus.

His purpose was to set people free from exile under the kingdom of *ha satan*, under the power of evil in all its forms, to regather the twelve tribes of Israel in a new Exodus into God's Kingdom. Also, there is no doubt that the gospel writers boldly attest, each in their own way, to Jesus' Spirit-empowered ministry of miracles, framing it as per their theological-gospel purpose.

QUESTIONS FOR REFLECTION AND DISCUSSION

1. Personalising Jesus' ministry and miracles, what does this chapter mean to you as his apprentice? What has God said to you?

2. Do you have a problem with supernatural miracles, or not? Why? Do you believe Jesus' healings, exorcisms, and miracles actually happened? Are they historically reliable accounts?

3. How would you summarise Mark's presentation of Jesus' ministry and miracles? What was new for you in this regard?

4. What is your view of Matthew's framing of Jesus' ministry and miracles? What stands out for you?

5. Luke-Acts is a biography and succession narrative. Do you agree with the framing of Jesus' ministry and miracles? If not, why?

6. Summarise John's view of Jesus' ministry and miracles. How can you be intimate with Jesus as he was with the Father, speaking his words, doing his works, seeing his wonders?

MYSTERY & PARABLES

Jesus' *mission and message* revealed his worldview, his underlying assumptions and beliefs, through stories, life questions, symbols, and praxis. Jesus' *ministry and miracles* represented his Kingdom praxis. He believed God was acting through him for Israel's deliverance from exile under oppressive (spiritual and political) powers. Jesus' *parables and teaching* are the story component that answered his worldview questions. This chapter, therefore, focuses on his storied teaching of *the nature of God's Kingdom* come in his person and ministry.

One of the pressing questions would have been the glaring disconnect that emerged between prevailing messianic expectations and Jesus' message and ministry of the Kingdom. "Kingdom of God" was code for a set of Jewish understandings and expectations (see p.91), derived from the Hebrew scriptures, Jewish apocalyptic literature, the current context, and popular persuasion. Despite Jesus' initial widespread acclaim through his authoritative teaching, healings and miracles, an elephant was in the room. How would Jesus establish God's Kingdom? Surely, by overthrowing the Romans?

The Kingdom that Jesus proclaimed and demonstrated did not exhibit the crucial signs Jews were looking for. There was little or no evidence that he prepared and organised his Kingdom movement to liberate the Holy Temple, Holy City, Holy People, and Holy Land. Jews expected the Messiah to bring political liberation, a national Kingdom. Jesus' Kingdom seemed to be a spiritual reality (John 18:36). Jews were looking for how and where the Kingdom would literally come, but Jesus said it was already "in your midst" (Luke 17:20-21).

Yet, both Jewish and Roman rulers considered Jesus a threat to the status quo. This was confirmed by the fact that he was betrayed by one of his own and was crucified as a blasphemer and false Jewish King. It confirmed the elephant in the room: what, exactly, was the nature of the Kingdom Jesus inaugurated? Because, clearly, it did not (seem to) deliver what was needed, what was expected. Where was it?

Jesus was aware of the question, the apparent contradiction. He called it "the mystery" (or secret) of the Kingdom of God, which he explained primarily through parables. This is attested to in all three synoptic gospels (Mark 4:11; Matthew 13:11; Luke 8:10). Jesus also taught the mysterious nature of the Kingdom, as he understood and enacted it, through direct statements. We need to examine both his indirect parables and direct teaching.

First, the gospel parables will be introduced ('parable research', as it is called) with Jesus' teaching method. Then "the mystery" of the Kingdom of God will be unpacked by discussing, a) some of the key parables and their meaning, and b) the direct statements of Jesus. We cannot examine all the parables for obvious reasons of space. See Snodgrass (2008) and Meier (2016) for a full scholarly examination. Some of the most prolific literature on Jesus is about his parables.

INTRODUCTION TO PARABLES

Meier (2016:2) sees the parables as one of four "enigmas" in Jesus Research. The other three are his relationship to Torah (next chapter), his self-designations (discussed earlier), and his death – what led to it and what it meant (a later chapter). The parables are an enigma due to the definition and number of parables, and which ones are authentic to the historical Jesus. Most scholars assume historical authenticity but disagree on their definition, number, and interpretation.

The fact that the Jesus of history was well-known as a storyteller is not in doubt. The issue is the historical parables of the historical Jesus; that is, which parables are authentic to Jesus? Which are from the early church? Or created by the gospel writers? How many parables are there? How do we define a parable? What did Jesus intend and mean by them? How do we interpret them? These, and more, are the kind of questions that historians ask, research, and debate.

I cannot here engage the technical debates that apply the historical criteria (in my introduction, p.28) to the parables, to decide which are from, or not from, the historical Jesus "with a good degree of probability", as Meier says (2016:48-57, his discussion in this regard). Thus, we don't claim absolute knowledge but work with the gospel parables as they are recorded and are intended to be understood.

Disagreement on the definition of 'parable' is due to the wide range of meaning of the Hebrew OT *masal* and Greek NT *parabole*. *Masal* is a short parable with a lesson/truth. *Parabole* means to "cast/throw down beside another", that is, to put ideas side by side to reveal wrong assumptions and make a point of truth. Rabbis would often illustrate a point by telling a parable. The common form is mini stories, but they can include similes, metaphors, comparisons, and allegories.

In the OT wisdom tradition parables can include proverbs, riddles, taunts, and aphorisms (wise sayings). Though these are not absent in Jesus' parables, the origin of his parables lies more in the prophetic tradition of mini stories. Such (prophetic) parables arise in the context of conflict, the rebuke of (national) leaders, and prophetic challenge in times of crisis. For example, Nathan confronted and rebuked King David via a narrative parable (2 Samuel 12:1-12. See also 2 Kings 20:39-42; Isaiah 5:1-7; Ezekiel 15:1-8, 24:1-14).

Intertestamental apocalyptic literature further expanded *masal* and *parabole*, using it for eschatological instruction, often through dreams/visions that needed angelic interpretation, as in 4 Ezra 4:13-21, 5:41-53, the "Parables" of 1 Enoch 37-71, and the book of Daniel.

This is the background to Jesus' parables. The noun *parabole* occurs only in the synoptic gospels, 48 times (17 x in Matthew, 13 x in Mark, 18 x in Luke). The only other two *parabole* occurrences in the NT, Hebrews 9:9 and 11:19, have the meaning of a 'sign' or 'type'. The gospel usages refer mostly to a *narrative parable*, sometimes with a similitude, aphorism, riddle, or analogy/allegory.

Depending on the criteria for defining a parable, scholars argue for between 34 and 46 parables in the gospels. The purpose of the (narrative) parable was to draw the listener in and provoke the mind by exposing incorrect assumptions. We can *define* Jesus' parables as,

> "A striking short story that employs figurative language... is meant to be puzzling enough to tease the mind into active thought and to personal decision. As a chosen rhetorical tool of such an eschatological prophet... many of Jesus' parables carry an eschatological tone, though the parable genre was flexible enough to serve more than one aspect of Jesus' mission and message" (Meier 2016:41).

This raises the question of interpretation. There are many differing views. We must ask what Jesus intended by the parables and what they meant to his hearers? Some parables lend themselves to analogous – even allegorical – interpretation, as in the Sower and the Seed, and the Wheat and the Tares (Matthew 13:3-9 cf. 18-23; 24-30 cf. 36-43). The interpretations given in these texts are debated as to whether they came from Jesus or were added by his followers. The overly allegorical method of interpretation was dominant from the 2nd to 8th centuries, resulting in many ingenious and fanciful views.

Most of the parables, however, begin with "the Kingdom of God is like...", indicating that they explain the eschatological nature, "the mystery", of God's Kingdom come in Jesus. This is the primary point being made or illustrated, the hermeneutical key that interprets the gospel parables.

In summary, we must not claim too much, but not too little, regarding Jesus' parables. We must not make them mean everything and thus nothing. Also, we must not press them all into one framework, either wisdom genre or prophetic-eschatological, though the latter is clearly Jesus' basic frame of reference for his parables.

JESUS' TEACHING METHODS

Besides Jesus' indirect method of parables, he taught (the nature of) the Kingdom through direct statements. This included asking questions, then giving answers. He used that method to teach his disciples, and to respond to Scribes and Pharisees, often asking a question when they confronted him with an issue of concern. Jesus' answers included straightforward explanations, similes, metaphors, memorable aphorisms, and pithy sayings. These are found in his teaching blocks, as in the Sermon on the Mount (Matthew 5 to 7) and the Sermon on the Plain (Luke 6). There we also find beatitudes ("Blessed be...") that Jesus spoke, drawn from Jewish wisdom and prophetic literature.

His direct teaching approach engaged *halakhic* debates of his day, i.e., the Torah interpretations regarding issues of life and purity under the Law – legal rulings – taught by Scribes and Pharisees. As with his parables, Jesus' relationship to Torah and its interpretation was determined by his understanding and fulfilment of the Kingdom – the Kingdom *halakha* or way of living that he modelled and taught.

Jesus' teaching method incorporated the rabbinic techniques in use from Hillel (1st century BC) to the Mishna and Talmud and beyond. There were four interpretative and teaching methods of scripture that rabbis practiced, summarised in the acronym *PaRDeS*, a Hebrew word meaning orchard or garden (commonly 'paradise'). It stands for four words representing four methods: *P'shat, Remez, Drash* and *Sod*.

P'shat, means simple, the text's plain sense or literal meaning the author wanted to convey. Jesus often used this teaching method without implying a deeper or secondary meaning, e.g., when he said he didn't come to "abolish the Law or the Prophets, but to fulfill them" (Matthew 5:17), he meant just that, nothing more, or less.

Remez, means a hint, a word or phrase that hints at a truth not conveyed by the plain sense *p'shat*. It was often a hint or allusion to, or a quote of, a portion of a text, to connote the truth intended by *the context*. Jesus' frequent use of this method revealed his remarkable memorisation and knowledge of the OT. For example, in his explanation of his prophetic enactment of God's judgement on the Temple (Matthew 21:13), Jesus cited a portion of Isaiah 56:7 ("a house of prayer for all nations") with a portion of Jeremiah 7:11 ("a den of robbers"). Isaiah's context spoke of the Temple being for Gentiles and not only for Jews. Jeremiah's context spoke of the religious leaders who believed their vested interests in the Temple would save them from judgement and the Temple from destruction. It did not! AD 70 was a repeat.

Drash (or *midrash*), means to search – search out meaning. Flusser (1987:61) defines it as "creative exegesis and understanding of the text of the Bible and its stories, an attempt to discover all the various senses implicit in the biblical verse." While some OT texts would be *p'shat,* others yield to multiple interpretations. The various possible meanings were debated by invoking authoritative rabbinic interpretations. A different authority marked Jesus' teaching. He did not quote or refer to other rabbis but spoke as if directly from God, commonly and uniquely saying, "Truly I tell you…" (Matthew 5:18f). *Midrashim,* the textual interpretations, took the form of, a) exegetical expositions and commentaries of OT texts/books, b) homiletical *midrash* in preaching/teaching and c) through parables. So, Jesus' interpretations of the six commandments in Matthew 5:21-48 would have been heard as *his midrash*. He both differed and agreed with other teachers in his *midrash* of various texts, and their application in life.

Sod, means secret. Teachers would find certain mystical, or secret, or hidden meaning in words and texts through the numerical value of the Hebrew letters, including unusual spelling or unusual words. It could lead to fanciful interpretations and esoteric teachings. There is no evidence that Jesus used this method, though he did speak of "the mystery" of God's Kingdom. In Revelation, John used a (legitimate) form of *sod*, working with numbers and letters to communicate hidden meaning. Keener (2014:757-8) shows how informed Jewish readers would have known that 666, "the number of the beast" (Revelation 13:18), was code for the Roman Emperor Nero (AD 58-68), a most violent persecutor of Christians.

THE MYSTERY OF THE KINGDOM OF GOD

Back to the elephant in the room. What, exactly, was the nature of God's Kingdom that Jesus proclaimed and enacted? Why was he not liberating Israel from her Roman enemies? Where was his Kingdom? Why, and how, must one be "born again" (from above) to "see", let alone "enter", the Kingdom of God (John 3:3-7)?

Jesus had a much more nuanced understanding of the Kingdom from the Hebrews scriptures and the times, as per his mission and message, than the Jewish expectation of his day. In his view, the establishment did not know "what would bring you peace (*shalom*)... it is hidden from your eyes... because you did not recognize the time of God's coming to you" (Luke 19:42-44). Jesus knew and predicted they would reject and kill him, bringing God's judgement on Israel – the AD 70 destruction. But all who put their faith in him entered, in a real experiential way, into the Kingdom he inaugurated.

Jesus called the true nature of God's Kingdom a "mystery". His disciples asked him, "Why do you speak to the people in parables?" He replied, "Because the knowledge of the secrets (*mysterion*) of the kingdom of heaven has been given to you, but not to them" (Matthew 13:10-11). What did Jesus mean?

First, mystery means the unknown, that which baffles the mind. In Greek, *mysterion* referred to secret knowledge of the gods and the initiation rites of eastern (Gnostic) mystery religions in the Greco-Roman world. Jesus used the Hebraic idea of "mystery": that which was hidden in God in times past – his mysterious wisdom, secret plan – made known to prophets (Amos 3:7) and revealed in the messianic age. Jews saw one coming of Messiah and his Kingdom. Jesus saw it as a two-part event that came and was unfolding in/through him. On closer inspection, his view was even more nuanced than that. This was God's secret plan, hidden in the OT scriptures, now revealed in Jesus' (prophetic) mission, message, and ministry of God's Kingdom.

Second, we will examine what the parables teach in explanation of this mysterious nature of the Kingdom. We will also cite Jesus' direct teaching statements that reveal the nature of the Kingdom.

Third, though rabbis often made their point through illustrative parables, they believed only their closest disciples could handle their more secretive teachings, reserved for private instruction. Similarly, Jesus gave "the knowledge of the secrets of the Kingdom of Heaven" (Matthew 13:11) *to his disciples.* He taught the crowds through parables to draw their mind into his Kingdom story, so that those who believed would see his intended meaning ("the mystery"), correcting their assumptions. But those who did not believe would simply hear them as stories. That, paradoxically, confirmed believing hearts in the revelation of the truth being communicated, and, at the same time, it confirmed unbelieving hearts in their fixed assumptions and their blindness to the truth.

In explaining, "This is why I speak to them in parables..." (Matthew 13:13-15), Jesus quoted Deuteronomy 29:4 and Isaiah 6:9-10. He saw the Jews in his day like, a) Israel in the wilderness who saw God's mighty acts but still did not believe ("though seeing, they did not see, though hearing, they did not hear"); and b) like the people in Isaiah's day who would see and hear, but due to "the hardness of their hearts" would not see the truth and repent and be healed. Isaiah's message would confirm them in their unbelief.

That is why Jesus often ended his parables with, "Whoever has ears to hear, let them hear" (Mark 4:9). And that's why he said to his *believing* disciples, "*But* blessed are your eyes because they see, and your ears because they hear... the knowledge of the secrets of the kingdom of heaven has been given to you" (Matthew 13:16 cf. 11).

The Mystery in the Parables – Present and Future

For Jesus, God's Kingdom was *the action* of his "rule and reign" (*Kingship*) defeating evil to set people free. The parables explain the nature of the coming and work of God's Rule and Reign.

The first parable Jesus taught, recorded in all three synoptic gospels, is The Sower and The Seed (Mark 4:3-9, 13-20; Matthew 13:3-9, 18-23; Luke 8:5-8, 11-15). It illustrates the above discussion, borne out in Jesus' explanation of the parable. Contrary to the dominant Jewish assumption, Jesus taught that God's Kingdom entered this age through messengers, not militant fighters. Jesus and his followers proclaimed the Kingdom, sowing "the seed" as it were, with different responses that revealed peoples' hearts. For some hearers, the (word of the) Kingdom makes no impression, confirming their unbelief. Others receive it joyfully, but it does not take root because when difficulties and opposition come, the person falls away from the Kingdom's influence. For others, life's worries and materialism's deceitfulness quickly choke out whatever impression the Kingdom makes on them. But for those who hear and receive the word of the Kingdom with true faith, it takes root and produces fruit.

The point is: the Kingdom has come as good news and is active in this age, with mixed responses. It calls to all, but those prepared to respond to the Kingdom with hearts full of faith benefit from it.

Matthew's next parable (13:24-30) is The Wheat and The Weeds. Jesus also interpreted it for his disciples (13:36-43). The Kingdom comes into this age in Jesus and his messengers, producing good seed: believers, citizens of the Kingdom. Contrary to the Jewish expectation, it does not end this age, but operates in tension 'alongside' this present evil age. Unbelievers, citizens of Satan's kingdom, are not 'taken out' but continue to do the will of evil on earth as in hell, side-by-side with believers who do the will of God on earth as in heaven. They will be separated in the final judgement at the end, when the Son of Man comes with his angels to consummate the Kingdom.

The point is: God's Kingdom *has* come and *will* come (again), with salvation for all who believe and judgement for all who do not believe. The mystery is that it's present and active without ending this age. The future consummation of the Kingdom will end this evil age, separating the wicked from the righteous, who will shine forever in the Kingdom.

It calls for faith-full-ness, integrity, and perseverance in the tension of co-existence, in God's intervening 'alongside' Kingdom.

Similarly, the parable of The Net and The Fish (Matthew 13:47-50). The Kingdom of God comes like a net that catches all kinds of people, only to be 'sorted out' at the end. The Kingdom has come without putting an end to this age, thus good and bad exist side-by-side till the final judgement at the consummation of the Kingdom.

The parables of The Mustard Seed and The Yeast (Matthew 13:31-33; Mark 4:30-32; Luke 13:18-21) – also The Growing Seed (Mark 4:26-27) – corrected the assumption that the Kingdom will come with a revolutionary 'big bang' through human effort. These parables illustrate that, though the Kingdom's coming and presence in Jesus seems insignificant, it has a power in and of itself for irresistible growth. Its small beginnings relentlessly advance to affect the whole world, giving shelter and belonging for Jews *and* Gentiles.

The Hidden Treasure and Costly Pearl (Matthew 13:44-46) speak of the hidden but inestimably valuable nature of the Kingdom in its presence and work in the world. Once discovered, one willingly sacrifices everything to enter and possess the Kingdom in its fullness. It calls for seeking and sacrifice to gain the Kingdom.

In summary, these and other parables teach that the Kingdom *has come* in this age, in principle and power, and *will come* in fullness and finality at the end of the age – a revealed mystery for Jews.

A Further Mystery in the Parables – Imminent and Delayed

There are other parables that illustrate the imminent coming of the Kingdom. *Imminent* means the Kingdom is impending, about to happen. It can break through at any time, which calls for readiness, alertness, and expectation. Note that this is different to *immanent,* meaning that which is inherent in something, as in the statement that Kingdom theology is immanent (inherent) in Jesus.

Jesus told parables of the (revealed) mystery that the Kingdom of God is imminent, close, about to come. This is found in the series of parables in Matthew 24:36-51, The Days of Noah, The Two Men and Two Women, The Thief in The Night, The Faithful and Wise Servant. They illustrate that Jesus believed the Kingdom can manifest at any moment. It can come without notice and surprise us, breaking into our lives when we least expect it. Therefore, we must "keep watch... (and) must be ready" (24:42,44).

Jesus exposed the false assumption that Israel knew and would recognise the signs of the Kingdom's coming and that they would be prepared and ready. They did not interpret "the signs of the times" (Matthew 16:3). He rebuked the idea that people can live as they want, presuming on God. Those who do not expect the Kingdom's imminence, its impending breakthrough, live their daily lives in self-indulgence. Thus, "you did not recognize the time of God's coming to you" (Luke 19:44). As in the generation in Noah's time, they would be swept away in judgement (Matthew 24:39).

Jesus admittedly tells these and other parables in the context of the consummation of the Kingdom when he, the Son of Man, will return on the clouds of glory (24:30,36, "that day or hour no one knows, not even the angels in heaven, nor the Son, but only the Father"). However, as we see below, Jesus also taught through direct statements (*p'shat*) that the Kingdom was imminent. *The point* of these parables is, a) the Kingdom can indeed manifest at any moment, and b) we must be expectant and ready for such breakthrough, and c) this expectation will fundamentally affect how we live our daily lives.

Then there is a development of thought: though the Kingdom is imminent, it is also delayed. The Bridegroom and Ten Virgins, and The Master and The Servants with Talents are parables that teach the delay of the Kingdom's coming in Matthew 25:1-30.

They illustrate a further mystery of the Kingdom, that it is, or can be, delayed: "The bridegroom was a long time in coming..." (5), and "After a long time the master of those servants returned..." (19). Bridegrooms were known to delay their coming, often arriving late to meet the bridesmaids who escorted him to the bride for the wedding feast. Similarly, masters were known to delay their return, for various reasons, after being away on a long trip.

These parables begin with, "At that time the kingdom of heaven *will be like... it will be like...*" (1,14). Again, in the context of his return, the Kingdom's consummation, Jesus revealed the 'delayed nature' (as it were) of God's Rule and Reign. Without discussing the details of these two parables, *the essential point is* that the Kingdom of God is/has been *delayed* – part and parcel of the mystery of it being *present, imminent*, and *future* simultaneously.

The implication is that the delay of the Kingdom calls for, a) vigilance and readiness ("keep watch", 13), b) waiting and patience, keeping busy with what the King has entrusted to us (16-17), and c) for faithful perseverance as we wait for Kingdom breakthrough, for the coming of the King. While waiting, the five wise virgins kept oil with their lamps, and thus "were ready and went in with him to the wedding banquet" (10). While the King delayed his coming, the two faithful servants used their talents – the money entrusted to them. Thus, they were ready to enter, celebrate, and rule when the Kingdom came: "Well done, good and faithful servant! You have been faithful with a few things; I will put you in charge of many things. Come and share your master's happiness!" (21,23).

The Mystery in Jesus' Direct Teaching

Jesus operated in the underlying Jewish worldview of "this present age" and "the age to come" (Mark 10:30). He saw God's covenant with Israel – in fact, all Hebrew scripture – in terms of promise (this age) and fulfilment (the coming age). That was common to Second Temple Judaism. All God did with Israel and the nations was in keeping with his promise(s), which would ultimately be fulfilled on the Day of *Yhwh* – the coming of his Messiah and his Kingdom.

Jesus, however, saw himself as that Messiah, The One promised in the scriptures. He believed he was fulfilling the OT promise: "I have come to fulfill the Law and the Prophets" (Matthew 5:17). But "the knowledge of the mystery of the Kingdom" was more than *promise* in the OT and *fulfilment* in him, in the NT. It was also *consummation* at the end of the age. This two-stage coming of the King and Kingdom was new in Judaism. More so that God's Kingship ("Heaven", "the age to come") entered this present evil age *without bringing it to an end*.

Theologians describe this phenomenon as the overlap of two ages – a new cosmic-spiritual reality in history – the "already" *and* "not yet" of God's Kingdom. Dunn (2003:405) argues that this eschatological reality is *the* "one central feature" in understanding the Kingdom, "the trigger" and key idea (the 'already and not yet') in the re-emergence of Kingdom theology in recent decades.

However, Jesus was even more nuanced. He taught that,

1. The Kingdom had come, was *present,* i.e., is active here and now.

Jesus said, "If I drive out demons by the finger of God, the kingdom of God *has come* upon you" (Luke 11:20). "The coming of the kingdom of God is not something that can be observed, nor will people say, 'Here it is,' or 'There it is,' because the kingdom of God *is in your midst*" (Luke 17:20-21, "among you" NRSV)). Jesus said the Kingdom *"has been* forcefully advancing" (Matthew 11:12, NIV margin note), i.e., we receive, experience, and enter the (present) Kingdom by assertively believing and following Messiah Jesus.

2. The Kingdom was about to come, is *imminent*, i.e., can manifest any moment. Jesus preached, "The time has come, the kingdom of God *has come near*" (Mark 1:15). Or *"is at hand"* (ESV), i.e., it is close, within reach. As Jesus approached Jerusalem, people "supposed that the kingdom of God was to appear immediately" (Luke 19:11). It is impending, about to happen. This meant faith and expectation of Kingdom breakthrough at any time.

3. The Kingdom is yet to come, is *delayed*, i.e., will come later. We have noted parables that taught the Kingdom's delay, in the context of Kingdom expectation and Jesus' return (second coming). This means "occupying" the time in working faithfully with what is entrusted to us, while waiting patiently in constant readiness for the breakthrough of the Kingdom, for the coming of the King.

4. The Kingdom will come, is *future*, i.e., will be consummated at the end of this age. The sure hope of believers. "At that time people will see the Son of Man coming in clouds with great power and glory" (Mark 13:36). That will be "at the renewal of all things, when the Son of Man is seated on the throne of his glory, and you (the twelve apostles) will also sit on twelve thrones, judging the twelve tribes of Israel" (Matthew 19:28). Jesus said at his last Passover meal, "I will not drink again from the fruit of the vine until that day when I drink it new in the kingdom of God" (Mark 14:25). "That day" refers to when the end will come, and Jesus will return.

When will it come? When the "gospel of the kingdom" has been "preached as a witness to all nations, *then the end will come*" (Matthew 24:14). Therefore, Jesus' great commission: "Go and make disciples of all nations... and I am with you always, *to the very end of the age*" (Matthew 28:19-20).

The Mystery, Hebraic Thinking, and Kingdom Worldview

In short, God's Kingdom is present, imminent, delayed, and future. All are true at the same time. But how can this be? To the western mind this makes no sense because the four statements/polarities logically contradict and cancel each other. That is either/or thinking. Either the Kingdom has *already* come (called realised eschatology) or it has *not yet* come (future eschatology). You cannot have both – let alone claim it is also *near* and *delayed*!

To the Hebraic mind, it is holding opposites in creative tension. It is both/and, or bi-polar thinking. Technically, Meier calls it "Semitic dialectical negation" (1994:142/3): putting two opposing (dialectical) ideas side by side, neither of which is to be taken absolutely, but in tandem with each other. If taken in isolation, the ideas/statements negate each other. But held in tension, they reveal one truth.

For example, "among those born of women there has not risen anyone greater than John the Baptist, yet whoever is least in the kingdom of heaven is greater than he" (Matthew 11:11). These two *apparent* contradictory statements/polarities (no one is greater than John, yet some are greater than John) represent two sides of one truth: John was the forerunner of the Kingdom that *has come* in Jesus.

Another example: "No one accepts his (Jesus') testimony. Whoever has accepted it has certified that God is truthful" (John 3:32-33). No one accepts it, yet people accept it – two opposing sides of the truth of acceptance. See also John 1:11-12, 8:15-16, 12:37,42.

The four *realities* of the Kingdom that Jesus taught are all true simultaneously. Together they explain and embody The Truth of the Kingdom. The presence ("already") *and* future ("not yet") of the Kingdom are *radical* polarities, and the nearness and delay are *moderate* polarities (Morphew 2019:114-125). Taking each strand *seriously*, held in creative tension, we see the Kingdom's full glory and power in Jesus. We see his prophetic view of history, God's mysterious plan revealed, represented in the diagram below.

Morphew (2019:122) summarises its significance like this:

> "This event that took place in Jesus Christ burst the confines of ordinary human thinking and expectations. No Old Testament prophet could have conceived of something like this happening. It completely transcended the expectations of Jesus' generation.

Biblical scholars and theologians have written numbers of books to explain what happened, but even those explanations that do full justice to every strand of the New Testament witness only provide a human model to explain the inexplicable."

We can summarise Jesus' Kingdom teaching and praxis with this statement: *God's Kingdom breaks through from the future into the present in successive interventions until God's will is done on earth as in heaven.* Though it occasions real spiritual warfare, it is revolutionary and world-changing! Figure 3 represents Jesus' Kingdom worldview (or framework) in which he lived, taught, and ministered, in which we also live.

Figure 3. Jesus' Kingdom Worldview

```
                 Kingdom of God      Future age
         ←─ ─ ─ ─ ─ ─ ─ ─ ─ ─ ─ ─ ─ ─ ─ ─ ─ ─→
             │  │  │  │           C
             │  │  │  │           o
             │  │  │  │           n
             ▼  ▼  ▼  ▼           s
                                  u
        OT           NT           m
      Promise    Fulfillment      m
             ▼                    a
           JESUS                  t
                                  i
                                  o
                                  n
   ──────────────────────────────────→
   "The present evil age" (Galatians 1:4)  THE END
```

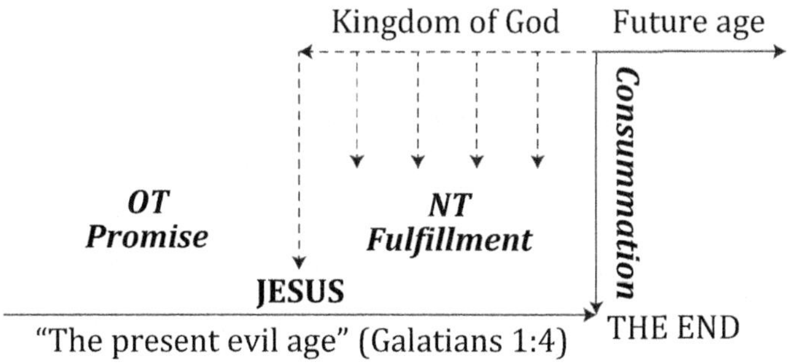

In Conclusion: Kingdom People and Kingdom Living

We have already crossed from historical study to biblical and practical theology. However, some concluding comments are needed.

The people of the Kingdom, all who believe in Jesus, are likewise a "mysterious" community: God's present, imminent, delayed, and future people. We experience the Kingdom in Jesus, by his Word (truth) and Spirit (indwelling presence), as present and active, yet near and about to break through. We also experience it as delayed, and yet to come at the end of this evil age, i.e., our certain hope of future consummation.

This is Christian living "between the times", between Jesus' first and second coming ("the last days", Acts 2:17; Hebrews 1:2). Scholars describe it as the "eschatological tension" of the "already" and "not yet". My book, *Doing Spirituality* (2019), explains what it means *to live eternally now in the tension* of two ages that overlap and coexist, which God uses to spiritually (trans)form us into Christlikeness.

Human nature, however, avoids tension. We cannot live with mystery. We want resolution; we see logical answers. Thus, we tend to either/or. Either Kingdom now or Kingdom not yet. However, the more we move to the "already" polarity, *without acknowledging or facing – and even denying – the "not yet"*, the more triumphalist, presumptuous, and arrogant we become in our theology and praxis. And the more we move to the "not yet" polarity, *without acknowledging and pursuing the "already"* – not seeking first the Kingdom (Matthew 6:33) – the more defeatist, hopeless, and fatalist we become in our theology and praxis.

The biblical idea embraces the opposing realities simultaneously without the need to reconcile or harmonise them logically. We cannot avoid the reality of eschatological tension; it confronts and adjusts us when we are wrong. The spiritual warfare that it occasions is a daily reality. Some deny or transcend it, with its warfare, by imposing the already – in forms of Kingdom now, triumphalist perfectionism – on their reality, in the name of "the finished work of the cross". Others try to nullify or escape the tension by accommodating and "making peace" with the not-yet, succumbing to its warfare, in the name of "whatever will be will be" till Jesus returns.

Some propose "the radical middle". It will fail if that means living *between* the polarities, integrating "the good" of both in a middle way, thereby trying to neutralise the tension. It will result in passive acceptance of the status quo, especially in times of difficulty, and when people are not healed. The phrase, "it's because of the already and the not yet," certainly explains some realities, but can be an easy excuse to rationalise our resignation to "little faith" (Matthew 6:30, 8:26).

Correctly understood, the mystery of the Kingdom is living in ongoing tension, which, in practice, is living in healthy ambivalence or indifference to the status quo. We neither deny nor accept it. We are *in* the world but not *of* the world (John 17:14-16). Our posture, therefore, is to push into the Kingdom assertively (Matthew 11:12), trusting God for his breakthrough, without trying to make something happen. We do not auto-suggest or engineer a spiritual experience, hype, or manipulate people into faith.

We do this while, at the same time, being honest about what happens or does not happen, exercising grace in waiting and patience in suffering. We endure in faith, letting God be God, without playing God. This realism of the "not yet" reality results in compassionate pastoring *and* persevering faith, *with* prophetic hope.

In short, the "already" of the Kingdom is not presumptive action but assertive faith in expectation of Kingdom breakthrough. And the "not yet" is not passive acceptance but patient perseverance in realistic hope of Kingdom come.

Consequently, Kingdom life is living in all polarities at the same time. We live on the expectant edge of the "already" *and* on the patient edge of the "not yet", with persistent faithfulness in hope of Kingdom come – now, sooner, later, delayed, or at the end.

The reality is that either way, or every way, we win!

QUESTIONS FOR REFLECTION AND DISCUSSION

1. In your personal view, what has been different, new, or difficult to understand and accept in this chapter?

2. Why did Jesus teach the crowds through parables?

3. How do you define a biblical parable – its character and purpose?

4. In your own words, what is "the mystery of the Kingdom of God" that Jesus taught? What can you agree with, or disagree with, as presented in this chapter?

5. To what degree has Jesus' Kingdom worldview, represented in the diagram, become your paradigm for living? How do you handle the "eschatological tension" of the Kingdom?

6. What is your 'heart condition' in receiving and working with God's Kingdom? What must you do to cultivate your heart to maximise the Kingdom's presence, power, and fruit?

LAW & LOVE

As mentioned in the previous chapter, we need a closer examination of Jesus' relationship to Torah. We now portray *Yeshua ha Notzri*, the 30-year-old rabbi, as teacher and interpreter of Torah. Jesus was, in fact, not only a rabbinical teacher, but a Sage filled with God's wisdom, and a Prophet filled with God's power, despite his young age.

THE HISTORICAL JESUS AND THE HISTORICAL TORAH

Torah was God's covenant and commandments to Israel, the Mosaic Law that legislated and determined every aspect of Jewish life. Broadly, it referred to God's inspired word/instruction to Israel and the nations, called "the Law and the Prophets" (Matthew 5:17). That, in turn, was used to cover the Hebrew scriptures, the *TaNaKh* – an acronym derived from the names of the three sections of the Hebrew Bible: *Torah* (Law or Instruction, also called the Pentateuch), *Nevi'im* (Prophets), and *Ketuvim* (Writings or Wisdom Literature). Jesus frequently quoted texts from all three categories of the 'Old Testament', as Christians call it. Jews revered every word as God-given and eternal. Every "jot or tittle" – the smallest letter and least stroke of the pen – was believed to be inspired by God's Spirit; it can never change or fall away (Matthew 5:18).

Most broadly, Torah was/is God's revealed will for humanity: how to live life as God intended, under his Kingship, doing his will on earth for human completion, societal flourishing, and cosmic shalom.

We will examine Jesus' relationship to and interpretation of Torah, *especially regarding The Law*, in light of some of the burning issues of his day – the *halakhic* debates on how Jews ought to live God's will in the context of Second Temple Judaism. These ways of holy living were summarised in, "Be holy because I, the LORD your God, am holy" (Leviticus 19:2). This command was the centre and summary of Israel's Holiness Code in Leviticus 17 to 26.

The Pharisees and Scribes, with whom Jesus clashed, went beyond Torah *observance*. Many Jews saw them as the 'holiness police' who insisted on legalistic *obedience* to all Moses' commands, including adherence to purity and ceremonial laws that distinguished Jews from Gentiles. They said, if Israel obeyed Torah, Messiah would come. This was later articulated in the Mishna and Talmud: if all Israel repented for one day, or obeyed God's commandments on the same day, or properly kept a single Sabbath, "forthwith the son of David will come" (see Neusner 2002:172-3).

John the Baptist and Jesus also preached repentance, *not* to get Messiah to come, but rather because Messiah *had* arrived and was inaugurating his Kingdom. Repentance and faith were needed to enter his Kingdom, entering God's new covenant. That *enabled* the required obedience from a heart made new and indwelt by the eschatological Holy Spirit through Messiah (Mark 1:8).

The Enigma of Jesus' Relationship to Torah

Like the gospel parables, scholars are divided on Jesus and Torah. Do all the *halakhic* (legal) disputes in the gospels, and Jesus' *midrashim* (interpretative answers), come from the historical Jesus? Did he oppose, rescind, or change the Law of Moses? Or any part of it? Any "jot or tittle" of Torah? Jesus' relationship to Torah is far from clear. Meier calls it an "enigma" and briefly summarises the range of divergent views and positions of biblical scholars (2009:1-5), from...

- Jesus being plain anti-*halakhic* and anti-Torah,
- To him rejecting Torah and its purity requirements,
- To being secretly a libertine teaching freedom from the Law,
- To being sovereign over the Law and thus abolishing it as a system of legalistic salvation,
- To subverting it by fulfilling it,
- To transcending it by distilling its essence,
- To upholding Torah, faithfully teaching it within the acceptable range of opinions held by 1st century Jews, with some exceptions (e.g., food laws, discussed below, Mark 7:15-19).

In short, Jesus' relationship with Torah was paradoxical, having both *continuity* (consistent with many aspects, and agreement with other Torah teachers) and *discontinuity* (changes in some aspects, with different interpretation to other teachers). The enigma we must unravel is how Jesus could at the same time affirm the Law as "the normative expression of God's will for Israel, and yet in a few individual cases or legal areas (e.g., divorce and oaths) teach and enjoin what is contrary to the Law, simply on his own authority" (Meier 2009:3, Meier's brackets).

Jesus' nuanced approach was due to his understanding and praxis of God's end-time Kingdom, the *'hermeneutical lens'* through which he interpreted Torah. His teaching – claiming God's direct authority – was his messianic *halakha* or way of holy living under God's Kingship, to do God's will on earth as in heaven (Matthew 6:11). Hence, Jesus' approach to Torah was controversial. It subverted the status quo, to the point of him being accused of undermining, even rejecting Torah, by placing himself above it, which was blasphemous.

We look at Matthew's presentation of *Yeshua ha Notzri* as the new Moses, the Messianic teacher of Torah and Teacher of the Messianic Torah. I first give an *overview* of how Jesus interpreted "the Law and the Prophets" (Matthew 5:17) as fulfilled in him, with application to some issues in his day. Then I examine his *essential* interpretation of The Law and the Prophets as the *love* that fulfils God's commands (Matthew 22:34-40). This is Jesus' hermeneutics of love, his love ethic – the essence of living Kingdom life.

THE NEW MOSES TEACHING THE MESSIANIC TORAH

I won't repeat what I explained earlier regarding Matthew presenting Jesus as the new Moses leading a new Exodus into the promised Kingdom of Heaven. Sufficient to say that his gospel structure of five teaching blocks connoted the five books of Moses (pp.143-4). The first block of Matthew 5 to 7, the Sermon on the Mount, is 'the beginning' (Genesis) of Jesus' Messianic Torah on life in the Kingdom, which he proclaimed and inaugurated. Here I examine Matthew 5 to help us understand Jesus' relationship to and interpretation of Torah.

Jesus "went up on a mountainside and sat down. His disciples came to him, and he began to teach them" (5:1-2). Matthew's Jewish readers would have noticed his intended allusion to Moses. Moses, who went up the mountain to receive the Torah, then sat down and taught Israel covenantal life in *Yhwh's* rule and reign. Jesus taught the Messianic Torah that Moses predicted in Deuteronomy 18:18-19, in fulfilment of the new covenant in the Messianic Kingdom that Moses, Jeremiah, and Ezekiel anticipated (discussed below).

Jesus' Beatitudes and Witness to the World (Matthew 5:3-16)

Drawing on Jewish wisdom literature, Jesus began by pronouncing "blessed be's" (5:3-11), indicating the social reversal that the Kingdom brought in Second Temple Judaism. The *anawim* – the spiritually bankrupt, oppressed poor, humble, mournful, even cursed – are blessed due to the Kingdom encountering them. Those considered blessed with the good life of material security, position and power, were generally not entering the Kingdom.

Jesus' "blessed be's" also echo the blessings Moses pronounced on Israel if she obeyed Torah (Deuteronomy 28:1f). Jesus' "woe be's" in Matthew's last teaching block (23:13-29) echo the curses Moses pronounced on Israel if she disobeyed and rejected God's "covenant of love" (Deuteronomy 28:15f cf. 7:9,12).

However, Jesus' "blessed be's" differed; they did not depend on obedience. They were not *prescriptive qualifications* or character requirements for Kingdom living. Rather, they were *descriptive conditions* of the kinds of people who enter and live in the Kingdom that Jesus was inaugurating, i.e., his disciples who came to be taught.

To enter and live in the Kingdom, one does not have to be poor in spirit, or mournful, or meek, or hungry for justice, or merciful, or pure in heart, or a peacemaker, or persecuted. The blessing is not in the condition but in the Kingdom. It is the Kingdom come in Jesus that meets and transforms us in our 'condition', making us "blessed" (*makarios*, "happy, to be envied").

It is those "blessed be's" that are witnesses to life in the Kingdom, as "the salt of the earth" and "the light of the world" (5:13-16). By applying these two images – references from Torah and the prophets – to those blessed in his Kingdom, Jesus reinterpreted Israel's calling and mission in him and his followers.

Salt was a sign of covenant integrity as God's flavouring agent and preservative in society: "the salt of the covenant" and "the covenant of salt" in Leviticus 2:13; Numbers 18:19; 2 Chronicles 13:5; Ezekiel 43:24. Jesus asked, if the salt (covenant Israel) loses its saltiness (integrity of covenant life that made them and the world palatable to God and preserved it from sinful decay), "how can it be made salty again? It is no longer good for anything, except to be thrown out and trampled underfoot" (Matthew 5:13). The last phrase referred to God's judgements, quoting Isaiah 5:5, 28:3, 63:3. *Therefore, the "blessed be's" are the salt of the new covenant as a witness to life in God's Kingdom come in Jesus.* They flavour society with "the righteousness" of the Kingdom (Matthew 6:33), making society acceptable to God by preserving it from corruption.

The light referred to Israel's mission: "I will make you to be a covenant for the people, a light for the Gentiles... that my salvation may reach to the ends of the earth" (Isaiah 42:6, 49:6). Jesus saw Israel's failed mission ("we have *not* brought salvation to the earth", Isaiah 26:18) fulfilled in his disciples: "You are the light of the world" (Matthew 5:14). Thus, they must not hide their light – the Kingdom life of the new covenant, God's light to the nations – under a basket, as Israel did. "Let your light shine before others, that they may see your good deeds and glorify your Father in heaven" (Matthew 5:16).

Jesus' followers, the "blessed be's", fulfil Israel's covenant integrity and missional destiny because the Kingdom has come.

Kingdom Fulfilment and the Surpassing Righteousness (Matthew 5:17-20)

Then Jesus said, "Do not think that I have come to abolish the Law or the Prophets; I have not come to abolish them *but to fulfil them*" (Matthew 5:17, my italics). Clearly, he did not come to reject or replace the Hebrew Bible. He honoured and upheld Torah and the Prophets, saying, "not the smallest letter, not the least stroke of a pen, will by any means disappear from the Law *until everything is accomplished*" (18, my italics). His principle of interpretation was the fulfilment and accomplishment of scripture in the coming of his Kingdom.

He added that "whoever practices and teaches these commands will be called great in the Kingdom of Heaven. For I tell you that unless your righteousness surpasses that of the Pharisees and the teachers of the law, you will certainly not enter the Kingdom of Heaven" (20). The righteousness of the Pharisees and Scribes was Torah obedience, which meant (outward) conformity to the letter of the Law to enter God's Kingdom. *Their* righteousness was seen by legalistic adherence to the Law and the Prophets, as in *their* interpretation and application.

The "surpassing righteousness" that Jesus taught was the (inner) transformation of *the heart* that fulfils the spirit of the Law – seen in his six contrasts that follow (5:21-48, below). The righteousness Jesus taught *assumed the promised new covenant* in the coming of the Kingdom. Let me elaborate on this important assumption.

Jeremiah (31:31-33) said *Yhwh* would make a new covenant with his people in a new Exodus out of exile, "*not* like the covenant I made with their ancestors". That "covenant of love" (Deuteronomy 7:12; 1 Kings 8:23) was written on stone tablets, accepting or accusing Israel, depending on obedience or disobedience. It failed, not because it was faulty, but "because *they* broke my covenant, though I was *a husband* to them" (Jeremiah 31:32 cf. Hosea 2:19-20). The fault was with Israel (Hebrews 8:7-8), with their unfaithful and hard *hearts*. When the *Messiah-Bridegroom* comes (John 1:29-30), God will put his Law in their minds and write it on their *hearts*, enabling them to obey Torah. This was God's intention (Deuteronomy 6:6f cf. 30:11-14). "The righteous" were those who had God's Law in their hearts (Psalm 37:31, 40:8, 119:11). David prayed for a new heart (Psalm 51:10).

The heart was the core/centre of human personhood, equivalent to the spirit/mind/will, from which all of life flows (Proverbs 4:23f). Ezekiel 36:24-27 gives a further angle. *Yhwh* says,

> "I will sprinkle clean water on you, and you will be clean; I will give you a new heart and put a new spirit in you; I will remove from you your heart of stone and give you a heart of flesh. And *I will put my Spirit in you and move you to follow my decrees and be careful to keep my laws*" (my italics).

Messiah Jesus is the Spirit-bringer, baptizing all who repent and believe with/in the promised eschatological Spirit (Mark 1:8,15). The new heart and spirit of the new covenant, cleansed and regenerated by God's life-giving Spirit, motivates and enables us from within to do God's will on earth as in heaven. Based on this Ezekiel text, Jesus told Nicodemus he had to be "born again" (from above) by "water and

Spirit" to see and enter God's Kingdom (John 3:3-5).

It answers what *Yhwh* said to Moses, "Oh, that their *hearts* would be inclined to fear me and keep *all* my commands *always*, so that it might go well with them and their children forever!" (Deuteronomy 5:29, my italics). God's commands are for human flourishing, but it assumes hearts that are inclined to do his will. Moses foresaw Israel's disobedience and consequent exile, *and* her restoration in a new exodus (Deuteronomy 30:1-5). Then, when God restores Israel, "The LORD will circumcise your hearts... so that you may love him with all your heart and with all your soul... you will obey the LORD and follow all his commands" (30:6-8 cf. 10:16).

The circumcision of the heart is the conversion of the new covenant to love God and obey his commands – the enabled fulfilment of 'the Shema' – to love God with all your heart and obey his commandments (Deuteronomy 6:4-6). This is precisely what Jesus assumed when he said, "teaching them to obey everything I have commanded you" (Matthew 28:20 cf. Deuteronomy 30:2; 1 Kings 8:36,58,61).

Six Contrasts of Kingdom Righteousness (Matthew 5:21-48)

Jesus then taught and illustrated the surpassing righteousness of the "blessed be's" who enter and live in the Kingdom by the new covenant. His choice of six Mosaic laws was probably related to issues in his day. His interpretation went beyond the rabbinical practice of 'building a fence' around the Law to protect its intention from being violated. He went to the heart, interpreting the commands by their fulfilment in his Kingdom, in his new covenant *halakha* (way of holy living).

Jesus claimed unprecedented divine authority by repeating, "but *I* tell you", "truly *I* tell you". This recalled Deuteronomy 18:18-19, "I will raise up for them a prophet like you (Moses)... I will put my words in his mouth. He will tell them everything I command. I myself will call to account anyone who does not listen to my words that the prophet speaks in my name." Jesus did not refer to respected rabbis as authorities to validate his teachings. He spoke as if directly from God in his interpretation of Torah and the Prophets.

1. *Murder and anger* (5:21-26). Jesus taught that "You shall not murder" is not about outward acts of violence, but inner anger, seen in contempt and name-calling. Unresolved anger, in Jesus'

mind, is tantamount to murder. It violates the dignity of 'the other' made in God's image and imprisons one in unforgiveness and resentment, extracting a considerable payment. Jesus' society was angry. Ours is filled with rage and violence. So, the command intends to immediately resolve anger in relationships by seeking forgiveness and reconciliation, even before worshipping God (see also Matthew 18:15-18). To do that is Jesus' surpassing righteousness of the new covenant heart.

2. *Adultery and lust* (5:27-30). It's not about "You shall not commit adultery", but about lust: to "look at a woman (or man) lustfully". Jesus referred to Exodus 20:17, "You shall not covet (desire) your neighbour's wife" – Moses' explanation of 20:14, "do not commit adultery". *Cultivating* lust/fantasy of the mind is adultery/idolatry of the heart. The intention not only leads to, but is, in effect, the outward act: "you have already committed adultery with her in your heart". The renewed heart stops lust at the root, restraining, not repressing, sexuality (sexual awareness) for its God-given purpose. We are moral beings, God's image-bearers, not animals driven by sexual instinct. Lust leads to sexual immorality, causing untold societal damage, even hell on earth. Jesus' "gouge out your eye/cut off the offending part" is deliberate exaggeration to teach his disciples radical treatment of temptation and sin.

3. *Divorce and remarriage* (5:31-32). The practice of divorce and remarriage, often "for any and every reason" (Matthew 19:3), was legitimised by "giving a certificate of divorce" (5:31; Deuteronomy 24:1-4). Rabbis debated this. Hillel said a man could divorce his wife for any reason, and both could remarry. Shammai argued only for adultery, which was the woman's immorality under Jewish law. Remarriage was not adulterous. Jesus said that "sexual immorality" (*porneia* 5:32, 19:9) breaks the marriage: not only the woman's adultery; also the man's cultivated lust – the moral equivalent of adultery (5:27-30). Jesus, therefore, taught that if one divorces one's spouse without valid grounds, the marriage is not truly dissolved, and subsequent remarriage – by the man and/or the woman – is adulterous (5:32, 19:8-10).

4. *Oaths and truthfulness* (5:33-37). It's not about swearing and making oaths to validate the truth of one's words. It's about being

truthful, a person of your word. Jesus' OT quote on not breaking your oath, but fulfilling it to the Lord, joined Leviticus 19:12; Numbers 30:2; Exodus 20:7. Jews commonly swore by all sorts of things, but not directly by God, to manipulate others into believing their words. Rabbis debated which oaths were binding. But Jesus argued that whatever one swears by is ultimately God's (see Isaiah 66:1f). So, don't make any oaths – that fulfils the spirit of the Law (Deuteronomy 23:22; Ecclesiastes 5:5). Jesus did away with oaths, teaching his disciples to tell the truth: "Simply say 'Yes' or 'No'; anything beyond this comes from the evil one" (5:37).

5. *Retaliation and response* (5:38-42). Jesus' quote of "eye for eye and tooth for tooth" (Exodus 21:24) is the well-known *lex telionis,* the law limiting retaliation to the injury received. One could either be a passive victim and do nothing, or get vengeance, which would be upheld in court. But Jesus taught a third way: the response of the new covenant heart is redemptively different. His disciples are to value people and relationships above possessions and security, by responding from love in creatively unselfish ways that expose "the evil person" for their injustice, calling them to repent.

6. *Enemies and love* (5:43-48). Beyond retaliation is the law of love (Leviticus 19:18). Jesus quoted it, "You have heard it was said, 'Love your neighbour and hate your enemy.'" 'Hate your enemy' was added by some groups. Essenes taught hatred for people outside their community (1QS 1:4,10; 2:4-10, Wise *et al* 2005:117-8). Zealot-Sicarii's hated the Romans and Jewish collaborators. Shammai added "and hate your enemy" to Leviticus 19:18, saying it was implied: having loved your neighbour (Jewish), you could then hate your enemy (non-Jews). "Enemy" was defined as those outside your group. In contrast, Leviticus 19:33-34 taught, in the context of v.18, love of foreigner "as a native-born, as you love yourself". Thus, by teaching "love your enemies" through doing good to them (5:44-47), Jesus upheld the spirit of the Law (Exodus 23:4-5; Proverbs 25:21-22). The renewed heart fulfils Torah, making Jesus' disciples different to the world (Matthew 5:46-47).

Matthew 5:48 concludes the six contrasts that illustrate surpassing righteousness: "Be perfect, therefore, as your heavenly Father is perfect". Luke says, "Be merciful, just as your Father is merciful"

(6:36). They both quote and interpret, taking the future imperative form of Leviticus 19:2, "Be holy because I, the LORD your God, am holy". Literally, "you *will be* holy/perfect/merciful *as* I am, *because* I am". "Perfect", Greek *teleios*, means mature, full-grown, complete. Merciful can be translated as compassionate. Thus, holiness is not moral purity *per se*, but maturity, wholeness, and completion in *God's love*. Jesus' six contrasts show the perfection of love in his Kingdom, enabled by the new covenant heart and Spirit that he imparts.

Concluding Comments

For Jesus, the heart of the matter is the human heart. We all live from our heart, whether we know it or not (Proverbs 4:23). How we live shows outwardly what has formed us inwardly. A good or bad person is known by what they say and do, seen in Jesus' repeated teachings on the heart-mouth, root-fruit, inside-outside cup reality (Matthew 7:15-20, 12:33-37, 15:17-20, 23:25-28). That is precisely why he spoke as *Yhwh* offering the new covenant heart, "Come to me all you who are weary and burdened, I will give you rest" (Matthew 11:28-30, quoting Jeremiah 31:25f). "Take my yoke upon you and *learn from me*, for I am gentle and humble *in heart*, and you will find rest for your souls. For my yoke is easy and my burden is light".

His easy yoke/light burden is his Kingdom new covenant, not the heavy burden of legalistic obedience to the letter of the Law that the Pharisees and Scribes laid on Jews (Matthew 12:1f, 23:4; Luke 11:46). They clashed with Jesus on *both* the written *and* oral Torah. The latter was the authoritative (legally binding) rabbinical teaching passed on from *verbal instructions* Moses gave beyond his written Torah. This is what the rabbis believed, later recorded in the Mishna and Talmud. Jesus referred to it as "the traditions of the elders" that he challenged (Mark 7:3,5,8, "You let go of God's commands and hold on to human traditions") with his interpretation of *the written* Torah.

Jacob Neusner states that Jesus drew disciples to himself, not to Torah, placing himself above Torah (2000:65-6). Jesus would have replied, "You study the Scriptures diligently because you think that in them you have eternal life. These are the very Scriptures that testify about me, yet you refuse to come to me to have life" (John 5:39).

Jesus' messianic interpretation pointed to himself as fulfilling the spirit and intention of Torah. He intensified the ethical requirements of Torah, seen in the six contrasts above, while relaxing other aspects of the Law. And controversially so, e.g., Jesus relaxed Sabbath keeping. He taught that the Sabbath was made for humans, for their benefit, not the other way round. Therefore, Jesus concluded, "the Son of Man is Lord of the Sabbath" (Matthew 12:1-13). In contrast, Neusner says only God is Lord of the Sabbath (2000:87).

A second example is that Jesus relaxed ceremonial purity laws, as in kosher food and eating practices (Matthew 15:1-20). In fact, food and fellowship (with whom one ate) were contentious issues that dominated debates among Jesus' first followers, seen in Acts 11 and 15, Galatians 2, 1 Corinthians 8, and Romans 14. They wrestled with how much newness there was in the new covenant, e.g., if the food laws were no longer binding, how does one avoid contamination by impure pagan food? The deeper question in the gospels and the early church letters was the relationship of Christ-followers to the Law of Moses, which this chapter has addressed from Jesus' perspective.

JESUS' LOVE ETHIC

Teachers of Torah commonly sought to reduce God's *mitzvot* – all the commandments – to their *essence*. The thought was that if they could correctly identify and interpret God's primary intent in the *mitzvot*, obeying *that intent* would mean keeping all of Torah.

Proposed Reductions of the Law to its Essence

This is seen in Hillel, 1st century BC, who said, "'What is hateful to you, to your fellow don't do'. That's the entirety of the Torah; everything else is elaboration. So go, study" (Neusner 2002:104). Neusner says that Hillel's phrase is "a reworking" of Leviticus 19:18. Debates on reducing the commandments to their essence were evident in Jesus' day and continued after AD 70, throughout Rabbinical Judaism.

Neusner (2002:25-7) gives an example from the Mishna, about AD 250, from Rabbi B.R. Simelai (trimming his details): "Six hundred and thirteen commandments were given to Moses, three hundred and sixty-five negative ones, corresponding to the number of the days of the solar year, and two hundred and forty-eight positive commandments, corresponding to the parts (bones) of a man's body. David came and reduced them to eleven". Then Simelai listed eleven commandments in Psalm 15. Isaiah reduced them to six in 33:25-26. Micah reduced them to three in 6:8. Then "Isaiah again came and reduced them to two: (i) Keep justice and (ii) do righteousness" (56:1). Simelai concluded, "Habakkuk further came and based them on one, as it is said, 'But the righteous shall live by his faith (2:4)'".

Even in Jesus' day, the more common view was that the Holiness Code of Leviticus 17 to 26 was a summary of the Law, essentially what *Yhwh* required of Israel to be holy as he is holy. That, in turn, was summarised in Moses' ten commandments in Exodus 20. And that was reduced to Leviticus 19:18, to love your neighbour as yourself. The idea was that love of the (visible) neighbour is evidence – the fruit of the root – of love of the (invisible) God. Jesus' followers understood and taught this, seen in 1 John 4:20.

Paul, a messianic rabbi and apostle of Jesus, taught that "the entire law is fulfilled in keeping this one command: 'Love your neighbour as yourself'" (Galatians 5:14). He listed some of the ten commandments, saying that they and "whatever other commands there may be, are summed up in this one command: 'Love your neighbour as yourself.' Love does no harm to a neighbour. Therefore, *love is the fulfilment of the law*" (Romans 13:8-10, my italics). Paul's conclusion directly represents and restates Jesus' love ethic, from whom Paul learnt.

Jesus' Unique Answer to the Debate

Jesus' answer to reducing the Law to its essence was unique. I will work from Mark 12:28-31, the earliest gospel, and integrate some comments from Matthew 22:34-40.

> One of the teachers of the Law came and heard them debating. Noticing that Jesus had given them a good answer, he asked him, "Of all the commandments, which is the most important?" "The most important one," answered Jesus, "is this: 'Hear, O Israel: The Lord our God, the Lord is one. Love the Lord your God with all your heart and with all your soul and with all your mind and with all your strength.' The second is this: 'Love your neighbour as yourself.' There is no commandment greater than these."

The opening question is evidence of this trend in Jesus' day. Matthew's version makes it a little clearer, "One of them, an expert in the law, tested him with this question: 'Teacher, which is the greatest commandment in the Law?'" (22:35-36).

Jesus' answer used a rabbinic technique called *gezera sawa* (in the Tosepta, Mishna, Meier 2009:493-4): joining two texts from different books for mutual interpretation if both share a common keyword or phrase. Jesus, 1) cited word for word Deuteronomy 6:4–5 (Israel's creedal *Shema*: "Hear, O Israel... *love* the LORD your God with all your...") and Lev 19:18 ("*love* your neighbour as yourself"); 2) joined them back to back; 3) prioritized them first and second; and then, 4) drew a conclusion by affirming their absolute superiority, "There is no commandment (singular) greater than these (plural)."

Matthew's conclusion to the question, "which is the greatest commandment" (singular), is "all the Law and the Prophets hang on these two commandments" (plural, 22:40). Jesus' conclusion in both Mark and Matthew reveals bi-polar thinking ('Semitic dialectical negation', defined on p.162): two apparent contradictory ideas, joined and held in tension, explain each other to reveal one truth. In other words, both commandments (plural) are "the greatest" (singular), revealing the one truth of *love* that fulfils the Law *and* the prophets.

Matthew's conclusion is key: love is not only the *primary* ethic in the whole of Torah and the Prophets but also *fulfils* them. "Hang on", means "depends on", "is summed up in", and "is fulfilled in". This recalls Matthew 5:17, Jesus came to *fulfil* the Law and the Prophets in his scriptural interpretation and life-praxis of love.

Therefore, we must explain what love means as Jesus used it by quoting and joining these two commands into one law or ethic of love. But first, we must note Meier's conclusion to his exhaustive examination of Jesus' love commands (2009:478-646). He shows that Jesus' answer and its manner (the four points above) is unique, in that it is unprecedented and unparalleled in all Jewish literature: the OT, Apocrypha, intertestamental writings, Philo, Essenes (Dead Sea Scrolls), Josephus, the rest of the NT, and the Mishna and Talmud.

Similarly, the *positive* form of the Golden Rule on the lips of Jesus ("In everything, do to others what you would have them do to you, for this sums up the Law and the Prophets", Matthew 7:12; Luke 6:31) is unique to the NT. The origin, in its *negative* form ("Do not do to others what you do not want them to do to you"), is from Greek historian

Herodotus (484-20 BC). It is then used in Greco-Roman literature and religious texts. It entered Judaism in the diaspora, as seen in Hillel's purported summary of Torah, "What is hateful to you, do not do to your fellow" (see Meier 2009:551-557, he argues that it's not clear either way if the positive form actually came from the historical Jesus).

The Context and Meaning of Jesus' Love Ethic

What did Jesus mean by love, by his ethic of love as he understood it from the two Torah texts? He would have interpreted their meaning in the context in which they were used.

The context of Leviticus 19:18 is the Holiness Code, i.e., to love is to be holy as God is holy (19:2). The immediate context is 19:17, "Do not hate a fellow Israelite in your heart. Rebuke your neighbour frankly so you will not share in their guilt". To not rebuke your neighbour in their wrongdoing is to hate them, to share their guilt. To frankly rebuke their sin is to love them as yourself, securing their wellbeing. Love discriminates to promote people's highest good. 19:18 is also defined by 19:34-35, to love the foreigner among you as yourself, treating them as native-born (mentioned earlier).

The context of Deuteronomy 6:4-5, Israel's creedal confession, is *God's* love that is first referenced as the basis of Israel's existence and her (returned) love of God. 4:37 states, "Because he (*Yhwh*) *loved* your ancestors and chose (them)... he brought you out of Egypt by his Presence and his great strength" (see Isaiah's interpretation of this, 43:4). This is confirmed in Deuteronomy 7:7-9 (my italics),

> "The LORD did not *set his affection on you* and choose you because you were more numerous than other peoples, for you were the fewest of all peoples. But it was *because the LORD loved you...* he is the faithful God, *keeping his covenant of love* to a thousand generations of those who love him and keep his commandments".

God chose to love (*ahav*, 4:37, 7:8,13, 10:15, 23:5, 33:3) Israel. His love was the basis of their (required) reciprocal love (*ahav*, 6:5, 7:9, 10:12, 11:1,13,22, 13:3, 19:9, 30:6,16,20). *Ahav* is relational love, affection, goodwill, care, and compassion, which is grounded in God's "covenant of love (*hesed*)" (5:10, 7:9,12; 1 Kings 8:23; Nehemiah 1:5, 9:32). *Hesed* is God's loyal/faithful love, translated "unfailing love" in the NIV.

Jesus' first followers, the NT writers, used *agape* in Mark 12:30-31 and Matthew 22:37-39, the least used word for love among three others in the Greco-Roman world (Lewis 1960, Wright 2010:156-9). They filled *agape* with messianic meaning, as in Jesus' modelling of *ahav* and *hesed:* selfless love, even sacrificing one's interests and well-being in willing the highest good of God and others.

Jesus believed *that* love, God's love for us that grounds and enables our love for God and others, fulfils the Law and the Prophets. We love because God first loved us (1 John 4:19). Jesus received *that* love as the essence of Torah, as a subjective reality. He taught from personal experience: "As the Father has loved me, so have I loved you" (John 15:9). His consciousness and being were so filled and formed by *Abba's* love that it became his love for others. God's love incarnate.

Jesus prayed to his Father, "You loved me before the creation of the world... I have made you known to them, and will continue to make you known in order that the love you have for me may be in them, and that I myself may be in them" (John 17:24,26). Jesus prayed – and continues to pray for us as our High Priest – that we have that same consciousness and experience of the Father's love in us, and through us, so that we reveal God to the world around us, as he did.

The Standard and Source of Love

According to John's gospel, on the night before Jesus was crucified, he gave this crucial instruction to his sent ones (apostles),

> "As the Father has loved me, so have I loved you. Now remain in my love. If you keep my commands, you will remain in my love, just as I have kept my Father's commands and remain in his love. I have told you this so that my joy may be in you and that your joy may be complete. My command is this: Love each other as I have loved you. No one has greater love than this, to lay down one's life for one's friends" (15:9-13).

First, note "as... so". Greek *kathos*, "as", has two nuances. It means "since" or "on the basis that", i.e., the *source* of love. And "just as" or "to the degree that", i.e., the *standard* of love (Meier 2009:564-5). Thus, God's love for Jesus was the *source* and *standard*, the *means* and the *measure* of his love for his disciples and others. It is the spiritual kind and quality of love that enables love to be experienced and exercised up to the standard of its source, God, who is love.

Second, Greek *meno*, "remain", means to "abide" (ESV) as in abode or dwelling. Not periodic visits or encounters, but mutual indwelling that produces *a state of being* (14:23 cf. 17:20-23). Jesus found his home in, continuously dwelt in, the Father's love. God's love 'homed' in Jesus' heart, mind, soul, and body – fulfilling the *Shema* Israel (Deuteronomy 6:4-5) – from which God lived into the world as love. Jesus used *meno* eleven times in John 15:1-17 to teach that his 'being-in-love' with God is the source and standard of our love for God and others, which fulfils the Law and the Prophets.

Third, love and obedience are inseparable and reciprocal. Love leads to and enables obedience to God. Obedience expresses and nurtures love of God – our mutual dwelling in God and God in us. *As Jesus "remained" in his Father's love by keeping his commands, so we "remain" in his love by keeping his commands.* Jesus' dwelling in God's love by obedience is the means and measure of our dwelling in Jesus' love by obedience. This is the nurturing of our 'being-in-love' that is naturally expressed and overflows in our 'doing-in-love'.

Fourth, the joy of Jesus completes us. We know the joy – his joy – of love and obedience that becomes our abiding heart condition.

Fifth, his (new) commandment to "love each other *as I have loved you*" (12, my italics), is an entire operating system upgrade. He transformed the (old) command, "love your neighbour *as* you love yourself" (Leviticus 19:18), by replacing self-love with "*as* I have loved you". If self-love is our source and standard for loving others, we will surely fail in what God requires of us. Sin has corrupted self-love. We are essentially self-centred, mostly loving others in self-serving ways. Some people are so broken, they reject and hate themselves, and thus reject others. They are unable to love others "as yourself".

Jesus embodied divine love as the measure and means of the love that frees and enables us to love as he loved. We must, however, believe and receive that love to experience its power that transforms the water of human love into the wine of divine love. Our limited and broken love is infused with and becomes the instrument of God's love. To reject God's love in Jesus, as Israel did to *Yhwh* in their "covenant of love", is to exile oneself from God.

Jesus' "new commandment" to love one another and all others "*as I have loved you*", is *the* distinctive mark of our apprenticeship to him.

"By this will everyone know you are my disciples" (John 13:34-35). It is *the* witness to the world of who God is.

Sixth, Jesus' definition of love is to selflessly lay down our life for our friends, including our neighbour (whom Jesus defined as the one in need, Luke 10:25-37) and our enemies (Matthew 5:44f).

Lastly, Jesus' "*as... so...*" teaching and modelling of divine love functions at four interactive levels, or overlapping circles of love, in John's gospel (see Venter 2019:192-8 for a detailed discussion),

- Father–Son love: the source and standard of all true love.
- Son–disciple love: the incarnate model of God's love.
- Disciple–disciple love: the witnessing Kingdom community of God's love.
- Disciple–world love: the world revolution of God's love.

Concluding comments

The historical Jesus knew and taught that this love – God's love enabling our love for God and others – fulfils the Law and the Prophets. Jesus' Kingdom 'hermeneutic of love' was his interpretative key to the Hebrew scriptures and to life. It was his Kingdom 'ethic of love', his way of holy living (*halakha*) that does the will of God on earth as in heaven. Furthermore, this love – the love of God, his *Abba*-Father – led Jesus to his suffering and death. His self-sacrificing life and death were the ultimate embodiment of God's love for Israel and all humanity: the cross-carrying Messiah-King who triumphs over evil through suffering love.

QUESTIONS FOR REFLECTION AND DISCUSSION

1. What is your essential takeaway from this chapter? How will you implement it in your life?

2. How would you describe Jesus' relationship to Torah, 'The Law'?

3. What is the "surpassing righteousness" that Jesus taught? How can you illustrate it in your life, as Jesus did in his context?

4. Define what love means, a) in your culture, b) as Jesus modelled and taught it; i.e., describe Jesus' hermeneutic and ethic of love.

5. Do you believe God loves you? How do you receive and experience God's love? How can it become your daily reality, your identity, as it was with Jesus?

SUFFERING & CRUCIFIXION

We've come to the climax of the story, the focal point of the portrait. If the Passover-Exodus is the Mount Everest, *the* defining paradigm, in the Jewish mind, then Jesus' death and resurrection is more so for his followers and the world. Few doubt, historically speaking, that Jesus was executed on a Roman cross. But his bodily resurrection is a different matter, of a different order, doubted by many historians.

God's self-sacrificing love in *Yeshua ha Notzri*, discussed in the previous chapter, led to his suffering and death. Hence, *The Crucified God* (Moltmann's phrase, 1974). From conception, his *given name* identified his destiny, "You shall call his name *Yeshua*, for he will save his people from their sins" (Matthew 1:21, I now use *Yeshua* to highlight his identity and destiny). From birth, a shadow of death hung over him (Luke 2:34-35). From twelve, his passion "to be about my Father's business" (Luke 2:49 KJV) led him, ultimately, to the cross.

Yeshua was more than a rabbi, more than a wise sage, more than a miracle-working prophet. He saw himself as Israel's representative King, doing for Israel what she could not do for herself: atone for sin. His worldview, beliefs, and aims pointed to this dark vocation of suffering love and sacrificial death, in hope of resurrection.

I tell *Yeshua's* story of passion (suffering and death) from Mark's gospel, integrating other material where needed. This is, again, an exercise in Hebraic historical narrative theology. Mark presents *Yeshua* as the Messiah, The Son of God (1:1 cf. 8:29). We have seen, throughout this portrait of *Yeshua,* how he defined the meaning of Messiah in his Kingdom mission, message, and ministry, contradicting the common expectation of a military King coming to establish a political Kingdom, as David did. *Yeshua* redefined the warrior-King idea *through suffering and death* in his victorious triumph over political, spiritual, and cosmic evil powers. This is called the *Christus Victor* tradition, which Gustav Aulen (1970) has expounded.

MARK'S GOSPEL STRUCTURE

Mark has 16 chapters, bracketed by an *inclusio*, a repeated opening and closing statement like two book ends holding the body of the story. Chapter 8 is the central turning point of *Yeshua's* story.

Scholars point to Mark's use of "torn open" at the beginning and end of Jesus' ministry: the heavens at his baptism (1:10) and the Temple curtain at his death (15:38). In baptism, *Yeshua* identified with Israel in her sin, symbolising a new Exodus into God's Kingdom through death and resurrection. In his atoning death, it was literally fulfilled. The torn veil opens the way for all into God's holy presence. In other words, the Kingdom of God broke through with great power in *Yeshua's* ministry and death, defeating the earthly and cosmic evil powers that separated humanity from God (see pp.59-61).

Yeshua's revealed *identity* in the verses that follow these two texts is part of the *inclusio*. When the heavens were torn open, God declared, "You are my Son, the Beloved, with whom I am well pleased" (1:11). When the Temple veil was torn, the centurion confessed, "Surely this man was the Son of God" (15:39). Both confirm the gospel's opening, "The beginning of the good news about Jesus the Messiah, the Son of God" (1:1), and the centre, "You are the Messiah" (8:29).

This center disclosure divides Mark's gospel in two: the 'messianic secret' and the 'messianic suffering'. Both halves unfold the breakthrough of the Kingdom with the revelation of *Yeshua's* identity and the consequent clash of authority: opposition by the authorities to his Kingdom authority, leading to his suffering and death.

The Messianic Secret (Mark 1-8)

Scholars have used the phrase 'messianic secret' (Wrede 1971) to refer to *Yeshua's* purposeful hiding of his identity, especially in the first half of Mark's gospel. If so, why did *Yeshua* hide his identity?

In Mark's first story of Kingdom breakthrough, demons reacted to *Yeshua's* authority, disclosing his identity, as "the Holy One of God". He silenced them and drove them out (1:21-28). This became the pattern, "he would not let the demons speak because they knew who he was... the Son of God" (1:34, 3:11-12). He told some who received healing miracles, "don't tell anyone" (1:44, 5:43, 7:36). He also ordered his apostles to keep his real identity secret (8:30, 9:9). After he stilled the storm that threatened to drown them, the disciples asked, "Who is this?" (4:41). That is the key question that the gospels answer.

But word of *Yeshua's* healings spread, and large crowds came to him (1:28,45; 3:7-8, 6:53-56). Jewish authorities began to oppose him due to his popularity, associations, miracles, and teaching (2:6-7,16,24; 3:2,22). They plotted to kill *Yeshua* early in his ministry (3:6; Matthew 12:14; Luke 6:11). Luke recorded how he was almost forced off a cliff after his synagogue teaching (4:28-30), and later King Herod wanted to kill him (13:31). John highlighted the plots to kill *Yeshua* and his awareness of them (5:18, 7:1,19; 8:37,40; 11:53-54). The political-religious authorities were surrogates for *ha satan* and his powers that opposed Jesus. They sought to kill him.

Wrede (1971:17-8, 228) said that Mark made up the messianic secret, believing *Yeshua* did not claim Kingship. Most scholars today disagree (Sanders 1985:321-2, Keener 2009:256-67), citing the fact that Jesus taught about the *Kingdom*; he would play the principle role with his apostles judging the twelve tribes of Israel (Matthew 19:28); he was executed as a would-be *King* ("The King of the Jews" is used six times of him at his trial and crucifixion, Mark 15:2,9,12,18, 26,32); and that his disciples expected him to return to establish the *Kingdom* (Matthew 16:27-28; Acts 1:6, 3:17-23).

Yeshua probably hid his real identity due to the dangers of popularity, with premature exposure of threat by the authorities. Wanting to evidence his messiahship differently, he believed he would become King through suffering and death, not by force. It was a matter of strategy to allow claims of his Kingship only toward the end of his ministry, not to risk wrong classification as a revolutionary and premature death. *Yeshua* delayed his martyrdom for the right time and place, Passover in Jerusalem (Mark 10:32-34; Luke 13:32-35).

In short, Jesus defined his role as Messiah while waiting on God to establish the Kingdom and install the King, rejecting any attempt to claim it for himself, or allow others to force him into it (John 6:15).

The Messianic Disclosure (Mark 8:27-30)

Yeshua strategically chose the time and place to disclose his identity: about halfway into his ministry, at Caesarea Philippi, north of Galilee beneath Mount Hermon. The city was first named Paneas after the Roman god Pan (its shrine was there) – mostly a Gentile area. Jewish King, Herod Philip, rebuilt and renamed it Caesarea Philippi in honour of Tiberius Caesar and himself (his royal residence was there). *Yeshua* probably chose to reveal himself as "The Messiah" among the mix of Jews and pagans, the gods and powers of the empire.

Mark places this story in the context of Jesus opening the eyes of a blind man, who first saw obscurely, then "saw everything clearly" (8:22-26). So, when *Yeshua* first asked, "Who do people say I am?", the answer was that they saw him obscurely as one of the prophets (8:27-28). Then he asked, "Who do you (his disciples) say I am?" Peter's eyes were opened to disclose *Yeshua's* real identity (Matthew 16:16-17).

Peter's confession, "You are the Christ", did not mean *Yeshua* was divine (God); rather that he was *the* promised Ruler. Messiah meant a human King, Anointed by God in the sense of the promised "Son of David, Son of God" (2 Samuel 7:14, Psalm 2:7 cf. Mark 10:47). This is seen in Matthew's rendering of Peter's disclosure: "You are the Messiah, the Son of the living God" (16:16, confirming Mark 1:1).

All three synoptic gospels record, a) this story, as the turning point in *Yeshua's* ministry; b) with him immediately telling his apostles to keep his identity secret; c) explaining that "Messiah" meant suffering and death for him (and his followers); d) followed by his transfiguration experience with God's heavenly voice again affirming his identity (Mark 8:27–9:1-7; Matthew 16:13–17:1-5; Luke 9:18-36).

The Messianic Sufferings (Mark 8:31f–10:52)

The second half of Mark's gospel leads into *Yeshua's* suffering and death, ending with his burial in Mark 15. I divide this second half into what scholars call the three predictions of *Yeshua's* passion, with growing opposition (8:31f–10:52), then his last week in Jerusalem (11:1f–14:52), and his trial and death (14:53f–15:47). Mark 16 is the story of *Yeshua's* resurrection, discussed in our next chapter.

First prediction of Yeshua's passion (8:31-38). With the disclosure of his real identity, "He began to teach them that the Son of Man must suffer... be rejected by the elders, chief priests, and teachers of the law, that he must be killed and after three days rise again" (Mark 8:31). Note that Jesus joined "Messiah" and "Son of Man", alluding to Daniel

7 and 9: the Son of Man suffers with/for God's people and is then entrusted with the Kingdom (7:13-27), and "The Anointed One" is "put to death" to "atone for wickedness" (9:24-27; see pp.106-111).

Mark's text listed the collaborating (Jewish) powers that opposed *Yeshua* and would kill him. However, Peter, the spokesperson for the twelve apostles, didn't understand or accept a suffering Messiah. So, *he* opposed *Yeshua*: "took him aside and began to rebuke him. But Jesus turned, looked at his disciples and rebuked Peter. 'Get behind me, Satan! You do not have in mind the concerns of God, but merely human concerns'" (8:32-33). This was a dramatic confrontation. Behind the political-religious opposition, and that of his disciples (one of his twelve would betray him), was the devil himself.

After speaking words of revelation inspired by the Spirit of God (Matthew 16:16-17), Peter spoke words of his vested human interests inspired by *ha satan*. The disciple's place was behind his master, following him, not in front of the master, rebuking him. Hence, *Yeshua* taught that following him, apprenticeship to him, also meant suffering and death: "Whoever wants to be my disciple must deny themselves and take up their cross and follow me. For whoever wants to save their life will lose it, but whoever loses their life for me and for the gospel will save it" (Mark 8:34-35).

Another mention of Yeshua's passion (9:9-13). Scholars do not consider this a prediction *per se*. However, coming down the mountain after his transfiguration, he referred to the Son of Man's resurrection from the dead. His disciples then discussed what that meant. *Yeshua* added, "the Son of Man must suffer much and be rejected... they have done to him everything they wished, just as it is written about him". The written prophetic texts formed *Yeshua's* beliefs and expectations of his suffering, death, and resurrection.

Second prediction of Yeshua's passion (9:30-37). Passing through Galilee, "Jesus did not want anyone to know where they were, because he was teaching his disciples. He said to them, 'The Son of Man is going to be delivered into the hands of men. They will kill him, and after three days he will rise.' But they did not understand what he meant and were afraid to ask him about it". Instead, they discussed who was the greatest among them. Vested interests and human ambition again. *Yeshua* intervened, teaching the way of insignificance and humble service, his way of suffering and death for the Kingdom to come.

Third prediction of Yeshua's passion (10:32-34). "They (*Yeshua* and his disciples) were on their way up to Jerusalem" for the Passover, as was their custom. Knowing it would be their last Passover together, he led up front with such purpose that his disciples were "astonished" and "afraid". So, "again he took the twelve aside and told them what was going to happen to him". The Son of Man will be delivered to the Jewish authorities who will condemn him to death. They will hand him over to the Gentiles who will kill him. Three days later he will rise. *Yeshua* wanted it to happen at Passover. All synoptic gospels attest to this prediction. Luke added that "the disciples did not understand any of this. Its meaning was hidden from them, and they did not know what he was talking about" (18:31-34 cf. Mark 10:32-34).

Mark 10:35-45 gave James and John's response (also in Matthew 20:28-30). They asked *Yeshua* to sit in his Kingdom at his right and left hand. This was selfish ambition, a grasp for power. *Yeshua* said they didn't know what they were asking. Could they drink his cup (of God's judgement, Psalm 75:8; Isaiah 51:17-23; Jeremiah 25:15-29) and be baptised with his baptism (of suffering and death, Matthew 3:13-15 cf. Luke 12:50; Psalm 69:2,14-15)? "These places", he said, are for those whom God has "prepared" (Mark 10:40) with the character that can be trusted with such authority, formed through suffering servanthood. *Yeshua* did not know who it would be. And, he said, it was not his to give. He surrendered all to his Father in absolute trust of God giving the Kingdom. What he *did* know was that his disciples would indeed suffer, because of him (10:39).

He contrasted the way of worldly rule with that of God's Kingdom. "The rulers of the Gentiles lord it over them" (10:42), i.e., the empire was structured on coercive power – officials asserted hierarchical authority to get things done. Those who didn't submit felt the full force of Rome. Rule was by political power through position and prestige, title and turf, honour and submission. All who desire and grasp for these, in any form, operate in the spirit of the oppressive empire.

"Not so with you" (10:43). Emphatic! *Yeshua* called his disciples to be like him, the "slave of all" (10:44), serving from the bottom up. He redefined greatness, prominence, and leadership in his upside-down Kingdom as the most selfless, vulnerable, socially inferior: *diakonos* (servants) and *doulos* (slaves). Rule in God's Empire is by spiritual authority, backed by God's power, derived from self-sacrificing

servanthood: no coercion or control, no titles or prestige.

Yeshua was the example: "For even the Son of Man did not come to be served, but to serve, and give his life as a ransom for many" (45). The last phrase referred to Isaiah 53:10-12. *Yeshua* linked Daniel's Son of Man to Isaiah's Servant of *Yhwh*. In Daniel 7:14,27, the Son of Man is "served" (Aramaic *pelach,* the language *Yeshua* spoke) by all nations, *after* God gave him the Kingdom. Knowing that, *Yeshua* said, "*even* the Son of Man *did not come to be served, but to serve"* by suffering with/ for God's people. He united Daniel 7:21-22, 25-27 with Isaiah 52:13-53:1-12, believing he, the Son of Man, was the suffering servant who will redeem Israel and the nations by his sacrificial death. A "ransom" was the price paid to "redeem" slaves. *Yeshua* became "the slave of all", giving his life as a ransom to bring freedom from slavery to sin, sickness, demons, and death, to free "many" – all who trust in him – from the powers of the empire and *ha satan*.

THE LAST WEEK IN JERUSALEM

Yeshua came to Jerusalem with his *talmudim* (apprentices) for his last Passover. He looked at the city from the Mount of Olives and made preparation for his entry (Mark 11:1f). The sequence and timing of events that took place in his final week need to be clarified. I only discuss the events related to his death.

Wept over Jerusalem (Matthew 23:37-39; Luke 19:41-44)

Matthew and Luke add that *Yeshua* wept, probably while looking over the city: "Jerusalem, Jerusalem... how often I have longed to gather your children as a hen gathers her chicks under her wings, and you were not willing". Alluding to OT texts like Deuteronomy 32:11, Psalm 17:8, 57:1, 91:4, *Yeshua* expressed God's passionate love to gather and protect Israel under his wings of the Kingdom.

The image was also a known event in farm life: when a fire swept through the barnyard, a hen would save her chicks under her wings, willing to sacrifice her own life. Wright says (1996:570-1), "Jesus believed he would suffer the fate that was hanging over Jerusalem; indeed, that he desired to take it upon himself so that she might avoid it". *Yeshua* predicted the fiery destruction of Jerusalem because Israel did not know "what would bring you peace... you did not recognize the time of God's coming to you" (Luke 19:42-44).

Triumphant Entry into Jerusalem (Mark 11:1-11)

Prominent figures and prophetic types had a triumphant entry into Jerusalem for the feasts. The point of *Yeshua's* entry was his Kingship. He deliberately rode on a colt of a donkey, echoing the prophecy that Matthew recalled, "Say to Daughter Zion! 'See your King comes to you, gentle and riding on a donkey, and on a colt, the foal of a donkey'" (Matthew 21:5 cf. Zachariah 9:9). He did not come as a conquering military King on a white horse, as the Roman governor would have entered Jerusalem. "Your King... will proclaim *shalom* to the nations" (Zachariah 9:10). He came as the "Prince of Peace" (Isaiah 9:6).

Though Mark didn't refer to Zachariah's prophecy, he highlighted *Yeshua's* humble Kingship by emphasising the choice of "a colt" on which "no one has ever ridden" (11:2-6). The spreading of garments and waving palm branches represented royal homage (2 Kings 9:13, 1 Maccabees 13:51). People shouted Psalm 118:25-26, "Hosanna!" ("O save"), "Blessed is he who comes in the name of the Lord". Jews had those messianic words in mind as they sang the Hallel (Psalms 113–118) during Passover. It was an expression of hope for the imminent restoration of the Davidic Kingdom: "Blessed is the coming kingdom of our father David!" (Mark 11:10). Because Passover commemorated deliverance from slavery by God's victory over Pharaoh. The crowd hoped *Yeshua* would save them in a new Exodus out of oppressive Roman occupation.

Prophetic Acts (Mark 11:12-22)

Then *Yeshua* did a prophetic act in the temple. Mark framed that with cursing a fig tree in front of his disciples. Scholars agree that both were enactments of God's judgement in the prophetic tradition.

The fig tree's cursing symbolised God's judgement on Israel, as she had not borne the fruit of her calling to be a royal priesthood and light to the nations, to bring salvation to the ends of the earth (Exodus 19:5-6; Isaiah 26:18, 42:6-7). *Yeshua* believed he and his followers would fulfill Israel's Kingdom call. The fig tree with its fruit symbolized Israel (Jeremiah 24), used parabolically earlier in Luke 13:6-9: the fig tree's owner looked for fruit for three years – the span of *Yeshua's* ministry – but found none. So, it would be cut down.

The enactment of judgement in the Temple was decidedly public and provocative. *Yeshua* entered the Temple courts and drove out the money changers, sellers and buyers of sacrifices, and overturned tables. He quoted two texts for his action (Mark 11:17): "Is it not written: 'My house will be called a house of prayer for all nations'? (Isaiah 56:7). But you have made it 'a den of robbers' (Jeremiah 7:11)". The Temple was meant for all nations (1 Kings 8:41-43), with a separation between priests and people. "But in Jesus' day the Temple was also segregated by ethnicity and gender for purity reasons, with Jewish women on a lower level outside the Court of Israel and non-Jews in the outermost court" (Keener 2014:157). The outermost court was overrun by commerce to the loss of worship.

Yeshua and most others saw the Temple system and its leadership as corrupt and abusive. Jeremiah rebuked Judah's trust in "the Temple of the LORD" as a safe haven for her sin, calling it "a den of robbers" – it would be destroyed (17:1-20). That happened in 586 BC, forty years after Jeremiah began prophesying (626, 1:1-2). In AD 70, the Second Temple was destroyed, forty years after *Yeshua's* prophecy.

All four gospels attest to his prophetic act, showing its significance (Matthew 21:12-16; Luke 19:45-47; John 2:19-22). John's account has Jesus interpreting it as the Temple of his body, i.e., predicting (again) his death and resurrection. The authorities saw his act as a direct attack on the temple establishment and immediately "looked for a way to kill him" (Mark 11:18). *Yeshua* foreknew his death *and* provoked it, knowing that his protest would trigger his martyrdom, "for surely no prophet can die outside Jerusalem" (Luke 13:33-35).

Prophecy of The End (Mark 13:1-37)

All three synoptic gospels (cf. Matthew 24–25; Luke 21:5-36) attest to *Yeshua* answering, in that last week, "when will these things happen?" (Mark 13:4), i.e., the destruction of Jerusalem and the Temple, *and* the end of the present age. I will merely summarise *Yeshua's* prophecy.

Yeshua listed signs – conflict, deception, troubles, suffering – leading to "the end", the destruction of Jerusalem *and* the end of the age. Both 'ends' would be immediately preceded by great suffering, a final war. The Jewish–Roman war, AD 66–70, ended in Jerusalem's destruction. *Yeshua* predicted in AD 30 that it would happen in "this generation" (13:30), commonly understood as forty years. Keener says, "no one before AD 66 was as accurate concerning the timing as Jesus was" (2014:162).

However, it's clear that *Yeshua* taught "the signs" as characterising all of life until the coming of the Son of Man (13:24-31). He called them "*the beginning* of birth pangs" (13:8), not the birth itself, *Yeshua's* second coming. If he was so accurate regarding the end of Second Temple Judaism, how much more his prediction of the end of the age? The bottom line for *Yeshua's* apprentices was not the times and dates, but readiness to follow him to the cross, sharing in his sufferings. "Everyone will hate you because of me, *but the one who endures to the end will be saved*" (13:13). As Bonhoeffer said, "To endure the cross is suffering, the fruit of an exclusive allegiance of Jesus Christ... The cross means sharing the suffering of Christ to the last and to the fullest... When Christ calls a man, he bids him come and die" (1963:98-9).

Parable of the Vineyard and the Tenants (Mark 12:1-12)

Yeshua taught a parable in the Temple that further provoked "the chief priests, the teachers of the law and the elders (who) looked for a way to arrest him because they knew he had spoken the parable against them" (12). All three synoptic gospels record this parable (Matthew 21:33-46; Luke 20:9-19). Moving from the fig tree, *Yeshua* used the vineyard as a symbol of Israel. He clearly drew on Isaiah 5:1-7 for his parable, applying it to himself and the current context.

Yhwh planted Israel and entrusted her to tenants, her leaders. But they presumed ownership and abused their authority. When God sent prophets, the leaders rejected and even killed them. When God sent his Son, they said, "This is the heir. Let's kill him, and the inheritance will be ours" (12:7). *Yeshua* verbalised their thinking: by killing him the Kingdom will be theirs. But it would result in their judgement and "the vineyard given to others" (12:9). "Therefore, the kingdom of God will be taken away from you and given to a people who will produce its fruit" (Matthew 21:43), *Yeshua's* followers. Hence, he said to them, "I confer on you a kingdom, just as my Father conferred one on me, so that you may eat and drink at my table in my Kingdom and sit on thrones, judging the twelve tribes of Israel" (Luke 22:29-30).

He ended the parable by quoting Psalm 118:22-23 (sung during Passover), believing that his rejection would be his exaltation: "The stone that the builders rejected has become the cornerstone". In other words, *Yeshua* saw himself, from the context of the Psalm (118:17-21, 25-27), as "the cornerstone" of a new Temple of "the righteous".

Interrogation of the Lamb (Mark 11:21f–12:37)

After the Temple act, the interrogation by the authorities began. All three synoptic gospels record days of questioning by various Jewish authorities, seeking evidence to have him executed. I only comment on three questions related to *Yeshua's* Kingship and death.

The first was about the source of his authority (11:27-33). It was a clash of ultimate authority and power, both spiritual and political. *Yeshua* answered with a counter question that clearly implied his authority was "from heaven", i.e., directly from God.

The question of whether they should pay the imperial tax to Caesar (12:13-17) was "a trap" set by the Pharisees and Herodians, who were normally enemies. The former were ardent nationalists, and the latter were supporters of Roman rule. If *Yeshua* said "No", the Herodians would report him to the Roman governor to be executed for treason (the Romans had brutally put down a tax revolt in AD 6, led by Judas of Galilee). If he said "Yes", the Pharisees would denounce him as disloyal to the nation.

Yeshua's profound answer, "Give to Caesar what is Caesar's and to God what is God's", silenced both in amazement. By distinguishing between Caesar and God, Jesus did two things. On the one hand, he protested the idolatrous claims of Caesar's image on the coins, rebuking the Herodians' idolatry, while not denying the paying of taxes. On the other hand, he promoted full allegiance to God by all human beings – God's image bearers – as he did by giving his life and body to do God's will. Thus, *Yeshua* rebuked the Pharisees' hypocrisy, while not endorsing paying taxes.

The last question was asked by *Yeshua*: Whose son is the Messiah? (12:35-37). If Torah teachers say Messiah is David's son, and rightly so, then why does David say by the Holy Spirit, "The Lord said to my Lord, 'Sit at my right hand until I put your enemies under your feet'"?

(Quoting Psalm 110:1). If David calls him "Lord", how can he be his son? Was *Yeshua* implying divine identity? Mark's readers would have connected it to his earlier use of "Lord" as "God" (12:29-30). Matthew concluded, "No one could say a word in reply, and from that day on no one dared to ask him any more questions" (22:46).

Scholars note these confrontations took place on the same days that the Passover lambs were scrutinized for any blemish, to be the perfect sacrifice. Thus, *Yeshua's* interrogation was a careful symbolic examination and preparation as "the lamb of God, who takes away the sin of the world" (John 1:29).

THE FINAL PASSION NARRATIVE

Mark's climactic narrative of the final passion of "The King of the Jews" is 14:1f–15:47. It's framed by the devotion of a woman who anointed his body for burial on the Wednesday (14:1-11), and by the devotion of a man who buried his body on the Friday (15:42-47).

Anointing of Yeshua (Mark 14:1-11)

Mark further framed the incident of *Yeshua's* anointing (3-9) with the final decision to arrest and kill him (1-2, 10-11).

That last week's events ended with: "the chief priests and the teachers of the law were scheming to arrest Jesus secretly and kill him" (1-2). This opening is answered and empowered in the closing frame: "Judas Iscariot, one of the Twelve, went to the chief priests to betray Jesus to them. They were delighted to hear this and promised to give him money. So he watched for an opportunity to hand him over" (10-11). What began early in *Yeshua's* ministry – the charge of blasphemy, a capital offense (2:7), and plotting to kill him (3:6), with mention of Judas' betrayal (3:19) – reached its climax.

By framing *Yeshua's* anointing in this way, the authority's evil scheme and Judas' vile betrayal are dramatically contrasted with the woman's "expensive" and "beautiful" devotion (14:3-9).

This unnamed woman anointed *Yeshua* "with very expensive perfume, made of pure nard" (3), worth a labourer's annual income. Once the neck of the alabaster jar was broken (probably a family heirloom passed on from mother to daughter) it was all used. The intense fragrance filled the house. The scent probably remained with him for a day or two, reminding him of her extravagant devotion, strengthening him in his intense suffering until his death.

She anointed *Yeshua* as he "reclined at the table", indicating a feast; not "sitting" for a meal. Anointing the head of an important guest was customary at feasts (Psalm 23:5, 141:5; Luke 7:46). But this was extreme. "Some of those present" (Mark 14:41; Matthew 26:8 said they were *Yeshua's* disciples) viewed it as a scandalous "waste": the money could have been "given to the poor". *Yeshua* defended her, explaining her act as anointing "my body beforehand to prepare for my burial". Lane points out that, "This pronouncement indicates that Jesus anticipated he would suffer a criminal's death, for only in that circumstance would there be no anointing of the body" (1974:494).

Yeshua cherished it: "she has done a beautiful thing to me". In his mind her scandalous gift of love anticipated his death and burial. It was written into the gospel tradition, fulfilling his prediction that "throughout the world, what she has done will also be told, in memory of her" (9). She was/is a model of discipleship.

A comment on harmonising the timing, sequence, and content of similar events, e.g., *Yeshua's* anointing and the Passover meal.

On the anointing: Mark and Matthew (26:6-13) drew on the same source. John probably described the same event, but from a different source (12:1-8, Mary anointed *Yeshua's* feet a week before Passover). Luke's story (7:36-50) is a different event (Keener 2003b:858-61).

On the Passover meal or 'The Lord's Supper': the synoptic gospels agree *Yeshua* celebrated it with his apostles on Thursday night (early Friday, 15 Nisan, in the Jewish calendar – the day began after sunset). John 13 has Wednesday night, 14 Nisan, an early Passover or a *haburoth* (a meal of brothers)? This different dating "is one of the most difficult issues in passion chronology" (Lane 1974:496-8; see Carson 1991:455-8, Wright 1996:554-8). Also, were the elements of *Yeshua's* Passover meal pre- or post- AD 70 tradition in their order and meaning? See McKnight's study, 2005:243-92. What follows is the synoptic tradition, as in Mark's passion narrative.

Passover Supper (Mark 14:12-26)

On the Thursday afternoon, when the Passover lambs were sacrificed,

Yeshua sent his disciples to prepare for the meal. After sunset, as all the families in Jerusalem gathered for the Passover, they "reclined at the table". It was a feast that continued late into the night with the *Pesach Haggadah*: the 'retelling of the Passover', God's great deliverance, in hope of God doing it again. *Yeshua,* however, fused and interpreted it with the story of his own life and impending death, believing that he was fulfilling Israel's story in a new Exodus.

The drama began when *Yeshua* said, "one of you will betray me". The twelve were in consternation, "surely not me?" He explained, "it is the one who dips bread into the bowl with me" (18-20). The hospitality of table fellowship was an intimate bond in that culture, so Mark's readers would have been horrified at such betrayal. In John 13:18, *Yeshua* quoted Psalm 41:9, "my close friend, someone I trusted, one who shared my bread, has turned against me".

His explanation of the betrayal was an acknowledgement of *both* God's sovereignty *and* human responsibility: "The Son of Man will go just as it is written about him. But woe to that man who betrays the Son of Man! It would be better for him if he had not been born" (Mark 14:21). *Yeshua's* use of 'Son of Man' here again is significant.

During the meal, when the *seder* (order of service) was to break the bread, *Yeshua,* the host, said "the blessing", i.e., he gave thanks. He did not "*bless* the bread" (nor the wine) – Jews only bless God and people, not inanimate objects. It was the "unleavened bread of *affliction*" that was burnt over fire. The *Pesach* liturgy was, "This is the bread of affliction our ancestors ate when they came out of Egypt" – a symbol to remember the affliction of slavery under foreign gods. *Yeshua* broke it with an astonishing interpretation: "Take it; this is *my body*" (my italics). Luke 22:19 says, "This is my body given for you; do this in remembrance of me". In Aramaic, the phrase could mean "is" or "represents" (Keener 2014:166-7). *Yeshua's* words would be utterly repulsive and cannibalistic if taken literally, as seen in John 6:52f.

He meant that the bread *represented* his body. The fiery affliction of Israel, and the world, would be taken into his body, which was given and broken as the bread of life, for all who "take and eat". It echoed Isaiah 53:3-5 (NRSV), "He was despised and rejected... a man of suffering and acquainted with infirmity... Surely he has borne our infirmities and carried our diseases; yet we accounted him stricken, struck down by God, and *afflicted*. But he was wounded for our transgressions, crushed for our iniquities; upon him was the punishment that made us whole, and by his bruises we are healed".

"Then he took a cup, and after giving thanks he gave it to them, and all of them drank from it. 'This is my blood of the covenant, which is poured out for many', he said" (Mark 14:23-24). Another dramatic interpretation. "Blood of the covenant" is from the first covenant in Exodus 24:8. Four cups of wine came to be used in the Passover meal. Scholars debate how many were used in *Yeshua's* day and which cup he took. Mark and Matthew (26:27) say "a cup". Luke has two, one at the start of the meal (22:17) and one "after the supper... This cup is the new covenant in my blood" (22:20). Paul, in his record of "the Lord's Supper" written over a decade *before* Luke (probably using the same source), also said the cup was taken "after supper" as "the new covenant in my blood" (1 Corinthians 11:20,25).

Again, the wine was not literally *Yeshua's* blood – unthinkable for Jews. The standard *Pesach seder* interpreted the wine as a symbolic remembrance, with the wording taken from Exodus 6:6-7,

- "I will bring you out": first cup of sanctification, taken at the start of the meal.

- "I will free you": second cup of rejoicing (or deliverance), taken during the meal.

- "I will redeem you": third cup of redemption (or salvation), taken after the meal.

- "I will take you": fourth cup of blessing (or 'benediction'), taken at the end, closing the Passover meal.

Yeshua almost certain took the cup of redemption and interpreted it as his blood of the new covenant. They would've understood it, as covenants were ratified by blood sacrifice. God 'redeemed' Israel from slavery by the 'ransom' of substitutionary sacrifice. The blood of the lamb placed on their doors made God's judgement 'pass over' to the Egyptians (Exodus 12:13,23), whose first-born sons died, resulting in the Exodus. *Yeshua* saw himself as God's Passover Lamb, as did Paul (1 Corinthians 5:7). His blood meant the forgiveness of sin (Matthew 26:28) *and* the defeat of the evil powers, *with* the new Exodus into God's Kingdom – the new creation (see Wright 2016:178-94).

Jeremias quotes a midrash from *Pirqe R. Eli'ezer* who interpreted the Passover blood eschatologically as messianic atonement:

> "God said: 'I see the blood of circumcision and the blood of the Passover, and I reconcile you'. Again, by the atoning force of this blood, they were redeemed in Egypt and they will be redeemed in the days of the Messiah". (Then Jeremias adds) "It is this eschatological Passover sacrifice with which Jesus compares himself. By the atoning force of his sacrifice, he inaugurates the final redemption; and by the distribution of bread and wine he gives his disciples a share in the atoning force of his sacrifice" (1949:6,9).

Yeshua's "new covenant" reference to Jeremiah 31:31-34 confirmed it. He believed his impending death would ratify *that* new covenant. "My blood... is poured out for many" (Mark 14:24) is a quote from Isaiah 53:11-12. It showed that he not only saw his death as sacrificial, to atone for sin, fulfilling Isaiah 53, but he also had this great passage in mind (quoted above). He was praying it from memory, with the Hallel psalms (113–118), drawing courage and strength. He prayed "the cup of salvation" in the context of his death (Psalm 116:1f cf. 13-15):

> "I will lift up the cup of salvation
> and call on the name of the LORD.
> I will fulfill my vows to the LORD
> in the presence of all his people.
> Precious in the sight of the LORD
> is the death of his faithful servants.
> Truly, I am your servant, LORD."

Praying these and other texts with *Yeshua*, we walk with him to the cross. We enter his heart and mind to watch and pray with him in his fiery passion, offering himself as a martyr to turn away God's wrath from Israel. We taste his battle against the real enemy, *ha satan*, the power of darkness, demons, death, sin, and sickness – the focus of his ministry. We enter into his 'strange victory' through death.

After *they* drank the third cup, he vowed abstinence – he didn't drink from that cup – "I will not drink again from the fruit of the vine until that day when I drink it anew in the kingdom of God" (Mark 14:25). A profoundly emotional promise of only drinking again in the Kingdom come – when he returns as Paul said (1 Corinthians 11:26).

They then sang a Hallel psalm (116-118?) and walked out the city to a garden on the slope of the Mount of Olives.

This Passover meal, with *Yeshua's* interpretation, represented all he believed and lived in terms of his identity and destiny.

Gethsemane (Mark 14:27-42)

Gethsemane is the Hebrew for "oil press" – the garden was in an olive grove (John 18:1). There was more drama along the way as *Yeshua* told his apprentices they would fail him ("fall away") in his time of need. Peter, and the others, vowed that would never happen. But *Yeshua* assured them: after God vindicated him in resurrection he will regather and lead them to Galilee (Mark 14:27-28).

Yeshua went there to pray because he was "deeply distressed and troubled" at what would happen. He asked his apprentices to "watch and pray" with him, saying, "My soul is overwhelmed with sorrow to the point of death" (14:34). He was so overcome that he felt he could die. He "fell on the ground" crying out, "*Abba*, everything is possible for you. Take this cup from me. Yet not what I will, but what you will" (14:36). Three times he prayed that, wrestling with it for an hour, while twice checking up on his apprentices. They had fallen asleep. He rebuked them, "Couldn't you keep watch for one hour?" (14:37).

Yeshua used his most intimate term of affectionate respect for God. He needed *Abba* now more than ever, feeling he couldn't drink the cup of judgement. He probably prayed the words of Psalms 116:3-4f, 18:3-6, 69:1f, "with loud cries and tears to the one who was able to save him from death" (Hebrews 5:7 NRSV). The anguish was so intense that his body pressed sweat "like great drops of blood falling to the ground", and "an angel from heaven appeared and gave him strength" (Luke 22:43-44 NRSV, see margin note). Angels "attended to him" when Satan tested and tempted *Yeshua* for forty days in the desert at the start of his ministry (Mark 1:13). Now at the end of his ministry, angels attended to him in the garden in his hour of greatest need. The messianic battle against the powers of darkness peaked.

However, with each cry to *Abba* to be spared from the cup, he rallied, "Yet not what I will, but what you will" (Mark 14:36). The fruit of a long obedience in the same direction. By routinely saying at every point in his life, "not my will but yours be done", he formed the moral character to say "Yes *Abba*" in his greatest test. He knew that if he saved his life, he would lose it (8:35). *Yeshua's* obedience reversed the disobedience of humanity in Adam, and the disobedience of Israel, as his first followers taught (Romans 5:12-21).

Thus, after praying, he said to his apprentices, "*The hour* has come. Look, the Son of Man is delivered into the hands of sinners. Rise! Let us go! Here comes my betrayer!" (14:41-42).

Betrayal and Arrest (Mark 14:43-52)

Judas had left during the meal (John 13:21-30) to keep his word to the chief priests to betray *Yeshua*. Now was the "opportunity to hand him over" (Mark 14:10-11). Judas came to the garden "with a crowd armed with swords and clubs", sent by the authorities (14:43). *Yeshua* said, "this is *your hour*, and the power of darkness" (Luke 22:53 NRSV). Judas betrayed him with a kiss: a sign of affection in family and close friends, and of respect and honour by a disciple to a rabbi. Judas' kiss was painfully hypocritical, considering Proverbs 27:6, "Wounds from a friend can be trusted, but an enemy multiplies kisses".

They arrested *Yeshua* and led him away around midnight. "Then everyone deserted him and fled" (Mark 14:50). This fits the criterion of embarrassment: his disciples would hardly have made up their desertion if it were not true. The same applies to Judas' betrayal. Both are severely embarrassing to *Yeshua* and his closest followers.

The Trial (Mark 14:53f–15:1-15)

"It can be claimed, without fear of serious contradiction, that the trial of Jesus of Nazareth is the most notable in the history of mankind... From its fatal outcome stemmed the Christian faith as a large part of mankind... (with) terrible consequences for the Jewish people, held guilty by generations of Christians for the murder of Christ" (Brandon 1968:13). It is a topic of historical study and scholarly debate on its own. I simply highlight the main features without discussing all the legalities (see Wright 1996:519-28, Keener 2009:313-21).

The Trial had two parts. Before the Sanhedrin at Caiaphas, the High Priest's home (14:53-72); then before Pilate, the Roman governor, in the early hours of Friday morning (15:1-15). All four gospels attest to this. Luke 23:6-15 recorded Pilate inviting Herod's participation.

After Peter had "followed from a distance", he came into Caiaphas' courtyard (Mark 14:54). There he denied knowing *Yeshua* three times. This confirmed *Yeshua's* earlier prediction (14:29-30). Luke said that after the rooster crowed, "The Lord turned and looked straight at Peter", and Peter "went outside and wept bitterly" (22:61-62).

The gospels portray the Sanhedrin as "looking for evidence against Jesus so that they could put him to death, but they did not find any" (Mark 14:55). They had decided to kill him. The witnesses were false, and their accusations were contradictory (14:56-59). *Yeshua,* in turn, was silent (14:61), highlighted in all four gospels, echoing Isaiah 53:7, "He was led like a lamb to the slaughter... silent... he did not open his mouth". He only broke silence twice: when Caiaphas asked, "Are you the Messiah, the Son of the Blessed One?" (Mark 14:61), and when Pilate asked, "Are you the King of the Jews?" (15:2).

Yeshua's reply to Caiaphas and the Sanhedrin was, "I am. And you will see the Son of Man sitting at the right hand of the Mighty One and coming on the clouds of heaven" (14:62). The end of his 'messianic secret'. He openly acknowledged his messianic identity, stating that God would vindicate him as such. Keener says, "Jesus' statement is a claim to be not only a mortal messiah but the cosmic ruler of Daniel 7:13-14, the embodiment of Israel's call, who would come in glory and reign forever" (2014:170). Here again *Yeshua* linked texts. He joined Daniel 7 to Psalm 110 by quoting "sitting at the right hand", which he had quoted two days earlier (12:35-37). The Son of Man was indeed the Son of David, the Messianic King.

Caiaphas tore his garments at this, calling it "blasphemy... worthy of death" (14:63-64). Technically, it was not blasphemy: he did not speak God's sacred name, nor call himself God (as the rabbis defined blasphemy post AD 70). Behind it was, clearly, *Yeshua's* Temple action and their view of him as a deceiving prophet/false messiah, leading the nation astray (Luke 23:2,5,14; Matthew 12:24f, 27:63; John 7:47f). They then brought him to Pilate early Friday morning for him to ratify their decision and order the execution.

Yeshua's reply to Pilate was, "Yes, it is as you say" (Mark 15:3). "King of the Jews" is used five times of *Yeshua* in Mark 15. It was inscribed on his cross, the charge on which he was crucified (15:26). John said that *Yeshua* explained, "My kingdom is not of this world. If it were, my servants would fight to prevent my arrest by the Jewish leaders. But now my kingdom is from another place" (John 18:36). *Yeshua* had rebuked Peter earlier in the garden at his arrest, after Peter drew his sword to defend him: "Put your sword away! Shall I not drink the cup the Father has given me?" (John 18:10-11). He had redefined 'Messiah/Kingship' as one of peace-making, established through sacrificial love.

Pilate (and Herod, Luke 23:13-16) found no fault in *Yeshua* worthy of death. He wanted to punish and release him. But the crowd, with the Jewish leaders, demanded his crucifixion – they wanted him to die as one cursed by God (Deuteronomy 21:23 cf. Galatians 3:13). So, as was the custom, Pilate offered to "release a prisoner whom the people requested": Barabbas, "son of *Abba*", or *Yeshua*, true son of the true *Abba* (Mark 15:6f cf. 14:61). Bar Abbas was a revolutionary, a violent rebel, and did not claim to be a king. *Yeshua* was the King of Peace. They chose Bar Abbas, shouting for *Yeshua* to be crucified. Persistence and volume, "Crucify him", won the day. "Wanting to satisfy the crowd, Pilate released Barabbas to them. He had Jesus flogged and handed him over to be crucified" (15:15). Thus, he would die the death of a rebel to save rebels – he would defeat *ha satan* at his own plan.

This raises two critical questions. *Who was culpable for Yeshua's death?* Both Jews and Gentiles. That's not antisemitic. Josephus stated that Pilate "condemned him to the cross" at the accusation of Jewish leaders (1987:480, *Antiquities* 18.3.63-4). Consistent with the gospel record. *Why did Yeshuah die?* Ultimately, because he believed it was his (dark) vocation to save Israel (and the nations) from their sins.

The evidence shows that *Yeshua's* trial was messianic, about his Kingship. Wright says the trial "draws together the key elements of Jesus' prophetic Kingdom-announcement, focussing them on himself. He is the representative of the true people of YHWH" (1996:528).

The Crucifixion (Mark 15:16-41)

Roman crucifixion was the most feared criminal execution known in antiquity. An agonising and degrading death by eventual loss of blood or, more commonly, loss of breath (death by asphyxiation).

It began with flogging (Josephus 1987:617, *Wars* 2.14.306-8). Jewish law restricted it to forty lashes (Deuteronomy 25:3). The Romans had no limit, stopping in time to prolong and maximise the torture of the cross. All four gospels say *Yeshua* was scourged, probably with a *flagellum,* a whip with three thongs embedded with lead and bone. His flesh would've been left hanging in bloody strips, even exposing some ribs. He, almost certainly, thought of Isaiah's servant, "I offered my back to those who beat me" (Isaiah 50:6). And Psalm 129:3, "Plowmen have plowed my back and made their furrows long". He probably prayed these and other texts while being beaten.

After the flogging, the Roman soldiers placed a purple robe on his bleeding back and pressed a crown of thorns onto his head. Then knelt, saying "Hail, King of the Jews" (Mark 15:22). "Hail" was the greeting given to the Roman emperor. They mocked him mercilessly, then led him away to be crucified outside the city (15:16-20). *Yeshua* probably started to carry his cross (John 19:17), but he was too weak. The soldiers forced a passer-by, Simon of Cyrene, to carry it – attested to in the synoptics. The crucifixion site was called 'The Place of the Skull' (Golgotha, Mark 15:22) because many deaths occurred there. It could also refer to the shape of a rocky outcrop.

The condemned would have been stripped naked – shamefully humiliating for Jews – and his clothes divided up among the soldiers. Traditionally, pious women of Jerusalem (e.g., Mark 15:40-41; Luke 23:27) offered a narcotic mix to dull the excruciating pain, referred to in Proverbs 31:6-7. English 'excruciating' is from the Latin *crux,* cross, i.e., from Roman crucifixion. *Yeshua* refused the drink (Mark 15:23), choosing to endure the full force of 'the *crux* of the matter'. He was then nailed to the cross, probably through his wrists and heel bone, as seen in "the first authenticated evidence of a crucifixion in antiquity", uncovered by archaeologists in Israel in 1968 (Lane 1974:564-5).

The gospels describe *Yeshua's* crucifixion in remarkable restraint – the first readers would already know the full horror of that mode of execution. The main points are simply recorded. "It was nine in the morning when they crucified him. The written notice of the charge against him read: THE KING OF THE JEWS. They crucified two rebels with him, one on his right and one on his left" (Mark 15:25-27).

In the eschatological messianic battle or 'great tribulation', *Yeshua* first endured the wrath of people for three hours: insults, mocking, taunts and sneering, from the crowds, passers-by, chief priests, and soldiers, and one criminal, perhaps both, on a cross beside him (15:29-32; Matthew 27:36-40; Luke 23:35-43). Then, "at noon darkness came over the whole land until three in the afternoon" (Mark 15:33).

However it is explained, such darkness signified judgment, as in Egypt (Exodus 10:21-23) and in "the Day of the LORD" (Isaiah 13:9-11; Joel 2:1-2,10,31; Amos 5:18, 8:9-10). Thus, theologically, *that* end-time 'Judgement Day' happened in history when *Yeshua* drank "the cup" to "its very dregs" for Israel and the nations (Psalm 75:7-8; Isaiah 51:17). As a result, God's judgement passes over all who put their trust him. Hence, he endured the wrath of God for the last three hours in silent darkness on the cross, dying at three in the afternoon.

In the gospels, *Yeshua* spoke seven 'sayings' from the cross. The timing and sequence of the sayings may differ (as with his crucifixion, John 19:14, see Lane 1974:566-7). They give us insight into what took place and his responses. He spoke the first three sayings in the three hours of daylight and the last four just before he died, after three hours of deep dark silence. *Yeshua* spoke words of...

1. *Forgiveness:* "Father, forgive them, for they do not know what they are doing" (Luke 23:34). Spoken when they nailed him to the cross. He did not hold it against the soldiers. He gave mercy.

2. *Salvation:* "Truly I tell you, today you will be with me in paradise" (Luke 23:43). His response to the other criminal who asked him, "Remember me when you come into your Kingdom". He promised salvation to the rebel, saying he would enter paradise (i.e., God's Kingdom) that day when he died.

3. *Relationship:* "Woman, here is your son... Here is your mother" (John 19:26-27). Spoken to Mary, his mother, and to John, "the disciple whom he loved", while they stood at the cross watching. From then on John took *Yeshua's* mother into his home and cared for her. In his excruciating pain, *Yeshua* loved his mother, making an oral testament before witnesses to provide for her care and protection. In so doing, *Yeshua* honoured his mother, fulfilling the fifth commandment (Deuteronomy 5:16).

4. *Rejection:* "'*Eloi, Eloi, lema sabachthani?*' (which means 'My God, my God, why have you forsaken me?')" (Mark 15:34). This was at three in the afternoon. He was near death and "cried out in a loud voice", praying Psalm 22:1 in Aramaic. He expressed his rejection, even abandonment by God. It indicated that he was praying this psalm all along – of the righteous sufferer with hope of divine vindication.

By praying it with *Yeshua* on the cross, we sense the awful battle he endured, how demons came at him...

"Do not be far from me / for trouble is near / and there is no one to help / many bulls surround me / strong bulls of Bashan encircle me / roaring lions that tear their prey / open their mouths wide against me / I am poured out like water / all my bones are out of joint / my heart has turned to wax / it has melted within me / dogs surround me / a pack of villains encircles me / they pierce my hands and my feet / all my bones are on display / people stare and gloat over me / they divide my clothes among them / and cast lots for my garments / but you, LORD, do not be far from me / you are my strength / come quickly to help me" (Psalm 22:11-19).

5. *Distress:* "I am thirsty" (John 19:28). *Yeshua* said this "knowing that everything had now been finished, and so that the scripture may be fulfilled". He quoted Psalm 69:21, where vinegar was given, just as the soldier gave it to *Yeshua* (John 19:29), fulfilling the scripture. Thus, another psalm of the distressed righteous sufferer was on his lips. It shows how he prayed the psalms by heart till his last breath. After *Yeshua* was offered the drink, he cried out...

6. *Triumph:* "It is finished" (John 19:30). The mood shifted. The Greek *tetalestai* is a shout of victory: "It's done! It's accomplished!" This was probably Mark (15:37) and Matthew's, "he cried out *again* in a loud voice" (27:50), without the words. In John, it referred to *Yeshua's* prayer the night before, "I have brought you glory on earth by *finishing* the work you gave me to do" (17:4 cf. 5:36). He had completed his mission, won the battle, atoned for sin by paying the price of redemption. (Hence, Paul taught: "Having disarmed the powers and authorities, he made a public spectacle of them, triumphing over them by the cross", Colossians 2:15). The rest – his vindication – was now up to God. So, "With that, he bowed his head and gave up his spirit" (John 19:30). With this, John alludes to Genesis 2:2, *Yeshua* rested from all his work.

7. *Reunion:* "Father, into your hands I commit my spirit" (Luke 23:46). A quote from Psalm 31:5 in hope of vindication, as the next phrase says, "redeem me, O LORD, the God of truth... I trust in the LORD, I will be glad and rejoice in your love, for you saw my affliction and

knew the anguish of my soul" (31:5-7). He surrendered his spirit to God, "breathed his last" (Luke 23:46). He gave up his life, no one took it from him (John 10:17-18) – his culminating act of obedience to *Abba* (8:29, 14:31). Hence, the soldiers "found he was already dead, they did not break his legs" (19:32-33, the legs were broken so that the one crucified could not push up on the heel nail to support their body to take a breath – so they died).

When *Yeshua* breathed his last, Matthew reported, "At that moment the curtain of the Temple was torn in two from top to bottom" (27:51 cf. Mark 15:38, discussed earlier. It could also indicate the departure of God's presence from the Temple as in Ezekiel 10–11, for destruction in AD 70). Matthew added that there was an earth tremor, rocks split, and tombs opened. Some "holy people (were) raised to life" and appeared to others *after Yeshua's* resurrection (Matthew 27:51-53). This is apocalyptic language and events, with the darkness that covered the land, which indicated 'The Day of *Yhwh*', The End, when the dead will rise as in Daniel 12:2 and other prophetic texts.

Then the Roman centurion exclaimed, "Surely this man was the Son of God" (Mark 15:39 cf. Matthew 27:54; Luke 23:47). 'Son of God' was the title of the Roman emperor – also "Lord" (*Kyrios*), among others. So, the *centurion's* confession symbolised *Yeshua's* triumph over the empire and idolatrous imperial worship. It also symbolised Gentiles acknowledging *Yeshua* as the Son of God and *Kyrios*.

Finally, all four gospels record – thus widely attested – that women disciples witnessed the events and remained there to the end (Mark 15:40-41; Matthew 27:55-56; Luke 23:49; John 19:25). Extraordinary devotion, in glaring contrast to the male apostles, who all deserted *Yeshua* – except for John, the beloved disciple (John 19:26). Again, the historical criterion of embarrassment: the gospel writers would not make this up if it were not true to what happened.

The Burial (Mark 15:42-47)

The Romans usually denied crucified criminals a burial, leaving their bodies to be eaten by vultures and dogs – more so, messianic claimants. Jews demanded burial (Deuteronomy 21:23). Thus, exceptions were made by the Romans when prominent advocates asked to bury the body. Pilate granted Joseph of Arimathea's request.

He was a wealthy man and a member of the Jewish Sanhedrin. This reveals how diverse the ruling body was because Joseph and Nicodemus were secret followers of *Yeshua* (John 19:38-39 cf. 3:1f).

The synoptic gospels did not mention Nicodemus helping Joseph with *Yeshua's* burial. However, they all referenced the faithful women, once again, who watched the burial and saw where he was laid.

John's account is particularly touching. At around four or five in the afternoon, the two elders of Israel took *Yeshua's* body down from the cross. We don't know if they or their servants did it. But the blood was carefully washed from his many wounds. His body was tenderly anointed and wrapped in linen strips with "myrrh and aloes" (19:39). Myrrh for was embalming and aloes for perfume.

"Seventy-five pounds" (thirty-four kilograms) of myrrh and aloes was extravagant, to say the least. It was, a hundred times more costly than the lavish anointing days earlier by the woman whose pure nard perfume was worth a year's wage (Mark 14:3, Keener 2014:308). Only kings were buried like this (2 Chronicles 16:14). They laid his body in Joseph's new tomb that was "cut out of rock" (Matthew 27:60) in a garden close to where *Yeshua* was crucified. Then the entrance to the tomb was closed by a tomb stone. Pilate posted soldiers to seal the tomb stone further and guard the tomb (27:62-66).

The King was buried. Shabbat had begun.

The trauma was over. All was still, resting.

Except for *Yeshua's* followers who quietly grieved and wept in the dark silence of their homes: "We had hoped that he was the one who was going to redeem Israel" (Luke 24:21).

It was Friday, but Sunday was coming!

QUESTIONS FOR REFLECTION AND DISCUSSION

1. What one thing has stood out for you in this chapter? Talk to *Yeshua* about it and let it settle deeply in your heart.
2. Was *Yeshua* 'secretive' about his identity as Messiah? If so, why?
3. How does Mark's gospel structure embody and convey its message and meaning?
4. How do you think *Yeshua*, from a human point of view, planned and prepared to die in Jerusalem... even provoking his death?

5. Why did he die? What did he believe it would accomplish? In your view, did it accomplish what he intended?

6. Personalise and apply what *Yeshua* said from the cross. Reflect on and talk to *Yeshua* about one or more of the seven sayings that 'speaks to you' in your current life context.

RESURRECTION & ASCENSION

Scholars who dismiss Jesus' miracles do not take his resurrection and ascension seriously. This is due to their modernist worldview with its 18th/19th century scientific method of study grounded in Newtonian science with its fixed laws of nature. In my introduction I showed how that 'scientific method' was wrongly applied to the social sciences and then taken as the basis of so-called 'scientific history'. Hence, if those scholars reject the spiritual reality behind Jesus' miracles, which made them possible, how much more his *bodily* resurrection?

The shift to post Einstein science – quantum physics with different assumptions – sees the 'old' method as the naivete of modernism. Postmodern and contemporary science, with its view of atoms made up of energy, can conceive of a trans-physical (resurrected) body. Most third quest scholars work with these 'new science' assumptions and do not have the (old) dichotomy of 'science versus faith' and 'the natural versus the supernatural' (discussed on pp.129-31).

So, some scholars interpret (Jesus') 'resurrection' as an existence beyond death not dependent on a reconstituted body. Borg says, "I see the empty tomb and whatever happened to the corpse of Jesus to be ultimately irrelevant to the truth of Easter... that Jesus lives, and Jesus is Lord" (Borg & Wright 2000:129-37). Jesus' physical resurrection is of such a different order that such scholars say it's a matter of 'Christian faith' and 'Easter truth'. It's not subject to the rules of critical study. There is no historical analogy, credible verification, or multiple attestation. No proof. Historically, we do not and cannot know if he rose from the grave, transformed in a new physicality. Therefore, the accounts of Jesus' resurrection, they say, are early church faith stories – visionary appearances and hallucinatory experiences of him being spiritually present and alive as 'Lord' (*Kyrios*).

But third quest scholars argue for Jesus' bodily resurrection from historical probability, seen in Wright's dialogue with Borg (in Borg & Wright 2000:111-27), and in his monumental, *The Resurrection of the*

Son of God (2003). This book is the benchmark for scholarship on Jesus' resurrection and life after death. Wright's more accessible and popular work is *Surprised by Hope* (2008).

Was Jesus' resurrection an actual event in human history? How do we know he was resurrected, never again to die? Or was he resuscitated from death? Or was it a fabrication? What was the nature of his resurrected body? What is the significance and the implications of his resurrection? How did he ascend into heaven? What did that mean? Who then did Jesus' followers conclude he really was, and is? And, therefore, what was the gospel they preached from Jerusalem to Rome, to the ends of the earth? We answer these questions in putting our final touches to our portrait of the historical Jesus.

Once we accept Jesus' bodily resurrection, his ascension easily follows, making sense of his life and mission. In fact, *his resurrection vindicated his ministry and death, declaring him to be "The Son of God"* (Romans 1:4). "If Christ has not been raised, our preaching is useless and so is your faith" (1 Corinthians 15:14). To reject his resurrection, we must do mental gymnastics to explain the gospel evidence as scientific nonsense, or fables, or 'blind faith' and 'religious truth'.

HISTORICAL PROBABILITY OF JESUS' RESURRECTION

Know the Real Jesus is written on the basis that the gospels are reliable eyewitness accounts of historical events, though theologically framed and/or interpreted (Luke 1:1-4). We approach Jesus' resurrection the same way. Even Josephus wrote that "Jesus... was (the) Christ... he appeared to them alive again the third day, as the divine prophets had foretold" (1987:480, *Antiquities* 18.3.63-4). Some scholars say this was influenced by Christians, while, ironically, they accept his reference to Jesus "condemned to the cross" in the same sentence.

Resurrection, Resuscitation, or Fabrication?

We are talking about *resurrection*: the Jewish eschatology of the body being resurrected at the end of the age, as the prophets taught (Isaiah 25:6-8, 26:19-21; Ezekiel 37:1-14; Daniel 12:1-3). It is widespread in Jewish intertestamental literature, e.g., 1 Enoch 22:13, 61:5; Psalms of Solomon 3:12, 15:12-13; 2 Maccabees 7:9,14,23 (Keener 2009:585, note 107, has all the references). Most Jews in Jesus' day believed it, except for the Sadducees (Mark 12:18-27). Philo of Alexandria (20 BC –AD 50) rejected it, believing in the immortal soul, existing as a ghost after death. However, for Jews to accept that *that* (end-time) bodily resurrection had *already* been accomplished in one man, *Yeshua ha Notzri*, was unthinkable. The sheer impossibility of it!

Not *resuscitation.* Jesus was not raised to life on the third day as in resuscitation from death. Jesus did three such miracles in the gospels (Luke 7:11-17, 8:49-56; John 11). But those people died again. Such resuscitations, as Jesus commanded his apprentices to do in his name ("raise the dead", Matthew 10:8), were/are *a* temporal defeat of death in Kingdom come. Jesus' resurrection was *the* permanent defeat of death in Kingdom consummated in *embodied* eternal life.

Not *fabrication.* An immediate issue at Jesus' burial, highlighted by Matthew. Jewish leaders asked Pilate to secure the tomb because "that deceiver said, 'After three days I will rise again.'... his disciples may come and steal the body and tell the people that he has been raised from the dead. This last deception will be worse than the first" (27:62-66). On the Sunday when Jesus rose and the tomb guards "reported everything that had happened... they gave the soldiers a large sum of money, telling them, 'You are to say his disciples came during the night and stole him away while we were asleep'... this story has been widely circulated among the Jews *to this very day*" (28:11-15, my italics). If his followers had fabricated Jesus' resurrection, surely the authorities would have found his corpse to refute the lie that he was risen.

Reasons for the historical probability of Jesus' resurrection

We can argue from the gospel evidence for the historical probability of Jesus' bodily resurrection on the following grounds.

1. *No corpse.* The fact that the Jewish and Roman authorities never produced any evidence, no body, to disprove the report/claim that Jesus was risen and alive. Indeed, the Jewish authorities would have had very strong motivation and every reason to do so.

2. *Prediction fulfilled.* Jesus believed and predicted that he would rise again "according to the scriptures", and his apprentices "did not understand" it (Mark 8:31, 9:9-10, 31-32, 10:34). He rose again just as he predicted – entirely beyond his manipulation or control.

Only God could do it. When it happened, his disciples still did not expect or understand it (John 20:9). That was embarrassing! They would not have made that up. And "according to the scriptures", in Jesus' mind, probably included other messianic texts like Psalm 16:9-11, 110:1; Isaiah 53:11-12; and Hosea 6:1-3.

3. *Supernatural phenomena.* The gospels report Jesus' resurrection taking place with angels appearing, an earthquake, the tomb stone rolling back, the tomb empty, and the soldiers running off in fright to tell the authorities. The middle eastern mind with a spiritual worldview could accommodate this – as in Jesus' miracles and the supernatural phenomena during his crucifixion and death.

4. *Women witnesses.* All the gospels attest that women first saw the tomb empty, and Jesus first appeared to them (Matthew 28:1f; Mark 16:1f; Luke 24:1f; John 20:1f). Their faithful devotion is truly remarkable. They were with Jesus all Friday, saw where his body was laid, and came early Sunday morning to anoint his body. The story has the marks of authentic eyewitness testimony: names are mentioned, they wonder who will roll away the tomb stone, the shock of seeing it already rolled away, the tomb empty, angels in attendance, and retelling what they saw and heard. That women first witnessed Jesus' resurrection was embarrassing, even offensive. Jewish and Roman law severely minimised women's testimony for suspicion of gullibility. What happened fits Jesus' counter-cultural ministry that challenged male status and prejudice – they would never have made it up. So, it meets the criterion of embarrassment.

5. *Men's reluctance to believe.* The women ran to tell the men, "He is risen". "But they did not believe the women, because their words seemed to them like nonsense" (Luke 24:11 cf. Mark 16:11,14). It makes the above point even more significant and embarrassing, reflecting historical reality. To invent the women's testimony and the men's response, and expect people to believe Jesus rose again, would be crazy! However, they depended on men's testimony for the public forum, seen in Paul's report in 1 Corinthians 15:5-8.

6. *Eyewitness appearances.* Our earliest source of Jesus' resurrection is Paul (1 Corinthians 15:3-8, AD 52/3). It predates the gospels by

a decade and more. Jesus appeared to Peter, the Twelve, to more than five hundred *"at the same time, most of whom are still living"*, and to James and all the apostles. It confirms the gospel stories (Matthew 28:8-11; Mark 16:12-14; Luke 24:13f, 36-44; John 20:19-31). Luke said Jesus "presented himself to them and *gave many convincing proofs that he was alive.* He appeared to them over a period of forty days" (Acts 1:3). All these references point to credible verification and multiple attestations.

7. *Bodily verification.* Jesus' many appearances over forty days were not spiritual visions or hallucinatory experiences. Rather, tactile encounters with the bodily Jesus, eating with him (Luke 24:30-31, 41-43; Acts 1:4; John 21:4-14). His first appearance to his apostles was the night he rose (Sunday), in a room "with the doors locked for fear of the Jewish leaders" (John 20:19,26). He "came and stood among them" – by implication, through the door or walls. He gave his regular greeting, *"Shalom aleichem"* (John 20:19; Luke 24:36). They initially thought he was a ghost, but he identified himself by his wounds, showing them his hands, feet, and side. They were overjoyed; it was *really* Jesus (Luke 24:37-41; John 20:20). To further 'prove' it was his corporeal self, he asked for fish and ate it (Luke 24:42). He invited 'doubting Thomas' to put his finger in his wounds to show he was bodily alive. Thomas' response, "My Lord and my God" (John 20:24-28), acknowledged Jesus' divinity.

8. *Transformation in the disciples.* Their radical change of heart and mind can only be explained by Jesus' resurrection. They had deserted him, were dejected and disillusioned, hid in fear of the authorities, not expecting him to rise from the dead, not believing the women's testimony about him. It suddenly all changed. His resurrection, 'proved' by his appearances, transformed them. These same disciples became bold witnesses of a risen Messiah in a few weeks. We see in Acts how they fearlessly preached Jesus risen from the dead, being willing to die for that truth, that reality.

9. *Paul's transformation.* The above is also seen in the Pharisee, *Rabbi Sha'ul*, "a blasphemer, persecutor, and violent man" (1 Timothy 1:13), "breathing out murderous threats against the Lord's disciples" (Acts 9:1). His transformation to Paul, the apostle who gave his life to preach Jesus as Lord, can only be explained by his

encounter with the risen Jesus (Acts 9:3-19). Paul explained, "he appeared to me also", *as Jesus did to those in the preceding list* in 1 Corinthians 15:5-8. Paul was martyred for *this* faith.

10. *Church growth.* The growth of Messianic Judaism, later called Christianity (Acts 11:26), into a global movement with 2.6 billion adherents can ultimately only be explained by Jesus' resurrection. Early church history, 1st to 4th century, shows how many Christ-followers who spread the good news of the Risen King, sought martyrdom for "the crown of righteousness" (2 Timothy 4:8). The blood of the martyrs is the seed of church growth, fired by faith in Jesus' death and resurrection. Like Paul, they firmly believed that his resurrection vindicated his death and all it meant.

11. *Lastly, 'The Lord's Day'.* Cranfield cites "the undisputed fact" that, despite the Sabbath being the holy day for Jews, both Jewish and Gentile Christ-followers quickly "came to regard the first day of the week as the special day for Christian worship... The Lord's Day" (in Dunn and McKnight, 2005:387, Acts 20:7; 1 Corinthians 16:2; Revelation 1:10; and Didache 14:1 in Holmes 1989:157). Such replacement of the Sabbath, which Jesus observed, is highly significant. It reveals extraordinary firm conviction of an event that took place on the first day of the week, so much so that it could be seen as transcending in importance God's Sabbath rest after completing his work of creation (Genesis 2:2).

MEANING AND SIGNIFICANCE OF JESUS' RESURRECTION

Mark and Matthew's resurrection accounts are brief, whereas Luke and John are longer. They drew on similar traditions, but also different sources. Paul's letters represent our earliest written source. So, I first comment on Paul's points relevant to the meaning and significance of Jesus' resurrection. I end with John's framing of Jesus' resurrection.

Paul's Understanding of Jesus' Resurrection (1 Corinthians 15)

Paul revised his Jewish view of eschatological resurrection in light of Jesus' resurrection. Though he referred to the resurrection in many of his letters, I work from his primary text, 1 Corinthians 15.

1. 1-4, Jesus' resurrection, including his death, is *"the gospel"* that Paul preached: *the* good news that God, in/through Messiah Jesus, has made all things right, and will make all things new. Jesus' death and resurrection were "according to the scriptures", i.e., like Jesus, Paul saw both as direct fulfilment of prophecy.

2. 5-8, Jesus' resurrection is based on historical reality, attested to by many who personally encountered the Risen Lord.

3. 12-19, answering the claim, "there's no resurrection", Paul said, "If there is no resurrection of the dead, then not even Christ has been raised". If so, our "faith is futile"; we "are still in our sins", and those who have died as believers are lost. The Christian faith is false.

4. 20-28, *however*, if he was bodily raised from the dead – as, indeed, he has been – then it means the following in God's plan,

    a) His resurrection is the "first-fruits" of the future "harvest", the end-time resurrection, now guaranteed to happen. And his risen body is the prototype of future resurrected bodies.

    b) His resurrection reverses human death "in Adam"; those "in Christ" will be "made alive", bodily resurrected as he was.

    c) That will happen "when he comes" – returns to earth. Paul also referred to this event in 51-52 and 1 Thessalonians 4:13-18.

    d) That's "the end". Jesus will reign with his resurrected followers, having defeated all his enemies – including "the last enemy", death – putting them "under his feet" (quoting Psalm 110:1). And "he hands over the kingdom to God the Father" and "subjects" himself to God "so that God may be all in all".

5. 35-53, *the nature of the resurrected body*. The "natural body" is transformed into a "spiritual body" (*pneumatikos,* 'of the Spirit'), never to die again. "Spiritual" does *not* mean "ghostly". Jesus described his resurrection body: "Touch me and see; a ghost does not have *flesh and bones* as you see that I have" (Luke 24:39). He didn't use the standard Jewish phrase for the natural mortal body, as Paul did: *"flesh and blood* cannot inherit the kingdom of God" (15:50 cf. Ephesians 6:12, Hebrews 2:14). That body is not fit for life with God in the eternal Kingdom, to rule with Christ in his new creation. It must be transformed into a body 'of the Spirit'.

The principle of life in the natural mortal body is *blood*: "the life of the flesh is in the blood". Thus, to "make atonement", blood must be shed, for "there is no forgiveness of sin without the shedding of blood" (Leviticus 17:11, Hebrews 9:22). Jesus gave his life, pouring out his blood as a once for all sacrifice to make 'at-one-ment' with God through forgiveness of sin. Then rose again in a transformed body with a transformed life-source.

The principle of life in the resurrection body is *Spirit*: Jesus' "flesh and bone" body, Paul's "spiritual body". It is not ethereal, but tactile and corporeal. Yet not mortal, nor subject to nature (natural laws), as in fallen creation. It is 'of the Spirit', of God's new creation order. Jesus' resurrection body is *literally* the most tangible reality of the future age that has *already* begun in this present evil age. The empty tomb is *the* turning point of human history.

Thus, in its substance and properties, the resurrection body is saturated by Spirit, completely subject to and governed by God's Spirit. The ultimate union of Spirit and matter, God and humanity, heaven and earth – as it was in Adam and Eve in the garden of delight before death entered their bodies, and all creation, through sin (Romans 5:12). But "the last Adam" reversed this through his resurrection – he is "a life-giving spirit" (1 Corinthians 15:45). Therefore, *only* the resurrected body is fully adequate for life in the coming ages. Because it is ruled by God's Spirit for rule with the risen King, in God's new creation, for eternity.

The characteristics of this in-Spirited trans-physical body are seen both in Jesus' post-resurrection bodily appearances, and in Paul's adjectives. Jesus could appear and disappear, ascend and descend, eat and not eat, walk through walls, not be recognised and then be recognised, and open people's minds to the scriptures. Though contradictory, these properties, *and more*, are all true and real at the same time. Paul's adjectives for the resurrection body are: "imperishable, glorious, powerful, spiritual, life-giving, image of the heavenly, immortality" (42-54). Greek "immortal" refers to a *disembodied* soul-life beyond death; but Paul uses and changes its meaning to Hebraic *embodied* eternal life.

6. 54-57, Paul ends with a triumphant declaration of Christ's victory over death, by joining Isaiah 25:8 and Hosea 13:14.

> "Death has been swallowed up in victory.
> Where, O death, is your victory?
> Where, O grave, is your sting?"

John's Framing of Jesus' Resurrection (John 20)

John framed his account of Jesus' resurrection as the first day of God's new creation, already begun in human history. He was the new Adam in the garden of new creation (see Wright 2003:440-8, 662-79).

John began his gospel alluding to Genesis 1:1, "In the beginning..." The Word, life, and light overcome the chaotic darkness with new creation (John 1:1-5), as in first creation (Genesis 1:1-5). John's gospel structure embodies this message. The prologue (1:1-18) and Jesus' resurrection (20-21) form an *inclusio* that brackets the gospel of Jesus' seven/eight miraculous signs (see pp.147-8). The structural centre is Lazarus' death and raising to life (11), anticipating Jesus' death and resurrection (19-20).

The first and seventh miraculous signs

John uses times and days to convey his message, e.g., "the next day" (1:29,35,43; 6:22), "the third day" (2:1,19-20), "two days" (4:40,43; 11:6), "the last day" (6:39,40,44,54; 7:37; 11:24), "six days" (12:1).

For example, "on the third day" a wedding took place where Jesus turned water into wine, his first miraculous sign (2:1-11). Then he cleared the Temple, saying it will be destroyed, but "I will raise it again in three days" (2:14-20). Both incidents pointed to his bloody death and bodily resurrection, his ultimate miraculous sign. "The third day" contained powerful echoes of Jesus' resurrection (Hosea 6:2 and Luke 13:32), "the last day" of *the* end-time resurrection. That, in turn, was "the first day of the week" (John repeats it twice, 20:1,19), i.e., Jesus rose on the first day of new creation.

Regarding Jesus' body and the Temple: in John's *inclusio*, Jesus' body is the Temple filled with God's glory (1:14) which rose again in the garden of new creation (20:1f). What the Temple was intended to do, Jesus did in his public ministry: the seven signs. He was the new living Temple, inaugurating God's new age of Temple-worship open to all, regardless of geography and ethnicity (4:20-26).

The seventh miraculous sign was the turning point to the ultimate sign, i.e., Lazarus' dramatic raising to life (11) was merely a signpost to the full reality of Jesus' resurrection (20). This is highlighted in the parallels and differences between the two stories. Lazarus was raised on the fourth day in the tomb (11:17,39) – *resuscitated*, only to die again (12:9-11). Jesus was raised on the third day – *resurrected,* never to die again. In both cases, the tomb stone was "taken away" from the entrance, one by human hands, the other by angels (11:41, 20:1). Both refer to "the strips of linen" and "head cloth" (11:44, 20:5-7, repeated in Jesus' case). Lazarus had to be freed from them after he exited the tomb. With Jesus, they lay "folded up" and "separate" from each other where he had laid. His body rose out of them, and they folded. God freed Jesus in the tomb from death itself with a trans-material body.

The centre of John's gospel is Jesus' climactic statement at Lazarus' resuscitation, fulfilled in Jesus' resurrection. Martha knew Lazarus would rise again in "the resurrection" at "the last day" (11:24). "The last day" stood before her! Jesus said, "*I am the resurrection and the life.* The one who believes in me will live, *even though they die*; and whoever lives by believing in me *will never die*" (11:25-26, my italics). This is the essence of his teaching on resurrection – both present (spiritual) *and* future (physical) resurrection (5:24-29, 6:39-40, 44, 50-54). *Because Jesus rose again,* he gives eternal life (*zoe aionios,* "life of the ages") to all who believe him. They are spiritually resurrected, having "crossed over from death to life" (5:24) – "even though they die". Jesus will physically resurrect them to consummated *embodied* eternal life in "the last day" – they "will never die".

Jesus said, the "time is coming and has now come when the dead will hear the voice of the Son of God and those who hear will live" (5:25). Therefore, some have said that when Jesus called, "Lazarus, come out!" (11:43), he was careful to call his name, otherwise many other dead bodies might have "come out"!

The ultimate (eighth) sign, Jesus' death

The final countdown to Jesus' death and resurrection began "six days before Passover" (12:1), when "the lamb of God who takes away the sin of the world" would be slain (1:29,35). On the Friday, the sixth day of that last week, Pilate presented Jesus, "Here is the man!", and then "Here is your King!" (19:5,14). Jesus represented humanity, "*the* man", echoing the first Adam presented as God's image on the sixth day of creation. Then he 're-presented' Israel, "*your* King", the end-time Messiah who imaged God's Kingdom. When the crowd, and creation, looked at "the man" (Jesus), they saw the embodiment of bloodied and brutalised humanity, made in the image of sin and death (19:1f). When they looked at "your King", they saw God's suffering servant made in the image of rebellious Israel, i.e., the evil empire.

Isaiah *saw* it in 700 BC: "*See*, my servant will... be raised and lifted up and highly exalted... they were appalled at him – his appearance was so disfigured beyond that of any human being and his form marred beyond human likeness – so he will sprinkle many nations and kings will shut their mouths because of him" (52:13-15). John said that Isaiah "saw Jesus' glory and spoke about him" (John 12:41).

Thus, on that Friday, he who knew no sin became sin for us, that we may become the righteousness of God in him (2 Corinthians 5:21). Having made "at-one-ment" with God, Jesus cried out on the cross, "It is finished!" (John 19:30). He completed the work God gave him to do (5:36, 17:4), i.e., he completed the work of creation by his seven – and now ultimate – miraculous signs. Then he "bowed his head and gave up his spirit" (19:30) – he rested. This clearly alluded to God resting on the seventh day after finishing his work of creation (Genesis 2:1-2, *synteleo*, to complete, is used twice in the LXX).

Jesus rested literally, it was now the Sabbath, and symbolically, he lay in the garden tomb waiting for "the next day". Death entered the first garden of creation through sin in Adam. That garden had no tomb because God never intended humans to die. Death entered the garden again, in Jesus' body of sin. It had "a new tomb in which no one had ever laid" (John 19:41), i.e., God intended to reverse death through Jesus' resurrection, so that humans may live eternally.

Completion, Jesus' resurrection

Jesus rose again "early on the first day of the week" (20:1): Sunday, the eighth day of creation, the first day of new creation.

Mary came to the tomb "while it was still dark" (20:1), symbolising human hopelessness entombed by evil, wrapped in the power of sin and death. However, she "saw the stone had been removed" and the tomb was empty! The life and light of "the Word made flesh", which "shines in the darkness" (1:1-5, 14), defeated death. It was the dawn of a bright and beautiful new creation.

Mary ran off to tell Peter and John. They ran to see if it was true. She stood outside the tomb, crying. Then she peered in and saw two angels "in white, seated where Jesus' body *had been*" (20:12). Mary was dressed in black, mourning. They were in white, representing a whole new story, "Woman, why are you crying?"

The glory of God that rested between two cherubim in the Temple was no longer behind the veil or tombstone. The glory was/is out in the garden, in the home, on the street. The 'missing body' that lay between the angels is the Resurrected Temple, the new Ark of the Presence, giving mercy and forgiveness, "life from above" to all who "receive him" (1:12). The stone has been removed, heaven has broken out on earth, new creation has exploded with life in a broken creation.

Then Mary "turned around" to see (whom she supposed was) "the gardener" of the garden (20:14-15). He called her name, "Mary". Then she knew it was Jesus, risen! Overcome with joy, she wanted to "hold onto" him. John clearly connotes a) Adam in the first garden as the gardener (Genesis 2:15), b) naming the woman (2:23 cf. 3:20), and c) the two "cling" (2:24 NRSV, "hold fast to", ESV). Jesus rose in a garden bursting with blossoms and new life – it was spring (the northern hemisphere). Thus, he was the new Adam in the new garden of God's new creation. He tends new creation, transforming broken creation. He reveals himself to all who look for him, calling us by name, uniting with us, giving us the joy of the *eschaton*.

Then, "On the evening of that first day of the week" (20:19), Jesus appears to his disciples locked in a room. John should have said, "on the second day" – the new day began at sunset. Instead, he emphasises *the day* of Jesus' resurrection as if it continues the next day, and the next, forever. On that evening, Jesus, fresh from The Resurrection, breathes into his disciples, saying, "Receive the Holy Spirit" (20:22). John used the phrase from the LXX in Genesis 2:7, God "breathed into (Adam's) nostrils the breath of life" (also Ezekiel 37:5-6). The new Adam breathes eternal resurrection life into new Adams and Eves, creating a new humanity: "born again", "from above" (John 1:12-13, 3:3-8), by The Resurrection Spirit.

That was when, technically, the church was born with eternal life. And given the new creation mandate: "As the Father has sent me, I am sending you. If you forgive anyone's sins, their sins are forgiven; if you do not forgive them, they are not forgiven" (20:22-23). What authority! What a co-mission! The renewal of the creation mandate, "Be fruitful and increase in number; fill the earth..." (Genesis 1:28). In other words, "take the New Garden of Eden to the ends of the earth".

To conclude. Jesus' resurrection is the "first-fruit", the prototype, and *the* guarantee of "the renewal of all things" (Matthew 19:28, the *palingenesia,* the 'again-birthing' of creation). His resurrection, and our resurrection at his coming, is the earth's liberation from its curse and bondage (Romans 8:19-22). God will create "new heavens and a new earth" in final fulfilment of Isaiah 65:17, 66:22.

Consequently, if God's spoken Word, "Let there be..." (Genesis 1:3), was the 'Big Bang' of creation, then God's resurrected Word, "He is risen!" (Mark 16:6), is the 'Big Bang' of new creation. That new creation is expanding and will exponentially expand throughout the eternal ages, never to reach the infinite end of who God is.

ASCENSION OF JESUS AND ITS MEANING

Once we accept the historicity of Jesus' resurrection and the nature of his Spirit-saturated body, it is easy to accept that he ascended into the heavens. Luke is the only NT writer that described Jesus' ascension, so we work from Luke-Acts, integrating other sources.

After his resurrection, Jesus appeared to his disciples many times over forty days. He ate with them and taught them (more) "about the Kingdom of God" (Acts 1:3), as in his three-year ministry. Luke's focus is Jesus preparing them to receive "the gift my Father promised... in a few days you will be baptised with the Holy Spirit" (1:4-5). That would be the mode of his Kingship/Kingdom: the power of the Spirit in them, through them, to the world around them. It answers why he appeared to his disciples, then disappeared, over forty days before ascending into the heavens. *He weaned them from dependence on his visible bodily presence and prepared them to live by his invisible indwelling presence*: the gift of God's enabling Spirit. To live by faith and not by sight.

Preparation for the Coming of the Spirit

His apprentices were to learn to live by faith in Jesus' heavenly rule, experienced in/through them on earth by his outpoured Spirit.

- A return to the garden before the fall when Adam and Eve lived by God's inbreathed Spirit and presence, exercising God's rule over creation. Their temptation was the idol of the visible, the lust of the eye and of the flesh (Genesis 3:4-7).

- A return to *Yhwh's* invisible Kingship over Israel. That is, till they demanded a visible "king to lead us, as all other nations have" (1 Samuel 8:5). It was a personal rejection of "me (*Yhwh*) as their King" (8:7). People crave a visible leader, a heroic saviour. God gave it to them – the 'compromise' of Israel's monarchy – warning them of the consequences. No fallen human being can ultimately substitute God's direct Kingship.

- Jesus was God's incarnate Rule on earth. As the new Adam and Israel's true King, he lived by the Father's invisible presence in the power of the indwelling Spirit. By faith, he only did what he saw his Father doing, and spoke what he heard his Father saying (John 5:19-20). He modelled life lived by God's invisible ruling presence. His followers are called to live like him.

In John 14-16, Jesus prepared his apprentices for his ascension. He must return to the Father *so that* the Spirit will come, *so that* they live by the Spirit – "another *Parakletos*" – counsellor, comforter, advocate, intercessor, and helper. He "will be with you forever. You know him, for he lives *with* you and will be *in* you" (14:16-17). Jesus was the *Parakletos with* them in his ministry, but he will send "another" to be *in* them, i.e., the Holy Spirit will be Jesus in and through them. Hence, Jesus must ascend so that the Spirit descends to live in them.

Commissioning before the Ascension

Thus, Jesus instructed his apprentices *not* to be focussed on "the times or dates" when the Kingdom will be consummated *in his bodily reign on earth* (Acts 1:6-7). Until then, while he ruled from heaven, they were his body on earth. Instead, they were to focus on receiving the dynamite (*dynamis,* "power") of the Spirit (1:8) that will explode them outwards as his Kingdom witnesses, from Jerusalem, to Judea and Samaria, to the ends of the earth. "Witness", *martureo,* in Acts 1:8 is 'martyr'. The indwelling Spirit will empower them to lay down their lives in witness to King Jesus, as he laid down his life in witness to his Father, to bring the Kingdom to Israel and the nations.

This was Jesus' commission to his community before ascending to heaven, summarising the version in Luke's gospel: "repentance for the forgiveness of sins will be preached in Messiah's name to all nations, beginning at Jerusalem. You are witnesses of these things. I am going to send you what my Father has promised; but stay in the city until you have been clothed with power from on high" (24:47-49). 'Clothed' was the language of identity. Jesus' apprentices would be mantled and marked by the Spirit's power to destroy the works of the devil as Jesus did (1 John 3:8), advancing his Kingdom to all nations. This is the love of Jesus that identifies us as his disciples (John 13:35).

In John, Jesus' commission is when he breathed his Spirit into his disciples, giving his new creation mandate, discussed earlier. John emphasised more the Spirit's work of regeneration, as did Paul in his letters. Luke's focus was the Spirit coming on God's people in power to do God's work, as in a) Jesus' mission, "The Spirit of the Lord is upon me because he has anointed me to..." (Luke 4:18), and b) Peter's explanation of Pentecost: the fulfillment of the promise to empower God's people with his eschatological Spirit (Acts 2:14-21, quoting Joel 2:28-31). Both works of the Spirit, the purification/new life *and* the anointing/empowering, come from the OT. John and Paul's emphasis versus Luke's emphasis, is not contradictory, but complementary, as Keener has carefully shown (2003b:1203-8. Also 1997, 2001).

Matthew's 'Great Commission', commonly called, recorded Jesus' last words before he ascended: "All authority in heaven and on earth has been given to me. Therefore, go and make disciples of all nations..." This refers directly to Daniel 7:13-14. Matthew is saying that Jesus' death, resurrection, and ascension into heaven literally fulfils Daniel's vision of the Son of Man's suffering and triumph. Jesus gave *"all* authority" to his community, "the saints of the Most High" (Daniel 7:18,27), who take his Kingdom to *"all* peoples, nations from every language", who, in turn, worship him (7:14).

In Mark 16:15-20 (verses not in the earliest manuscripts), Jesus' commission is to "Go into all the world and preach the gospel to all creation" with miraculous Kingdom signs and wonders. "After the Lord Jesus had spoken to them, he was taken up into heaven and he sat at the right hand of God. Then the disciples went out and preached everywhere, and the Lord worked with them and confirmed his word by the signs that accompanied it". Mark's account affirms all the elements in the other three commissionings.

Jesus' Ascension and its Meaning

Luke's eyewitness account is that Jesus "led them (his disciples) to the vicinity of Bethany, lifted up his hands and blessed them. While he was blessing them, he left them and was taken up into heaven" (Luke 24:50-51). Jesus went up in a cloud (Acts 1:9), and while they "were looking intently up into the sky as he was going", two angels dressed in white stood with them. They said, "This same Jesus... will come back in the same way you have seen him go into heaven" (1:11), i.e., he went up in a cloud and he will come back in a cloud. It again recalls Daniel 7:13f, Jesus' suffering, triumph, and return as "the Son of man coming in a cloud with great power and glory" (Luke 21:27).

This event was literal, not metaphorical. It was unsurprising to Jesus' apprentices, due to his resurrection, forty days of appearing and disappearing, and how he prepared them for his departure. Also, Jews knew Elijah was taken up into heaven. As explained earlier, Luke connotes Jesus as the Elijah (Israel's mighty prophet) taken up while Elisha watched (Jesus' prophetic community), giving his Spirit-mantle to Elisha (the Pentecost outpouring, Acts 2:1f). This made Jesus' ascension and outpouring of the Spirit one continuous event.

What, then, is the significance and meaning of Jesus' ascension?

Ruling King. The phrase most associated with Jesus' ascension is "exalted to... sat down at... *the right hand of God*" (Acts 2:33-34). In fact, Psalm 110:1 is the most quoted OT text in the NT. Jesus' ascension on a cloud was the Son of Man's coronation. He was given all authority in heaven and earth. Peter preached, "God has made this Jesus, whom you crucified, both Lord (*Kyrios*) and Christ (*Christos*)" (Acts 2:36 cf. 5:31, 13:33). The OT LXX translates *Yhwh* as *Kyrios*, and *Meshiach* as *Christos* (Messiah-King). Thus, Peter spoke of Jesus as the divine Lord of lords and King of kings. Hence, "All rule and authority, power and dominion, and every name that is invoked, not only in the present age but also in the one to come", is accountable to King Jesus (Ephesians 1:21). He rules from heaven till all his enemies are under his feet – when he returns to set up his Kingdom on earth. Then death, the last enemy, will be defeated in The Resurrection.

Coming Judge. Jesus' ascension means he is not only the Saviour-King of all who believe, but the Judge of all, "of the living and the dead" (Acts 10:39-43, 17:31). Paul also speaks of Jesus as the judge in 2 Corinthians 5:10. It's what Jesus taught: "the Father has given him authority to judge *because he is the Son of Man*" – to be exercised in full at the end, at The Resurrection (John 5:27-30 cf. Daniel 12:2). Jesus will return in judgement of all who reject him and his Kingdom. Again, Jesus' divinity is assumed (see below).

High Priest. Jesus' ascension fulfilled the role of the High Priest. Beside "the Son of David", Jewish messianic expectation included a High Priest, i.e., a Royal Priest. For example, the Essene community referred to the Messiah as Melchizedek, the divine High Priest of Genesis 14 and Psalm 110. The writer of 11Q13 in the Dead Sea Scrolls (Wise *et al* 2005:590-3) cited Isaiah 61:2, "this is the time decreed for 'the year of Melchizedek's favour'". He substituted Melchizedek for *Yhwh* in "the year of the LORD'S favour". Thus, *Yhwh* will come as Melchizedek in a jubilee year to institute the (eternal) Messianic Jubilee. This High Priest Messiah atones for sin and judges the wicked (the writer quoted Psalm 82:1-2). Hence, Wise *et al* conclude, "Clearly, Melchizedek was a focus of powerful salvific imagery among various Jewish groups in the period of the scrolls."

Hebrews 7-9 taught Jesus was the High Priest-Melchizedek-figure, the human-divine Messiah. He ascended into the Holiest of Holies, cleansing "the heavenly things" with his blood of atonement, having "obtained eternal salvation" (9:12, 23-26). A human body is in God's immediate presence, opening the way for others to enter. Jesus "appears *for us* in God's presence" (9:24), representing us. And he "empathizes with our weaknesses", giving "mercy and grace in our time of need" (4:14-16). How? By his indwelling Spirit. Thus, he "ever lives to intercede *for* us" at God's right hand (7:25), while his Spirit intercedes *in* us "according to the will of God", according to the mind of Christ (Romans 8:26-27, 34). Because Jesus is *the* God-man and the *only* true mediator between God and humans (1 Timothy 2:5).

Outpoured Spirit. Jesus' ascension was the outpouring of the Spirit fulfilling "the gift my Father promised" (Acts 1:4). In obedience to Jesus' instruction, his apprentices returned to Jerusalem after his ascension and waited prayerfully for the Spirit to come. It took nine days. Then, on the tenth, the day of Pentecost, the Spirit came upon them (Acts 2:1f). 'Pentecost' meant 'fifty' days after Passover – after his crucifixion and resurrection. Jesus literally fulfilled the Passover feast. Now he literally fulfilled Pentecost, the Feast of *Shavuot,* 'the harvest'. The Spirit's outpouring at Pentecost began the great end-time harvest of the nations into God's Kingdom.

Jesus' disciples all "spoke in tongues" (2:4), being filled with the 'prophetic' Holy Spirit. They supernaturally spoke in the languages from the Jewish diaspora at the feast, "from every nation under heaven" (2:5-11). People heard "the wonders of God" in their language and three thousand put their faith in King Jesus and entered the Kingdom. This reversed the Tower of Babel where God used "speaking in tongues", different languages, in judgment, to scatter human pride into "the nations" (Genesis 11). Now God uses it to gather, reconcile, and unite all the nations under Jesus' Kingship. This eschatological harvest continues to the ends of the earth, till Jesus returns on the clouds of glory.

CHRISTOLOGY AND THE GOSPEL WE PREACH

We now return to where we began. I asked two questions in my preface. Who was (is) Jesus, *really*? And who is the Jesus we preach, or what is the gospel? A concluding answer to both is appropriate.

Christology

To *Know the Real Jesus,* we have focused on the man of history in his humanity. Jesus was an end-time Jewish apocalyptic prophet who claimed to be *the* Messiah and was vindicated as such by being resurrected from the dead (Romans 1:4). It raises the question: was he divine? His first followers came to believe, certainly after his resurrection, that Jesus was human *and* divine – called 'early high Christology'. They identified *Yeshua ha Notzri* as the risen and exalted "Lord and Christ" (Acts 2:26). Hence, they confidently identified Jesus with the one true God of Israel.

Our Christology – study of his birth, ministry, death, resurrection, and ascension – leads us to conclude that he could not have done what he did, been who he was, if he was not divine – in some real sense. As Pope Benedict XVI (Ratzinger 2007:3-8) said, we cannot make ultimate sense of the evidence of the historical Jesus without assuming his divinity. Or else we would have to conclude he was a blasphemer, imposter, joker, or psychotic (insane).

What did it mean if Jesus had two natures, human and divine in one person? Did his followers impose it on him? Did *he* believe he was divine? When did he 'become' God? How did his followers reconcile him with the one true God of Israel in their Jewish monotheism? It's a big topic beyond the scope of this book. I merely offer a summary. I recommend reading opposing views debated side by side, as in Borg & Wright (200:145-68), and Ehrman, Bird & Stewart (2022).

See Bauckham (2009) and Fletcher-Louis (2015) for complete studies. Fletcher-Louis' argument is: "The historical Jesus believed himself to be uniquely included – as one who served as Israel's royal and priestly Messiah and as a fully divine person – within the identity of the one God (as the 'Son' of the 'Father')" (2015:xiv). Jesus' human-divine consciousness was represented and interpreted in the NT writings. I give a sample of references in the next section.

We must start with *Jewish* monotheism. God as "one" in the credal *Shema* (Deuteronomy 6:4) is not *yachid*, Hebrew for single or "one and only", used of Isaac in Genesis 22:2f. It was *echad*, a unity of one, as in "Let *us* make...", Genesis 1:26. Jews saw *Yhwh* as a composite unity, manifested in personified Spirit, Word/Law, Glory/Presence, and Wisdom – all involved in creation and covenant, through which God revealed himself. So, in this Jewish understanding, Jesus could identify himself and be identified with *Yhwh* as divine – though blasphemous for some. Note that this idea is fundamentally different to Roman imperial worship, or pagan multiple gods, or pantheism.

Overview of Selected References to Jesus' Divinity

Paul's 'Jesus-monotheism'. In the earliest NT manuscripts available to us, Paul adapted the *Shema* by placing Jesus in it: "there is but one God, the Father, from whom all things came and for whom we live; and there is but one Lord, Jesus Christ, through whom all things came and through whom we live" (1 Corinthians 8:6). Hence, the "one God" is the "one Lord", both "the Father" and "Jesus Christ".

Paul also used Isaiah's monotheism in 40-55 to celebrate Jesus' universal Lordship in Philippians 2:6-11. As *Yhwh* defeated the pagan gods, where "Before me every knee will bow; by me every tongue will confess" (Isaiah 45:23); Jesus triumphed over all evil powers, where "At the name of Jesus every knee should bow in heaven and on earth and under the earth, and every tongue confess that Jesus Christ is Lord, to the glory of God the Father" (Philippians 2:9-11). In this poem or 'credal hymn', Jesus was "in very nature God" in his eternal pre-existence. Yet he did not grasp and use that "equality with God" to "his own advantage". He "emptied himself" (*kenosis*) in his incarnation in a human body and was obedient to death, then vindicated as "Lord and Christ" over all. Paul also praises Jesus' pre-existence and role in creation and redemption as divine Wisdom, taken from Proverbs 8 (Colossians 1:15-20, all God's "fullness dwell in him").

The synoptics and Christology. Mark began his gospel with "the gospel about Jesus Christ, the Son of God" (Mark 1:1), which is "the gospel of God" (1:14). He described John's ministry by quoting Malachi 3:1 and Isaiah 40:3, "Prepare the way for the LORD, make straight in the desert a highway for our God" (1:2-3). Jesus is *Yhwh* coming to save his people in a new Exodus. Jesus forgives sin, but only God can forgive sin (2:5-12). As the sailors cry to their gods in Jonah 1:5, and to *Yhwh* in Psalm 107:23-30 – God stilled the storm – so the disciples cry to Jesus, who stills the storm (4:35-41, "terrified, they asked, 'Who is this? Even the wind and waves obey him!'").

Jesus is part of the divine identity. We see it in Matthew's gospel *inclusio*. At birth, Jesus is called Immanuel, "God is with us" (from Isaiah 7:14), and is worshipped (1:23, 2:2,11). He is then worshipped at his ascension while saying, "surely I am with you always, to the very end of the age" (28:17,20). Jesus is God with us, always.

In Luke-Acts, Jesus did on earth and continues to do from heaven, God's mission by doing God's deeds, just as *Yhwh* did by the power of his Spirit in the OT. In Luke 19:44, Jesus claimed his climactic trip to Jerusalem was a divine visitation, that God came to her, but she did not recognise it.

John's high Christology. Jesus' consciousness and claims of divinity proliferate John's gospel. Many scholars dismiss it as the later emergence of insipient 'Christian Trinitarianism'. Despite John's theological framing, others see John's gospel as a reliable account of the historical Jesus. Jesus is the eternal Word (*Logos*) who was with God, and was God (1:1,18). He "became flesh" (1:14): God was incarnate in Jesus. As "the Son", he revealed "the Father" (1:14-18, 5:19f). "Son of God" takes on divinity, e.g., "I and the Father are one" (10:28-30). It is also evident in Jesus' "I AM" declarations (6:35; 8:12, 24,58; 10:7,11; 11:25; 14:6; 15:1), echoing *Yhwh's* identity in Exodus 3:14. And "Son of Man" refers to Jesus' divinity: he "came from heaven" and will "ascend to where he was before" (3:13, 6:62).

The book of Hebrews. Though scholars debate the authorship and date of Hebrews, its high Christology is not in doubt. Chapter 1 describes Jesus' full divinity as God's Son, superior to the angels: "heir of all things... through whom he made the universe... the radiance of God's glory... exact representation of God's being, sustaining all things by his powerful word" (2-3). Chapter 2 describes Jesus' full humanity "made lower than the angels for a little while... so that by the grace of God he might taste death for everyone... to bring many sons and daughters to glory" (9-10). Both his divinity and humanity together uniquely qualify him to be the perfect messianic High Priest, described in chapters 4–10. I earlier elaborated on his role as High Priest.

Heresies and the church creeds. In the first few centuries, NT church letters and writings evidence contrary views of Jesus' identity. Bird (2017) examines the origin and falsity of the 'Adoptionist Christology' that arose. It claimed that Jesus was not originally God or divine, but that he was 'adopted' as God's Son (i.e., became God/divine) at his baptism, or transfiguration, or resurrection and ascension – or even at his birth. The arguments are laid out in the debate by Ehrman, Bird & Stewart (2022). Bird's other study of Christology lists and explains all the heresies that arose regarding Jesus' identity and nature as human and divine (2020:517-46). These variant views led to the assertion of the orthodox apostolic consensus – the above 'early high Christology'. That occurred through the first ecumenical councils where Christology was 'hammered out' in prayerful debate and consensus, then carefully worded in the early creeds (Apostolic, Nicaean, Athanasian, Chalcedonian).

The consensus, in short, was that Jesus was/is simultaneously fully human and fully divine, without confusion or assimilation of one nature into the other, or domination of one over the other.

The point of our historical Jesus study is that we don't start with our notion of God and define Jesus by it. We begin with Jesus. He came to reveal God. He (in)forms our notion of God and humanity, as in this quote from N.T. Wright,

> "If you want to know who God is, look at Jesus. If you want to know what it means to be human, look at Jesus. If you want to know what love is, look at Jesus. If you want to know what grief is, look at Jesus. Go on looking until you're not just a spectator, but you're actually part of the drama which has him as the central character." (https://www.azquotes.com/quote/882880)

The Gospel

This then leads to the second question, what is the gospel we preach? As I emphasised in my preface, the Jesus we see is the gospel we preach, which is the (S)spirit we impart. This is so serious that Paul warned, "If anybody is preaching to you a gospel other than the one we preached to you, let them be under God's curse!" (Galatians 1:8-9).

In short, Paul and the apostles preached the good news of King Jesus and his Kingdom come... and coming in fullness to wrap up and renew all things at the end of this present evil age.

The gospel has been notoriously reduced to doctrinal emphases, cultural formations, and feel-good fads in the epochs of the church. At the end of my lengthy introduction, I listed thirteen such variant 'gospels', each flowing from the 'Jesus' preached, imparting its particular spirit, for better or for worse. The reader may want to review them again.

As with Christology, the gospel – in its definition, meaning, and content – has become a hot topic of debate in our day. Wright (2012) and McKnight (2016) have written books on the authentic gospel of King Jesus. It's also been a Vineyard debate, with a view to retrieving the gospel of the Kingdom (see Morphew ed. 2020).

The biblical gospel, in summary, is the good news that,

- God is King and is becoming King,
- Through Jesus of Nazareth,
- In his birth, life, ministry, death, resurrection, and ascension,
- The Messiah, who rules and reigns now and forever,

- Forgiving sin, giving eternal life, healing and delivering from evil, bringing justice, putting things right, making all things new,
- For all who believe him, who declare allegiance to his Kingship in all of life,
- Leading to wholistic transformation: personally, politically, socially, environmentally, and ultimately, of all cosmic reality,
- In assurance of the King's return to establish his Kingdom on earth, where his will is done as in heaven.

I close with the words of King Jesus, "This gospel of the Kingdom will be preached in the whole world as a testimony to all nations, and then the end will come" (Matthew 24:14).

Let us obey the King.

QUESTIONS FOR REFLECTION AND DISCUSSION

1. What do you make of Jesus' resurrection? Do you believe he rose again? If so, how has it changed your life?

2. Do you agree with the arguments for the historical probability of Jesus' bodily resurrection? What would you argue differently?

3. How would you describe the nature of Jesus' post-resurrection appearances to his disciples? And the nature of his body?

4. In your understanding, why did Jesus appear and disappear over forty days?

5. What is the significance and meaning of Jesus' ascension?

6. Having looked at this portrait of Jesus, how would you answer the question, who was/is Jesus, *really*?

7. And what is your summary statement of 'the gospel', the good news of Jesus that you believe and preach?

BIBLIOGRAPHY OF REFERENCES

Allen, Charlotte 1999. *The Human Christ: The Search for the Historical Jesus,* Oxford and New York: Lion and Free Press.

Archer, Gleeson L, Jr. 1985. *Daniel,* in Gaebelein F.E (Gen. Ed.), *The Expositor's Bible Commentary, Volume 7,* Grand Rapids: Zondervan Publishing House.

Aulen, Gustaf 1970 (1931 First Edition). *Christus Victor: An Historical Study of the Three Main Types of the Idea of the Atonement,* London: SPCK.

Bauckham, Richard 2006. *Jesus and the Eyewitnesses: The Gospels as Eyewitness Testimony,* Grand Rapids: Eerdmans.
2009. *Jesus and the God of Israel: God Crucified and Other Studies on the New Testament's Christology of Divine Identity,* Grand Rapids: Eerdmans.

Bird, Michael F 2017. *Jesus the Eternal Son: Answering Adoptionist Christology,* Grand Rapids: Eerdmans.
2020 (Second Edition). *Evangelical Theology: A Biblical and Systematic Introduction,* Grand Rapids: Zondervan.

Bock, Darrell 2002. *Studying the Historical Jesus: A Guide to Sources and Methods,* Grand Rapids: Baker Academic.

Bonhoeffer, Dietrich 1963 (1937 first published, translated by John W Doberstein). *The Cost of Discipleship,* New York: MacMillan Publishing.

Borg Marcus 1987. *Jesus: A New Vision,* HarperSanFrancisco.
1994. *Meeting Jesus Again for the First Time: The Historical Jesus & the Heart of Contemporary Faith,* HarperSanFrancisco.

Borg, Marcus & Wright, N.T. 2000. *The Meaning of Jesus: Two Visions,* HarperSanFrancisco.

Bornkamm, Gunter 1960. *Jesus of Nazareth*, New York: Harper & Row.

Bosch, David 1991. *Transforming Mission: Paradigm Shifts in Theology of Missions*, Maryknoll: Orbis books.

Brandon, S G F 1968. *The Trial of Jesus of Nazareth*, London: Batsford Publishers.

Brown, Colin 1984. *Miracles and the Critical Mind*, Grand Rapids: Eerdmans.

Brown, Raymond E 1977. *The Birth of the Messiah: A Commentary on the Infancy Narratives in Matthew and Luke*, Garden City: Doubleday.

Bultmann, Rudolf 1961. *Kerygma and Myth: A Theological Debate*, New York: Harper & Row.

Caragounis, Chrys 1986. *The Son of Man: Vision and Interpretation*, Tübingen: Mohr Siebeck.

Carson, D A 1991. *The Gospel According to John*, Grand Rapids: Eerdmans.

Charlesworth, James H 1988. *Jesus within Judaism: New Light from Exciting Archaeological Discoveries*, London: SPCK.

Charlesworth, James H (ed.) 1983a. *The Old Testament Pseudepigrapha, Volume One: Apocalyptic Literature and Testaments*, Peabody: Hendrickson Publishers.
1983b. *Volume Two: Expansions of the Old Testament and Legends, Wisdom and Philosophical Literature, Prayers, Psalms, and Odes, Fragments of Lost Judeo-Hellenistic Works*, Peabody: Hendrickson Publishers.
1991 (ed.) *Jesus' Jewishness: Exploring the Place of Jesus in Early Judaism*, New York: Crossroad Publishing Company.
2006 (ed.). *The Bible and the Dead Sea Scrolls: Volume Three, The Scrolls and Christian Origins*, Waco: Baylor University Press.

Chilton, Bruce D 1984. *A Galilean Rabbi and his Bible*, Wilmington: Michael Glasser.
1996. *Pure Kingdom: Jesus' Vision of God*, Grand Rapids: Eerdmans.
2000. *Rabbi Jesus: An Intimate Biography – The Jewish Life and Teachings that Inspired Christianity*, London: Image Books.

Cohen, Abraham 1949. *Everyman's Talmud: The Major Teachings of the Rabbinic Sages*, New York: Schocken Books.

Crossan, Dominic J 1991. *The Historical Jesus: The Life of a Mediterranean Jewish Peasant*, HarperSanFrancisco.

Cullmann, Oscar 1952. *Christ and Time: The Primitive Christian Conception of Time and History*, London: SCM.

Dunn, James 2003. *Christianity in the Making, Volume I, Jesus Remembered*, Grand Rapids: Eerdmans.
2005. *A New Perspective on Jesus: What the Quest for the Historical Jesus Missed*, Grand Rapids: Baker.
2009. *Christianity in the Making, Volume II, Beginning from Jerusalem*, Grand Rapids: Eerdmans.
2019. *Jesus According to the New Testament*, Grand Rapids: Eerdmans.

Dunn, James and McKnight, Scot (eds.) 2005. *The Historical Jesus in Recent Research*, Winona Lake: Eisenbrauns.

Ehrman, Bart D, Bird, Michael F, and Stewart, Robert B 2022, *When did Jesus become God? A Christological Debate*, Louisville: Westminster John Knox Press.

Fletcher-Louis, Chrispin 2015, *Jesus Monotheism. Volume 1, Christological Origins: The Emerging Consensus and Beyond*, Toddington: Whymanity Publishing.

Flusser, David 1987. *Jewish Sources in Early Christianity*, New York: Adama Books.
2007. *The Sage from Galilee: Rediscovering Jesus' Genius*, Grand Rapids: Eerdmans.

Freyne, Sean 2004. *Jesus, A Jewish Galilean: A New Reading of the Jesus Story*, London: T & T Clark International.
2008. *Galilee, Jesus and the Contribution of Archaeology*, in The Expository Times, Volume 119 Number 12, pp. 573-581.
2014. *The Jesus Movement and Its Expansion: Meaning and Mission*, Grand Rapids: Eerdmans.

Funk, Robert W 1996. *Honest to Jesus: Jesus for a New Millennium*, HarperSanFrancisco.

1998. *The Acts of Jesus: The Search for the Authentic Deeds of Jesus,* HarperSanFrancisco.

Funk, Robert W & Hoover, Roy W 1993. *The Five Gospels: The Search for the Authentic Words of Jesus,* New York: Macmillan.

Gentry, Peter J 2003. *The Son of Man in Daniel 7: Individual or Corporate?,* in Michael A. G. Haykin (ed.), *Acorns to Oaks: The Primacy and Practice of Biblical Theology,* Toronto: Joshua, 59–75.

Hamilton Jr., James M 2014. *With the Clouds of Heaven: The Book of Daniel in Biblical Theology,* in Cardon, D.A. (Series Ed.), New Studies in Biblical Theology 32, Downer Grove: InterVarsity Press.

Heiser, Michael S 2015. *The Unseen Realm: Recovering the Supernatural Worldview of the Bible,* Bellingham: Lexham Press.

Hengel, Martin 1968 (1981 Second Edition). *The Charismatic Leader and his Followers,* New York: Crossroads Publishing.
1971. *Victory over Violence: Jesus and the Revolutionists,* Philadelphia, Fortress.

Holmes, Michael W (ed.) 1989. *The Apostolic Fathers, Second Edition,* (translated by J. B. Lightfoot and J. R. Harmer) Grand Rapids: Baker Books.

Jeremias, Joachim 1949. *The Last Supper,* The Journal of Theological Studies Volume OS-L; issue 1, pp.1-10.
1958. *Jesus' Promise to the Nations,* Naperville: Allenson.

Josephus, Flavius 1987, translated by William Whiston. *The Works of Josephus: Complete and Unabridged – New Updated Version,* Peabody: Hendrickson Publishers.

Kahler, Martin 1964 (1892 First Edition). *The So-called Historical Jesus, and the Historic, Biblical Christ,* Philadelphia: Fortress.

Kallas, James 1961. *The Significance of the Synoptic Miracles: Taking the Worldview of Jesus Seriously,* Woodinville: Harmon Press.
1966. *The Satanward View: A Study in Pauline Theology,* Philadelphia: Westminster Press.
1968. *Jesus and the Power of Satan,* Philadelphia: Westminster.
1975. *The Real Satan,* Augsburg: Fortress.

Kasemann, Ernst 1964. *Essays on New Testament Themes*, London: SCM.

Keener, Craig 1997, *The Spirit in the Gospels and Acts: Divine Purity and Power*, Peabody: Hendrickson Publishers.
2001. *Gift & Giver: The Holy Spirit for Today*, Grand Rapids: Baker Academic.
2003a. *The Gospel of John: A Commentary*, Volume One, Grand Rapids: Baker Academic.
2003b. *The Gospel of John: A Commentary*, Volume Two, Grand Rapids: Baker Academic.
2009. *The Historical Jesus of the Gospels*, Grand Rapids: Eerdmans.
2011. *Miracles: The Credibility of the New Testament Accounts*, 2 Volumes, Grand Rapids: Baker Academic.
2012. *Acts: An Exegetical Commentary Volume 1*, Grand Rapids: Baker Academic.
2014 (Second Edition). *The IVP Bible Background Commentary: New Testament – Second Edition*, Downers Grove: IVP.
2019. *Christobiography: Memory, History, and the Reliability of the Gospels*, Grand Rapids: Eerdmans.

Kloppenborg, J S 1994. *The Shape of Q*, Minneapolis: Fortress.

Koester, Helmut 1990. *Ancient Christian Gospels: Their History and Development*, London: SCM.

König, Adrio 1982. *Here I Am!: A Christian Reflection on God*, London: Marshall, Morgan & Scott.
1988. *New and Greater Things: Re-evaluating the Biblical Message on Creation*, Pretoria: University of South Africa.
1989. *The Eclipse of Christ in Eschatology*, Grand Rapids: Eerdmans.
2004. *Jesus, Name Above All Names: Revealing The Heart of Christianity*, Wellington: Lux Verbi.BM.

Kummel W G 1961. *Promise and Fulfilment: The Eschatological Message of Jesus*, London: SCM.
1974. *The Theology of the New Testament*, London: SCM.

Ladd, George Eldron 1959. *The Gospel of the Kingdom: Popular Expositions on the Kingdom of God*, Grand Rapids: Eerdmans.
1974a. *The Presence of the Future*, Grand Rapids: Eerdmans.
1974b. *A Theology of the New Testament*, Grand Rapids: Eerdmans.

Lane, William L 1974. *The Gospel of Mark*, The New International Commentary on the New Testament, Grand Rapids: Eerdmans.

Lewis, C S 1960. *The Four Loves*, London: Geoffrey Bles Publishers.

Mack, Burton L 1995. *Who Wrote the New Testament? The Making of the Christian Myth*, HarperSanFrancisco.

Mason, Steve 2009. *Josephus, Judea, and Christian Origins: Methods and Categories*, Peabody: Hendrikson Publishers.

McKnight, Scot 2005. *Jesus and His Death: Historiography, the Historical Jesus, and Atonement Theory*, Waco: Baylor University Press.
2016 (revised edition). *The King Jesus Gospel: The Original Good News Revisited*, Grand Rapids: Zondervan.

Meier, John P 1991. *The Marginal Jew, Rethinking the Historical Jesus, Volume I, The Roots of the Problem and the Person*, New York: Doubleday.
1994. *The Marginal Jew, Rethinking the Historical Jesus, Volume II, Mentor, Message, and Miracles*, New York: Doubleday.
2001. *The Marginal Jew, Rethinking the Historical Jesus, Volume III, Companions and Competitors*, New York: Doubleday.
2009. *A Marginal Jew: Rethinking the Historical Jesus, Volume IV: Law and Love*, New York: Doubleday, 2009.
2016. *A Marginal Jew: Rethinking the Historical Jesus, Volume V: Probing the Authenticity of the Parables*, Yale University Press.

Metzger, Bruce M (ed.) 1957. *The Apocrypha of the Old Testament, Revised Standard Edition*, New York: Oxford University Press.

Meyer, Ben F 1979. *The Aims of Jesus*, London: SCM.
1989. *Critical Realism and the New Testament*, Princeton Theological Monographs 17, Allison Park: Pickwick Publications.
1994. *Reality and Illusion in New Testament Scholarship: A Primer in Critical Realist Hermeneutics*, Collegeville: Liturgical Press.

Moltmann, Jürgen 1974. *The Crucified God*, London: SCM Press.

Montgomery, James A. 1972 (1st Edition 1927). *A Critical and Exegetical Commentary on The Book of Daniel*, Edinburgh: T & T Clark.

Morphew, Derek 1980. *A Critical Examination of the Infancy Narratives in the Gospels according to Matthew and Luke*, PhD thesis submitted

to Faculty of Arts at the University of Cape Town.
2019. *Breakthrough: Discovery the Kingdom, Fifth Edition*, Cape Town, Vineyard International Publishing (first edition 1991).
2020. *The Kingdom Reformation: Rediscover Jesus, Review Everything*, Cape Town, Vineyard International Publishing.

Morphew, Derek (ed. 2020, with Thomas Creedy, Woudineh Endayelalu, John Fischer, Thomas Lyons, & Neal Swettenham). *Atonement and the Kingdom: Reviewing Atonement and Retrieving the Gospel*, Cape Town: VIP.

Naugle, David K 2002. *Worldview: The History of a Concept*, Grand Rapids: Eerdmans.

Neusner, Jacob 1984. *Judaism in the Beginning of Christianity*, Augsburg: Fortress Press.
1990 (ed.) *Origins of Judaism, Volume II*, New York: Garland. 1993. *Rabbinic Literature and the New Testament. What We Cannot Show, We Do Not Know*, Eugene: Wipf and Stock.
2000. *A Rabbi Talks with Jesus*, McGill-Queen's University Press.
2002. *Judaism when Christianity Began: A survey of Belief and Practice*, Louisville: Westminster John Knox Press.

O'Collins, Gerald SJ. 2008. *Jesus: A Portrait*, London: Darton, Longman & Todd, 2008.

Pannenberg, Wolfhart 1991. *Systematic Theology Volume One* (translated by Geoffrey Bromiley), Grand Rapids: Eerdmans.
1994. *Systematic Theology Volume Two* (translated by Geoffrey Bromiley), Grand Rapids: Eerdmans.
1998. *Systematic Theology Volume One* (translated by Geoffrey Bromiley), Grand Rapids: Eerdmans.

Ratzinger, Jospeh (Pope Benedict XVI) 2007, *Jesus of Nazareth: From the Baptism of the Jordan to the Transfiguration* (translated by Adrian J Walker), London: Doubleday.

Reimarus, H.S. 1970 (1778). *Fragments*, edited by Charles H Talbert, Philadelphia: Fortress.

Robinson, James M 1959. *A New Quest for the Historical Jesus, Studies in Biblical Theology*, London: SCM.
1988. Editor, *The Nag Hammadi Library, Revised Edition*,

HarperSanFrancisco.

Sanders, E P 1985. *Jesus and Judaism,* London: SCM.
1993. *The Historical Figure of Jesus,* London: Penguin Books.

Schweitzer, Albert 1954 (1906). *The Quest for the Historical Jesus: A Critical Study of its Progress from Reimarus to Wrede,* London: A. & C. Black.

Snodgrass, Klyne R 2008. *Stories with Intent: A Comprehensive Guide to the Parables of Jesus,* Grand Rapids: Eerdmans.

Sommer, Benjamin D. 2009. *The Bodies of God and the World of Ancient Israel,* Cambridge University Press.

Stassen, Glen H & Gushee, David P 2003. *Kingdom Ethics: Following Jesus in Contemporary Context,* Downers Grove: IVP Academic.

Strauss, David Fredrich 1972 (1835 First Edition). *Life of Jesus Critically Examined,* Philadelphia: Fortress.

Twelftree, Graham 1985. *Christ Triumphant: Exorcism Then and Now,* Hodder and Stoughton.
1993. *Jesus the Exorcist: A Contribution to the Study of the Historical Jesus,* Tubingen: Mohr Siebeck.
1999. *A Historical and Theological Study: Jesus the Miracle Worker,* Illinois: InterVarsity Press.
2007. *In the Name of Jesus: Exorcism among Early Christians,* Grand Rapids: Baker.
2011. *The Cambridge Companion to Miracles,* Cambridge: Cambridge University Press.
2013. *Paul and the Miraculous,* Grand Rapids, MI: Baker Academic.

Van Voorst, Robert E 2000. *Jesus Outside the New Testament: An Introduction to the Ancient Evidence,* Grand Rapids: Eerdmans.

Venter, Alexander F 2004. *Doing Reconciliation: Racism, Reconciliation and Transformation in the Church and World,* Cape Town: VIP.
2010 (Revised Edition). *Doing Church: Building from the Bottom Up,* Cape Town: VIP.
2018 (Revised Edition). *Doing Healing: How to Minister God's Kingdom in the Power of the Spirit,* South Africa: Kingdom Treasures.

2019. *Doing Spirituality: The Journey of Character Formation toward Christlikeness,* South Africa: Kingdom Treasures.

Vermes, Geza 1961. *Scripture and Tradition in Judaism, Haggadic Studies,* Leiden: Brill.
1973. *Jesus the Jew: A Historian's Reading of the Gospels,* London: Collins.
1981. *The Gospel of Jesus the Jew,* New Castle: University of Newcastle on Tyne.
1983. *Jesus and the World of Judaism,* London: SCM.

Wise, Michael, Martin Abegg, & Edward Cook (eds.) 2005 (Revised Edition). *The Dead Sea Scrolls, A New Translation,* New York: Harper Collins.

Wrede, William 1902 (1971, translated by J. C. G. Greig). *The Messianic Secret,* Cambridge: James Clark.

Wright, N. T. 1992. *Christian Origins and the Question of God, Volume I, The New Testament and the People of God,* Minneapolis: Fortress.
1996. *Christian Origins and the Question of God, Volume II, Jesus and the Victory of God,* Minneapolis: Fortress.
2000. *The Challenge of Jesus,* London: SPCK.
2003. *Christian Origins and the Question of God, Volume III, The Resurrection of the Son of God,* London: SPCK.
2008. *Surprised by Hope: Rethinking Heaven, the Resurrection, and the Mission of the* Church, HarperOne.
2010. *Virtue Reborn,* London: SPCK.
2012. *How God Became King: Getting to the Heart of the Gospels,* London: SPCK.
2016. *The Day the Revolution Began: Reconsidering the Meaning of Jesus's Crucifixion,* HarperOne.

Young, Brad H 1995. *Jesus the Jewish Theologian,* Peabody: Hendrickson Publishers.

Yonge, C D (ed) 1993. *The Works of Philo: Complete and Unabridged,* New Updated Edition, Peabody: Hendrickson Publishers.

ENDORSEMENTS

Alexander has taken his extensive reading and condensed it brilliantly, leading the reader to a deeper understanding of Jesus in an unusually engaging way. Rich in content, it is at the same time dense with biblical references and scholarly insights while being a very accessible read throughout. Explanations of technical terms are given such that both the theologically educated and those for whom this is the first Christian book they have read, can follow with ease. There were moments as I read where I related to Wesley's experience of my heart being strangely warmed, and to the disciples on the road to Emmaus, who talked about their hearts burning as the scriptures were opened up to them. I highly commend this book to you.

John Wright, National Director, Vineyard Churches UK & Ireland

I keep turning back to Alexander's books again and again... they are so full of knowledge and wisdom. *Know the Real Jesus* is a book to sit down and read, and then to come back to again and again as a valuable study resource. In this book Alexander has done the hard yards of study and research for us and the result is a superb examination of the life and ministry of Jesus giving a fresh Kingdom perspective that will encourage and inform those who read it. Already we have plans to use it centrally in a study of The Historical Jesus with our Vineyard College students.

Peter Downes, DMin, Director of Vineyard College Australia

Alexander Venter has a rare gift and ability to combine rigorous scholarly method and deep spiritual insight. This work is a welcome addition to the growing library of scholarly work on the historical Jesus. In an age of fluid morals and the absence of objective truth, Alexander presents a persuasive portrait of the "most inspirational person to have ever lived". The reader cannot help but be impressed by the careful consideration of good scholarship on this important subject, and equally by the insight and personal spirituality that the author brings, which leads us into an inescapable desire to know and serve this Jesus. We heartily recommend this book and trust that it will find its way into the academy classroom, the study of devoted pastors, and the devotions of committed believers.

Paul R. Alexander, PhD, President of Trinity Bible College and Graduate School, North Dakota, USA, and Chair of World Alliance for Pentecostal Theological Education.
Carol A. Alexander, PhD, Dean of Trinity Bible College and Graduate School, North Dakota.

Books that combine knowledge of scholarly historical Jesus research with personal devotion to that Jesus are both rare and precious. Alexander Venter is well-positioned to offer such a combination, both from his years of research on the subject and his work in the Kingdom love and justice that Jesus preached, and his experience with the kinds of Kingdom miracles that Jesus demonstrated.

Craig S. Keener, F. M. and Ada Thompson Professor of Biblical Studies at Asbury Theological Seminary.

Oh man, what a good read! I highly recommend this work by Alexander Venter. It brings so much into focus, orientating the reader to the enduring essentials of the Gospel wrapped in the historical life, death and resurrection of Jesus. It equips us with clarity and confidence that come with being in his presence. It reminds me of the unlearned Galilean fishermen, Peter and John, who could face the Sanhedrin with faith and boldness because "these men had been with Jesus" (Acts 4:13). Reading this book is like being with Jesus. The world needs this!

David Pedersen, PhD, National Director of Vineyard Churches South Africa

The question of who Jesus truly was and what he aimed to achieve during his life on earth continues to spark curiosity among many. Despite numerous studies on this subject, the church has predominantly focused on Jesus as a divine being. This approach, however, poses a challenge because it presents only one perspective of Jesus while ignoring others. Understanding Jesus' mission and message and our place in it in today's world requires a holistic view of this complex figure from Nazareth. Alexander's book addresses this need by drawing on years of research on the historical Jesus and carefully selecting critical details about his life, mission, message, and times. *Know the Real Jesus* is a valuable resource for anyone, regardless of their level of familiarity with Jesus.

Quinton Howitt, PhD, Director of the School of Leadership and Theology, South Africa, and Adjunct Professor at Trinity Bible College

Our 21st century world has become a complex global village. It is an unprecedented mission opportunity, with difficult contextual questions that scream for urgent answers. Alexander Venter offers a well researched and biblically grounded theological resource to help Christ followers stay true to the life and work of Jesus, and to offer him in a compelling way to the nations as Saviour of the world. It is a must read for Christ followers everywhere in this our common village.

Moss Ntlha, General Secretary, The Evangelical Alliance of South Africa

Alexander Venter says that when he writes he feels the pleasure of God. This is very evident in the pages of this text in which he systematically reveals the reality of the authentic Jesus in a very refreshing picture that he gradually paints for the reader. That sense of pleasure is passed on chapter by chapter to those who read through the thoroughly absorbing, inspiring, and exciting outlines. Alexander stimulates the reader to view Jesus through new looking glasses, fresh lenses, to literally absorb the impact of history intertwined with the psycho-emotional-spiritual worldview of Jesus. For the layperson, this picture becomes a holistic reality in which gaps in knowledge and understanding may be filled, and the many false gospels can be confidently cast aside. For the scholar this text provides more than sufficient researched substance to add significant value to one's knowledge. Most importantly, we are provided with the thoroughly human, thoroughly divine Jesus who draws us to himself, encouraging us to relate to him in his growth, suffering, calling, prophetic knowledge, joy, and spirituality. This is a call to experience Jesus for who he truly is, to know the 'Jesus heartburn', the burning in our hearts as we see him more clearly as our Saviour and God.

Robin Snelgar, PhD, Professor Emeritus of Industrial Psychology at Nelson Mandela University, South Africa

There are many theological perspectives on Jesus – among others, the Jesus of Creedal dogma, leaving out his entire teaching on the Kingdom of God in the gospels; the Jesus of Christendom, informing new forms of Christian nationalism in the 21st century; and the miracle-working Jesus of a consumerist 'health and wealth' Pentecostalism. But what does history say about Jesus of Nazareth? There is much 'Kingdom-talk' in contemporary Christianity that refers to very different understandings of this Kingdom. How did Jesus of Nazareth, in his context of Second Temple Judaism, understand the Kingdom of God? And what does this imply for us, as his followers? Taking the four gospels as reliable eyewitness accounts of historical events, and drawing from the historical research of scholars such as John P. Meier, James D.G. Dunn, and N.T. Wright, Alexander Venter passionately paints an accurate portrait of Jesus of Nazareth – his life, self-understanding, mission and message. In doing so, Venter recovers Jesus' real message of the Kingdom, and thus recalibrates our understanding of Jesus and the purport of the entire Bible. *Know the Real Jesus* is a highly topical book, rich and profound, yet accessibly written for lay-readers and pastors alike. It is a must-read for all who seek a biblical understanding of Jesus and his mission – and our mission.

Ronald Westerbeek, Theologian for New Wine Netherlands

Alexander Venter's book is written with a clear and sincere passion for Jesus and will awaken your desire to see Jesus more clearly and become more like him. Prepare yourself for falling in love with Jesus again, or for the first time.

Flemming Mølhede, National Director of Vineyard Nordic

This latest book by Alexander Venter acknowledges the danger of projecting on to the authentic Jesus the kind of Jesus we want to see. We have seen many such Jesus' in history and contemporary Christianity. Venter's impressive attempts in this portrait of the historical Jesus surgically removes our cultural and theological cataracts to help us see Jesus more clearly for who he was and is. It reminds me of the Jesus that Alexander taught and lived when he crossed the Apartheid dividing walls of hostility in the 1980s to reconcile with blacks. As I read *Know the Real Jesus*, I found it is the Jesus we worshipped together as blacks and whites in Soweto. This is a scholarly articulation of the Palestinian Jesus who walked the dusty streets of Soweto as a teacher and healer, as a prophetic revolutionary and pastoral maverick, who was wastefully gracious, working wonders in our sick and sinful world. This Jesus has marked Alexander's life and character, becoming his hermeneutic and ethic in all of life. I therefore highly recommend this fresh view of Jesus as an indispensable contribution to the quest for the intriguing historical Jesus.

Trevor Amafu Peter Ntlhola, PhD, Vineyard Pastor and Chair of Emthonjeni Fountain of Life Orphan Village, South Africa

Despite the numerous challenges that face the church in today's cultural context, and though those challenges are real, I can think of nothing more important than wrestling with the identity of Jesus. With the growing post-Christian climate we find ourselves in, knowing how to answer questions related to Jesus life, ministry, death, and resurrection, are of the utmost importance. Alexander Venter has written a truly helpful book that covers the wide range of questions regarding Jesus and I'm excited to recommend it for readers I do not know as well as for those in the church I serve. As I read it, I felt more love for Jesus, more commitment to Jesus' mission, and more of a desire to see others experience the Kingdom of God.

Luke Geraty, Co-Lead Pastor at the Red Bluff Vineyard, USA, and host of the Sacramental Charismatic

Alexander Venter, a distinguished theologian, has embarked on a remarkable journey through the annals of history and the depths of faith to present a comprehensive portrait of the man whose life has influenced billions for over two millennia. This book is a testament to Alexander's dedication to bridging the gap between historical inquiry and spiritual devotion. But it is more than a historical account; it's a spiritual odyssey that invites readers to explore the timeless wisdom of Jesus. Alexander skillfully connects the dots between the historical figure and the transformative teachings that continue to inspire and guide countless lives today. Whether you are a seasoned scholar, a curious seeker, or someone seeking to strengthen your faith, *Know the Real Jesus* will captivate your mind and touch your heart. It's a book that will enrich your understanding of the historical Jesus and deepen your connection to the Jesus we follow today. Through its pages, you'll find both historical insight and spiritual nourishment—a rare and invaluable combination in the world of literature about Jesus of Nazareth.

Rose Madrid-Swetman, DMin, Associate Director of The Center for Transforming Engagement, and Teaching Pastor at The Practicing Church in Shoreline, USA

Alexander's contribution to freshly discovering the Jesus of the gospels and its impact on Christian discipleship and the church's mission is significant. It captures a delicate tension between the necessary technical aspects of the topic on the one hand, yet oozes tender devotion and desire to discover the man, Jesus, who walked the dusty byways of Israel on the other. *Know the Real Jesus* is a highly accessible read and sparks anew a deep passion for responding to Jesus' call to us today, "Come, follow me", to be further fashioned to live and love like him in these troubled times.

Ryan Matthews, Team Leader at Freedom House Church, South Africa, and Leader of Catalyst Connect Family of Churches

It is with great enthusiasm and reverence that I endorse Alexander Venter's *Know the Real Jesus: A Portrait of the Historical Jesus*. This book is thorough and precise showing of Jesus from history, from his birth till his ascension, emphasising the mystery of God's Kingdom. In Alexander's words, writing about God's intent, "Jesus' self-sacrificing life and death were the ultimate embodiment of God's love for Israel and all humanity: the cross-carrying Messiah-King who triumphs over evil through suffering love." In endorsing this book, we celebrate the wisdom and the inspiration Alexander has imparted. The historical context in which Jesus lived, the socio-political challenges he confronted, and the radical ideas he championed have sparked countless discussions. Alexander has enriched our understanding of history, philosophy, theology, and ethics, and inspires dialogue, introspection, and the pursuit of God's great love in Jesus. Let us recognize the profound significance of this writing that will shape our collective journey and may the Spirit of the historical Jesus guide us into a future of love, understanding, unity, and enduring peace.

Steve Olivier, MA Missional Leadership, Senior Pastor at Knysna Vineyard, South Africa

Printed in Great Britain
by Amazon